"Psychoanalytic Thinking *is a bold an[d]
diverse trends in contemporary psychoan[alysis and]
the history of the discipline. Carveth's fearless cr[itique of]
trends in psychoanalysis, past and present, is balanced by re[freshing]
reminders of the emancipatory power of truth, the dangers of postmodern
relativism, and the importance of differentiating between the superego
and conscience proper. And much, much else besides."*

Daniel Burston, Ph.D., Department of Psychology,
Duquesne University.

*"Internationally respected, Donald Carveth is one of the most original
and penetrating psychoanalytic theorists in Canada. Among his notable
contributions, he has added the concept of conscience to Freud's notion
of the super-ego to produce a picture of moral psychology much closer
to complete than Freud's. And he has made Lacan intelligible to English-
speaking students of psychoanalysis in a way that few if any others have
done. As is true of most prolific authors, Carveth's works originally
appeared in a great variety of different publications, some no longer
easily accessible. Having a large sample of his work available in one
volume is a cause for celebration."*

Andrew Brook, Ph.D., Chancellor's Professor of Philosophy
and Cognitive Science, Emeritus, Carleton University,
Fellow and Treasurer, International Psychoanalytic Association.

"The publication of Donald Carveth's Psychoanalytic Thinking *continues what I have come to regard as a 'Wittenberg moment' in the history of psychoanalysis, which began with his first book,* The Still Small Voice: Psychoanalytic Reflections on Guilt and Conscience *(2013). Like Luther in the Catholic world, Carveth has managed, with a trenchant logic that is rare in psychoanalytic writing, to 'nail' down something fundamental, which I hope will alter the course of psychoanalytic culture in a positive and integrative way."*

Charles Levin, Ph.D., Director, Canadian Institute of Psychoanalysis
(Québec English Branch), Editor-in-Chief, *Canadian Journal of
Psychoanalysis/Revue canadienne de psychanalyse.*

Psychoanalytic Thinking

Since the classical Freudian and ego psychology paradigms lost their position of dominance in the late 1950s, psychoanalysis became a multi-paradigm science with those working in the different frameworks increasingly engaging only with those in the same or related intellectual "silos." Beginning with Freud's theory of human nature and civilization, *Psychoanalytic Thinking: A Dialectical Critique of Contemporary Theory and Practice* proceeds to review and critically evaluate a series of major post-Freudian contributions to psychoanalytic thought.

In response to the defects, blind spots and biases in Freud's work, Melanie Klein, Wilfred Bion, Jacques Lacan, Erich Fromm, Donald Winnicott, Heinz Kohut, Heinrich Racker, Ernest Becker among others offered useful correctives and innovations that are, nevertheless, themselves in need of remediation for their own forms of one-sidedness. Through Carveth's comparative exploration, readers will acquire a sense of what is enduringly valuable in these diverse psychoanalytic contributions, as well as exposure to the dialectically deconstructive method of critique that Carveth sees as central to psychoanalytic thinking at its best. Carveth violates the taboo against speaking of the Imaginary, Symbolic and the Real unless one is a Lacanian, or the paranoid-schizoid and depressive positions unless one is a Kleinian, or id, ego, superego, ego-ideal and conscience unless one is a Freudian ego psychologist, and so on.

Out of dialogue and mutual critique, psychoanalysis can over time separate the wheat from the chaff, collect the wheat and approach an ever-evolving synthesis. *Psychoanalytic Thinking: A Dialectical Critique of Contemporary Theory and Practice* will be of great interest to psychoanalysts and psychoanalytic psychotherapists and, more broadly, to readers in philosophy, social science and critical social theory.

Donald L. Carveth is an Emeritus Professor of Sociology and Social and Political Thought and a Senior Scholar at York University, Toronto, Canada and a Training and Supervising Analyst in the Canadian Institute of Psychoanalysis. He is past Director of the Toronto Institute of Psychoanalysis and a past Editor-in-Chief of the *Canadian Journal of Psychoanalysis/Revue canadienne de psychanalyse*.

Psychological Issues

David L. Wolitzky
Series Editor

The basic mission of *Psychological Issues* is to contribute to the further development of psychoanalysis as a science, as a respected scholarly enterprise, as a theory of human behavior, and as a therapeutic method.

Over the past fifty years, the series has focused on fundamental aspects and foundations of psychoanalytic theory and clinical practice, as well as on work in related disciplines relevant to psychoanalysis. *Psychological Issues* does not aim to represent or promote a particular point of view. The contributions cover broad and integrative topics of vital interest to all psychoanalysts as well as to colleagues in related disciplines. They cut across particular schools of thought and tackle key issues, such as the philosophical underpinnings of psychoanalysis, psychoanalytic theories of motivation, conceptions of therapeutic action, the nature of unconscious mental functioning, psychoanalysis and social issues and reports of original empirical research relevant to psychoanalysis. The authors often take a critical stance toward theories and offer a careful theoretical analysis and conceptual clarification of the complexities of theories and their clinical implications, drawing upon relevant empirical findings from psychoanalytic research as well as from research in related fields.

The Editorial Board continues to invite contributions from social/behavioral sciences such as anthropology and sociology, from biological sciences such as physiology and the various brain sciences, and from scholarly humanistic disciplines such as philosophy, law and ethics. Volumes 1–64 in this series were published by International Universities Press. Volumes 65–69 were published by Jason Aronson.

Routledge titles in this series

Vol. 70
From Classical to Contemporary Psychoanalysis: A Critique and Integration
Morris N. Eagle

Vol. 71
Memory, Myth, and Seduction: Unconscious Fantasy and the Interpretive Process
Jean-Georges Schimek

Vol. 72
Identity and the New Psychoanalytic Explorations of Self-organization
Mardi Horowitz

Vol. 73
Myths of Termination: What Patients Can Teach Psychoanalysts About Endings
Judy Leopold Kantrowitz

Vol. 74
Manual of Regulation-Focused Psychotherapy for Children (RFP-C) with Externalizing Behaviors: A Psychodynamic Approach
Leon Hoffman, Timothy Rice, & Tracy Prout

Vol. 75
Psychoanalytic Perspectives on Conflict
Edited by Christopher Christian, Morris N. Eagle, & David L. Wolitzky

Vol. 76
Death and Fallibility in the Psychoanalytic Encounter: Mortal Gifts
Ellen Pinsky

Vol. 77
Core Concepts in Classical Psychoanalysis: Clinical, Research Evidence and Conceptual Critiques
Morris N. Eagle

Vol. 78
Core Concepts in Contemporary Psychoanalysis: Clinical, Research Evidence and Conceptual Critiques
Morris N. Eagle

Vol. 79
Psychoanalytic Thinking: A Dialectical Critique of Contemporary Theory and Practice
Donald L. Carveth

Psychoanalytic Thinking

A Dialectical Critique of Contemporary Theory and Practice

Donald L. Carveth

Routledge
Taylor & Francis Group
LONDON AND NEW YORK

First published 2018
by Routledge
2 Park Square, Milton Park, Abingdon, Oxon OX14 4RN

and by Routledge
711 Third Avenue, New York, NY 10017

Routledge is an imprint of the Taylor & Francis Group, an informa business

© 2018 Donald L. Carveth

The right of Donald L. Carveth to be identified as author of this work has been asserted by him in accordance with sections 77 and 78 of the Copyright, Designs and Patents Act 1988.

All rights reserved. No part of this book may be reprinted or reproduced or utilized in any form or by any electronic, mechanical, or other means, now known or hereafter invented, including photocopying and recording, or in any information storage or retrieval system, without permission in writing from the publishers.

Trademark notice: Product or corporate names may be trademarks or registered trademarks, and are used only for identification and explanation without intent to infringe.

British Library Cataloguing-in-Publication Data
A catalogue record for this book is available from the British Library

Library of Congress Cataloging-in-Publication Data
Names: Carveth, Donald L., 1944– author.
Title: Psychoanalytic thinking : a dialectical critique of contemporary theory and practice / Donald L. Carveth.
Description: New York : Routledge, 2018. | Includes bibliographical references and index. |
Identifiers: LCCN 2017050635 (print) | LCCN 2017061204 (ebook) | ISBN 9780203713105 (Master) | ISBN 9781351360548 (Web PDF) | ISBN 9781351360531 (ePub) | ISBN 9781351360524 (Mobipocket/Kindle) | ISBN 9781138560710 (hardback : alk. paper) | ISBN 9781138560727 (pbk. : alk. paper)
Subjects: LCSH: Psychoanalysis.
Classification: LCC BF173 (ebook) | LCC BF173 .C4247 2018 (print) | DDC 150.19/5–dc23
LC record available at https://lccn.loc.gov/2017050635

ISBN: 978-1-138-56071-0 (hbk)
ISBN: 978-1-138-56072-7 (pbk)
ISBN: 978-0-203-71310-5 (ebk)

Typeset in Times New Roman
by Wearset Ltd, Boldon, Tyne and Wear

For Nicholas

Plato seems to have received the decisive thought as to how a philosopher ought to behave toward men from the apology of Socrates: as their physician, as a gadfly on the neck of man.

Nietzsche (Kaufmann, 1968, p. 398)

Contents

About the author   xiii
Foreword   xiv
Acknowledgments   xxi

Introduction: on critique   1

1 *Civilization and Its Discontents*: a Kleinian re-view   26

2 Expanding structural theory: id, ego, superego, ego-ideal and conscience   42

3 Is there a future in disillusion?   66

4 Self psychology and the intersubjective perspective: a dialectical critique   99

5 Lacanian theory: appreciation and critique   131

6 The melancholic existentialism of Ernest Becker   161

7 Concordant and complementary countertransference: a clarification   168

8 Clarifying and deconstructing Winnicott   181

9 Neo-Kleinian theory: a dialectical re-vision   193

10 Beyond nature and culture: Erich Fromm's
existentialism 213

Postscript: dialectical thinking 230

References 237
Index 260

About the author

Donald Carveth, Ph.D., RP, FIPA is an Emeritus Professor of Sociology and Social and Political Thought and a Senior Scholar at York University in Toronto. He is a Training and Supervising Analyst in the Canadian Institute of Psychoanalysis and a past Director of the Toronto Institute. After completing a doctorate (Carveth, 1977, 1984a) comparing and contrasting sociological and psychoanalytic theories of human nature, he undertook clinical psychoanalytic training graduating from the Toronto Institute of Psychoanalysis in 1985. With Dr. Eva Lester and others he helped found the *Canadian Journal of Psychoanalysis/Revue canadienne de psychanalyse* of which he is a past Editor-in-Chief. He has published some eighty papers and reviews in various academic journals. Over the past decade his work has concentrated on issues of guilt, guilt-substitutes and the differentiation of conscience as a fifth component of the structural theory of the mind in addition to id, ego, superego and ego-ideal. His recent book, *The Still Small Voice: Psychoanalytic Reflections on Guilt and Conscience* was published by Karnac in 2013. He is in private practice in Toronto and may be found on the web at www.yorku.ca/dcarveth and on YouTube at www.youtube.com/user/doncarveth/

Foreword

The publication of Donald Carveth's *Psychoanalytic Thinking: A Dialectical Critique of Contemporary Theory and Practice* continues what I have come to regard as a "Wittenberg moment" in the history of psychoanalysis, which began with his first book, *The Still Small Voice: Psychoanalytic Reflections on Guilt and Conscience* (2013). Like Luther in the Catholic world, Carveth has managed, with a trenchant logic that is rare in psychoanalytic writing, to "nail" down something fundamental, which I hope will alter the course of psychoanalytic culture in a positive and integrative way.

Before I specify what I have in mind about Carveth's contribution to our discipline, allow me a few preliminary comments. In recent decades, there has been a great deal of discussion about the institutional illnesses and occupational hazards of psychoanalysis. Having participated in these discussions, I think of them as important exercises in professional self-reflection. But too often they also serve as foils for the promotion of a particular brand of psychoanalysis. Slochower (2017) says as much of her own school of relational psychoanalysis:

> Every psychoanalytic theory is organized around an implicit clinical ideal ... our ideal is formulated in ... argument with its theoretical predecessors and competitors. While these conversations can deepen our thinking, they frequently don't.... Instead they become fighting words.... We polarize, elevating the originality of our own contribution while minimizing, stereotyping, sometimes denigrating, the position of the psychoanalytic Other whose ideals collide ... with our own. Each pendulum swing seems inevitably to provoke a counter-move that itself overcorrects.
>
> (p. 282)

In the spirit of Slochower's call for us to reconsider the over-selling of our ideals and the over-correction of the Other's faults, Carveth has gone a step further. He has been a consistent champion of dialectical thinking in response to the chronic either-orism of the analytic profession. In all of his analytic writings, since his early paper on metaphor (Carveth, 1984), he has been calling our attention, in one way or another, to a blind spot in the psychoanalytic way of making arguments and building theoretical models. He can be very critical of psychoanalysis. But unlike Popper, Grünbaum or Crews, Carveth's critique comes from a place that is profoundly *within* psychoanalysis. He is not trying to tear psychoanalysis down. He is trying to defend it from itself, or more precisely, from its "schools."

In my view, Carveth's central move has been to insist on the idea that psychoanalysis is not a "separate" and "distinct" form of knowledge that possesses the unconscious as its unique object domain, exclusive of other disciplines. His body of work is remarkable for the way that he has consistently maintained and developed, from his clinical standpoint, a radical vision of the potential for psychoanalytic thinking to transcend its own developmental history. But in order to achieve this, he argues—in order to have a truly dialectical discussion about itself or anything else—psychoanalysis needs to recognize that it is part of a much larger human discussion, participating as one of the many arts and social and health sciences. Our style of discourse, our way of talking to each other, needs desperately to address (and to include) this public dimension of knowledge and human interests.

In taking this tack, *Psychoanalytic Thinking* confronts the dominant trend in institutionalized psychoanalysis, which I would describe as a medieval guild attitude, claiming exclusive access to the unconscious through a prescribed method, which only apprenticeship in the guild can teach. In recent years, for example, the International Psychoanalytic Association (IPA) has been riveted by scholastic debates about whether access to the unconscious, and the appropriate level of "regression," can be achieved at a frequency of three sessions per week, or only four or more. As readers will discover, Carveth's critique of this kind of professionalized theoreticism does not involve an abandonment of intrinsic psychoanalytic values. On the contrary, he demonstrates time and again that so many of the arguments we have been hearing that wrap themselves patriotically in the psychoanalytic flag are in fact rather anti-analytic in spirit. He continuously calls the profession to account for its clinical neglectfulness with respect to fundamental psychological issues that psychoanalysis itself had originally uncovered.

Among these neglected issues for Carveth, perhaps the most important is the question of ethics—not just in the sense of professional ethics, or deontological codes (for example, with regard to boundary violations)—but also the personal moral sensibility of the analyst, and—still more radically—the moral disposition of the patient. In reframing the problem of ethics in this way, and making it the focal point for the various angles of his argument, Carveth significantly adds to our understanding of what it means to be truly engaged with our patients (and for them to be engaged with us).

A persistent idealized trope of well-practiced analysis has involved the imagery of selfless understanding of the patient, which Freud originally defined in terms of the analyst's capacity to observe the patient objectively, albeit through personal access to unconscious communications, but without any countertransference interference. This rather implausible assumption of anonymous and abstinent neutrality morphed over time into the notion that in order to understand the patient, the analyst needs to become empathically merged, even to the point of virtual mimesis.

Carveth's contribution in this debate is to show that engagement with the patient requires more than a measure of where we are on the spectrum between our own subjectivity and that of the other, between separateness of mind and identification with the patient. Our position on this continuum necessarily varies with context, which is fine in principle, and not a deep epistemological problem. But what do we do when we find ourselves unwittingly forming an alliance with one part of a patient against another? Or when the patient divides us against ourselves in some surprising way? Because we are complicated and internally divided beings, inherently conflictual by nature, Carveth concludes that our technical language is insufficient to grasp the complexity of the analytic process. We need something more—and it is not some *thing* about human nature that Freud, Klein, Winnicott, Bowlby and all the others have missed. It is simply a way of thinking and speaking among ourselves, which we already had before the psychoanalytic revolution. It can be found with some effort in its most distilled form by working through the implicit framework of basic moral philosophy, and the spiritual traditions of East and West (which Carveth tries to do on our behalf).

Foreword   xvii

The important thing to understand while you are reading Carveth is that the "ordinary" ways of speaking to which he appeals, such as the word "conscience," which may sound psychologically naive, are the very forms of social interchange that the technical language of psychoanalysis was consciously intended to neutralize for scientific (read: professional) reasons. This tells us something we don't want to hear about the way we have positioned ourselves as a *métier*. I say this because at the core of the language we have been trying to displace with technical concepts, like the superego, is the traditional human sense of an irresolvable problem about social order and responsibility. Do we really want to disable this level of discourse among ourselves, let alone with our patients? Do we really believe that we have a model and a technique that bypasses the language of social and moral responsibility? Is this really the way to engage with our patients more deeply?

Behind the non-technical human discussion about the problem of social order and personal responsibility, there is always some version of the concept of the Good, as Plato believed. Freud taught us correctly that there is no way to pin down the objective content of such a concept, and he was right. But as Carveth eloquently demonstrates, this is not a reason to banish the Good as a frame of psychoanalytic discussion and treatment. Indeed, Melanie Klein elevated the idea of the internal "good object" to a kind of categorical imperative in psychoanalysis. Her analysand Donald Meltzer (1981), went so far as to argue for "a theological model of the mind," explaining that "every person has to have … a 'religion' in which his internal objects perform the functions of Gods … because these Gods do in fact perform functions in the mind" (p. 179). Unfortunately, the Kleinian discourse tends to have a distancing or objectivizing effect, partly because it is still tied intellectually to the Freudian metapsychological reduction of moral concepts to a schema of development organized exclusively around the pleasure-pain axis. Klein recognized that the superego is a defensive institution, not notably committed to ethical human relationships; but her followers remain trapped in Freud's pain-driven developmental model, which forces them to understand any notion of the Good that lies beyond the "ego destructive superego" (Bion, 1967, p. 107) as the product of a secondary thinking process (even though it will arise like a phoenix out of the ashen pain of mourning), undertaken by a liberated, educated ego (Britton, 2003).

For Carveth, the concept of the good has been rendered superficial and clinically less interesting, by this psychoanalytic habit of conceiving it essentially as a way of coping with pain and frustration. Winnicott (1965) had tried, brilliantly, to sidestep the whole problem by proposing the "good enough" as the basis of social adaptation, but this is still imagined as a compensatory compromise. The assumption that the Good, like social adaptation, is ultimately rooted in pain avoidance and tolerance of frustration, is a well-established corollary of classical Freudian metapsychology (Levin, 1992), which defines pleasure as the reduction of stimulus innervation, just as the superego concept implies. The superego sense of the Good, which Freud (1930) described in detail, is not much more than a by-product of our fear of castration (however, that is metaphorized), and our internalization of societal values and prohibitions, however we may believe they are transmitted. Given these assumptions, it should be no surprise that we seem to love and even relish the superego that punishes us, and that masochism is widely considered the fundamental psychic position (Laplanche, 1976).

By contrast, in Carveth's view, the ordinary non-technical, intuitive sense of the Good is an independent force and not only a phantasy construct related to the struggle with pain. He argues that even in the absence of a psychoanalytic theory to support it, faith in goodness as an independent value has always been indispensable for our clinical work. This "innate" sense of goodness, i.e., conscience (which does not play the punitive games of the superego) is a valuating-expressive modality that is grounded in the un-coerced forms of human pleasure that we associate with stimulus-seeking behavior in the infant (as opposed to pain avoidance), self-expressive exploration and above all the internalization of the caring and nurturing other—the original experience of attachment, even if compromised and insecure. These benign nuclei of conscience, which the inherently narcissistic organization of the superego fears, suppresses and attacks, are powerful healing agents, but they are often buried under layers of psychopathology, waiting for discovery and recognition for the first time, in forms of psychoanalytic intimacy that take the analytic couple yet further still than intersubjective engagement, empathic attunement and the co-creation of narrative truths.

However much we may wish, professionally or clinically, to avoid an appeal to this non-defensive concept of the Good, Carveth maintains that it will always be a factor in the best of the clinical work that we do. This is a radical argument, not least because it exposes a fundamental philosophical misunderstanding at the heart of the psychoanalytic identity. There is a history behind this misunderstanding, which analysts may not have been taught.

Psychoanalysis emerged in the late nineteenth century, of course, and remains one of the more cogent modernist responses to the collapse of traditional social order. Freud's superego powerfully condenses all of his mature, scientific understanding of the modern dilemma. It takes into account the relative devolution of collective symbolic processes, which had always depended upon a stable and unified cultural system of references. The devolution in question was onto the unsuspecting individual, who was thereby laden with angst-ridden responsibilities and intimidating demands for creativity. This new burden was the psychological consequence of the disenchantment of the world (aided by the mechanistic world-views of Newton, Descartes and Locke), and the replacement of this lost world by Weber's "iron cage" of industrialization, social atomization and the professionalized sub-division of community life into specialized functions, such as bureaucracy and psychotherapy. Traditionally, a sense of the Good had always been underwritten by a socially-sanctioned moral framework, usually of cosmic proportions; but this was now gone, and with the broad social destruction of the classical and medieval "great chain of being" (Lovejoy, 1936), Freud's patients became ill with the puzzle of moral responsibilities for which they were not prepared and for which society offered no universally understood response. This was the psychoanalytic moment in history.

Freud's work offered a skillfully engineered bridge into this cultural unknown. In order to achieve a historically significant role, he probably could not have avoided a self-contradictory stance, in which he simultaneously championed a scientific, quasi-mechanical, biologistic model of the soul, but also worked very hard to salvage the last vestiges of the magical, interconnected symbolic cosmos of the "ontic logos" (Taylor, 1989), whose remnants still scatter the social field today. In a world suddenly finding itself barren of genuinely unifying ritual and symbolic order, the "capacity to symbolize" found a new home in the Freudian psyche.

The same dialectic of symbolic internalization can be traced in the Judeo-Christian tradition, which split apart during the Reformation over the question of individual conscience. Like the Catholic Church in

Luther's time, Freud saw morality as a matter of established authority and natural necessity (Ananke). These were the dominating powers vested in the superego, which is established by submissive identification as the internal representative of the "external world" (however much it might be fueled by the "death instinct"). Carveth agrees with this analysis of the superego, while maintaining that "conscience" has a deeper personal root in the primary sociability shared by our species.

For a whole variety of reasons, and on many levels, Carveth's work provides psychoanalysis with the contemporary equivalent of a powerful spiritual insight. You will find his very clearly argued theses pinned on the door. I invite you to open it, and enter this book.

Charles Levin, Ph.D.
Director, Canadian Institute of Psychoanalysis (Québec English Branch)
Editor-in-Chief, *Canadian Journal of Psychoanalysis/Revue canadienne de psychanalyse*

References

Bion, W.R. (1967). *Second Thoughts*. New York: Aronson.
Britton, R. (2003). *Sex, Death and the Superego: Experiences in Psychoanalysis*. London: Karnac.
Carveth, D.L. (1984). The analyst's metaphors: a deconstructionist perspective. *Psychoanalysis and Contemporary Social Thought* 7, 4: 491–560.
Carveth, D.L. (2013). *The Still Small Voice: Psychoanalytic Reflections on Guilt and Conscience*. London: Karnac.
Freud, S. (1930). Civilization and its discontents. *S.E.* 21: 57–146. London: Hogarth.
Laplanche, J. (1976). *Life and Death in Psychoanalysis*. Trans. J. Mehlman. Baltimore: Johns Hopkins University Press.
Levin, C. (1992). Thinking through the hungry baby—toward a new pleasure principle. *The Psychoanalytic Study of the Child* 47: 119–137.
Lovejoy, A.O. (1936). *The Great Chain of Being*. Cambridge, MS: Harvard University Press.
Meltzer, D. (1981). The Kleinian expansion of Freud's metapsychology. *International Journal of Psycho-Analysis* 62: 177–185.
Slochower, J. (2017). Going too far: relational heroines and relational excess. *Psychoanalytic Dialogues* 27, 3: 282–299.
Taylor, C. (1989). *Sources of the Self: The Making of the Modern Identity*. Cambridge, MS: Harvard University Press.

Acknowledgments

Discussions with colleagues, students and friends too numerous to mention have informed my thinking over the years, but special acknowledgment is owed to my late mentor Eli Sagan (1927–2015); to Daniel Burston who, despite substantial reservations with respect to some of the positions I take here, did me the honor of reading, commenting upon and even editing several key chapters, which are far better as a result of his efforts; to Charles Levin, my friend and colleague who, in his capacity as Editor-in-Chief of the Canadian Journal of Psychoanalysis, has over the years provided me with very thoughtful responses to my writings and who, in his "Foreword" to this volume, has conveyed better than anyone else I know could hope to do the essential meaning of my work; to my son Nicholas for deepening and broadening my thinking by bringing perspectives from critical social work into our ongoing dialogue; and, of course, to Jeanie, always.

Chapter 1 is a revised version of "Freud's 'Civilization and Its Discontents': A Kleinian Re-View," *Clio's Psyche* 21, 3 (December 2014): 328–333 (reused by kind permission of the journal editor, Paul H. Elovitz; Chapter 1 also draws upon "Freud's and Our Paranoid Myth of 'the Beast'," *Canadian Journal of Psychoanalysis/Revue canadienne de psychanalyse* 20, 1 (Spring 2012): 153–157. Chapter 2 draws on both "The Immoral Superego: Conscience as the Fourth Element in the Structural Theory of the Mind," *Canadian Journal of Psychoanalysis/Revue canadienne de psychanalyse* 23, 1 (Spring, 2015): 206–223; and "Why We Should Stop Conflating the Superego with the Conscience," *Psychoanalysis, Culture & Society* (March 2017), Volume 22, Issue 1, pp. 15–32. Chapter 3 is a revised version of "Is There a Future in Disillusion? Constructionist and Deconstructionist Approaches in Psychoanalysis," *Journal of the American Academy of Psychoanalysis* 27, 2

(1999): 325–358. Revised with permission of Guilford Press. Chapter 4 is a revised version of a two-part paper, "Selfobject and Intersubjective Theory: A Dialectical Critique. Part I: Monism, Dualism, Dialectic," *Canadian Journal of Psychoanalysis/Revue canadienne de psychanalyse* 2, 2 (1994): 151–168; and "Selfobject and Intersubjective Theory: Part 2, A Dialectical Critique of the Intersubjective Perspective," *Canadian Journal of Psychoanalysis/Revue canadienne de psychanalyse* 3, 1 (1995): 43–70. Chapter 5 is a much revised and expanded version of a paper originally delivered to the Toronto Psychoanalytic Society in 1987 titled: "Why I Am Not a Lacanian Analyst" and published five years later as "Some Reflections on Lacanian Theory in Relation to Other Currents in Contemporary Psychoanalysis," *Journal of Psycho-Social Studies* 1, 1 (2002). Chapter 6 is a slightly revised version of "The Melancholic Existentialism of Ernest Becker," *Free Associations* Volume 11, Part 3, No. 59 (2004): 422–429. Chapter 7, originally entitled: "Racker's Error," appeared as "Concordant and Complementary Countertransference: A Clarification," *Canadian Journal of Psychoanalysis/Revue canadienne de psychanalyse* 20, 1 (Spring 2012): 70–84; to my surprise, despite its rather technical nature, it has perhaps been my most popular paper to date. The first part of Chapter 8 is adapted from "Dark Epiphany: The Encounter with Finitude or the Discovery of the Object in *The Body*," *Psychoanalysis & Contemporary Thought* 17, 2 (Spring 1994): 215–250; the second part of this chapter appears here for the first time, as do the Introduction and Postscript. Chapter 9 is a revised version of "Bion, Britton and the Neo-Kleinian Model of the Mind: A Dialectical Critique," *Canadian Journal of Psychoanalysis/Revue canadienne de psychanalyse* 24–25 (2017): 158–171. Chapter 10 is a slightly revised version of "Beyond Nature and Culture: Fromm's Existentialism," *The Psychoanalytic Review* 104, 4 (August 2017): 485–501.

Introduction
On critique

For me the original appeal of both the academic and psychoanalytic professions had to do with their avowed commitment to truth values. Freud (1915b), for example, wrote that "psycho-analytic treatment is founded on truthfulness. In this fact lies a great part of its educative effect and its ethical value" (p. 164). For Bion (1992), "Psycho-analytic procedure presupposes that the welfare of the patient demands a constant supply of truth as inevitably as his physical survival demands food" (p. 99). Educated in the humanities and social sciences in the 1960s and in psychoanalysis in the 1970s, I came to conceive of the systematic and rigorous (logical and empirical) interrogation of theoretical claims and systems, as central to the scholarly pursuit of truth, of equal importance to (and really inseparable from) empirical research and theory creation. As something of an angry young man, critique, or the careful scrutiny of theory for internal incoherence or contradictions and inconsistency with established bodies of fact, held considerable appeal, offering opportunities for (more or less) successful sublimation of aggressive drives into fundamentally prosocial intellectual creativity.

The decline of critique

For a time such critical work appeared normative and validated by colleagues and journals, even in psychoanalysis, though to a notably lesser extent than in other human sciences, except when directed at those who challenged the dominant classical and ego psychology paradigms. But by the late 1970s and early 1980s a sea-change had become evident. Just as the field of sociology became a manifestly multi-paradigm science where intellectual work involved less critical debates between competing paradigms than of conversation among workers within each sub-field, so in the wider world of the humanities and social sciences discussion seemed increasingly limited to those working within the different intellectual "silos," Marxists debating with Marxists, structuralists with structuralists, etc. In psychoanalysis, the emergence in the 1970s of revisionist perspectives, such as self psychology (Kohut, 1971, 1978), stimulated intense debate for several years, until partisans of the opposing points of view, like partners in a disintegrating marriage, pretty much abandoned efforts to communicate with one another.

While these developments were unfolding within disciplines, the emerging anti-foundationalism of post-structural and postmodern theory, the rejection of the very idea of fundamental and unitary truth, had a sweeping cross-disciplinary impact that undermined efforts to arrive at it and to offer critique of inadequate, one-sided or erroneous approaches to it. When the existence of truth is in doubt, its continued pursuit appears quixotic or presumptuous and critique begins to seem intolerant, impolite and even rude. In a world where there are multiple "truths" but no truth, multiple "narrative truths" but no "historical truth" (Spence, 1984), the nature of intellectual virtue shifts from skepticism to tolerance, from rigorous critique to relaxed and playful enjoyment of multiplicity—or, more often, to ideological insularity and either benign neglect of those who think differently, or malign, intolerant and moralistic attacks rather than intellectually probing and sophisticated critique.

Writing about the state of scholarship in North American universities in recent years, Paglia (2016) has pointed out that neglect of crucial training in "the methodology of research … based in logic and reasoning and the rigorous testing of conclusions based on evidence" has meant that:

> too many college teachers … lack even the most superficial awareness of their own assumptions and biases. Working on campus only with the like-minded, they treat dissent as a mortal offence that must be suppressed, because it threatens their entire career history and world-view.
>
> (p. 11)

"A tragic result of the era of identity politics in the humanities," she concludes, "has been the collapse of rigorous scholarly standards, as well as an end to the high value once accorded to erudition" (p. 14). At the very time psychoanalytic training was becoming available to scholars in the social sciences and humanities who might have infused more of the spirit of rigorous critique into a profession that had developed outside the university more as a guild than a scholarly discipline, this spirit was in marked decline among the newcomers, a fact that may have eased their entry and adaptation to a field that, from the beginning, had been as preoccupied with issues of identification and loyalty as with the critical appraisal of ideas.

In both academia and the institutions of psychoanalysis, as everywhere else, devotion to the truth is often compromised by a range of competing values. As sociologists understand, the institutions established in pursuit of various goals and ideals often take on a life of their own such that the survival and traditions of the organizations often displace their original mission. Max Weber (1922) described the "routinization of charisma" whereby the spirit and vision of great charismatic leaders come to be codified and administered by more or less unimaginative bureaucrats in the institutions (e.g., the Church) established in their name. However unfaithful the institution may prove to be with respect to the original vision, it may at least serve to preserve some of its remnants and signifiers, which might seed regeneration of creativity under fortuitous conditions. The IPA has sought, however inadequately, to preserve and communicate the spirit and insights of Freud and some of his creative colleagues (but notably not those it excommunicated) to subsequent generations. In something of an extension of Weber's insight, Bion (1970) suggested that the very devotion of the charismatic leader to the truth sometimes renders her or him a threat to the institution and *vice versa*. He refers in this connection to the danger of:

> the group's promotion of the individual to a position in the Establishment where his energies are deflected from his creative-destructive role and absorbed in administrative functions. His epitaph might be "He was loaded with honors and sank without a trace."
>
> (p. 78)

—a comment that may cast light on Bion's decision to leave England during his last years.

Whereas widespread perversion of the original ideals and goals of the university as a community of scholars became evident in recent decades due to its increasing corporatization and domination both by government and the private sector under the hegemony of neoliberalism, the displacement of truth values in psychoanalysis in favor of established ideologies and the interests of psychoanalytic societies, institutes and associations has been a factor almost from the beginning. Genuine critique has not often been welcomed in psychoanalytic circles where deference to founding fathers and mothers is *de rigueur*, criticism must be carefully muted, and departures from orthodoxy ingeniously disguised. Though his tone was always sober and objective, Fairbairn's (1952) lucid criticisms of the master's theories suffered undeserved neglect for many years. The important ideas of Ian Suttie (1935) remained largely unknown, not only because he died young and was not around to defend them, but because he had advanced his critique in a clear, direct and impassioned manner. Both orthodox and heterodox analysts have been masters of "the silent treatment," often refusing to engage with intellects who mount powerful challenges to their beliefs. Ferenczi was not the only critic to have his sanity unjustly impugned (Balint, 1958; Haynal, 1989). No wonder Edith Jacobson (1964), who was capable of writing clearly about clinical matters, so often lapsed into obscurity as she approached the dangerous area of critique of and departure from orthodoxy. Erik Erikson's (1950, 1968) ideas represent in substance a quite penetrating critique and revision of Freudian theory, but his need to disguise this fact through his adoption of an excessively polite and respectful tone made it difficult for readers to appreciate this (Burston, 2007). Whereas Roy Schafer (1976), a theoretical lamb in wolf's clothing, proposed radical changes in the *language* of psychoanalysis while adhering closely (at that time, if not later) to standard Freudian ego-psychological clinical theory and practice, Otto Kernberg (1975, 1976), a theoretical wolf in lamb's clothing, managed radical departures from orthodoxy by soothing and distracting his readers by careful adherence to the sacred tongue ("libido," "aggression," "drives" and "Oedipus complex"), sticking to the "letter" of theory while substantially altering the meaning of key concepts—such as redefining the "drive" not as investing object relations, but as constituted by them. Whether he did so self-consciously or not, Kernberg can be seen to have employed a kind of "Trojan Horse" strategy: by accepting the theory of primary narcissism rejected by the Kleinians who insisted on object relations from the beginning, he gained admission to the Freudian stronghold. Once inside, he brought a good deal of Kleinianism (splitting, projective identification, etc.) into the mainstream.

While the academic pursuit of truth and its practice of critique have always been vulnerable to the many influences stemming from careerism, favored ideologies, fashion, external political pressures, etc., for some time the institution of tenure provided professors with some degree of protection of their scholarly autonomy, particularly if they were able to publish their work, however disagreeable it was found to be in various circles. But professional psychoanalysts are not primarily researchers and writers, but practitioners, dependent for referrals and career advancement upon a relatively small circle of colleagues in the local society and institute. And psychoanalytic training has, for better or for worse, mostly taken a patriarchal, hierarchical and authoritarian form, dominated by a committee of largely self-selected training and supervising analysts.

The fact that a good many of the early analysts of prominence in the American Psychoanalytic Association had been card-carrying members of the Communist Party of the USA (CP USA) (Richards, 2016) is significant primarily because people with a Leninist mind-set could feel quite comfortable in the psychoanalytic organizations founded and operated by Sigmund Freud and his epigones. Freud founded his "Secret Committee" (Grosskurth, 1991) around the same time that Lenin was developing his approach to political organization along very similar hierarchical and undemocratic lines. The subtitle of the article in which Richards describes the erstwhile Marxism-Leninism of a number of prominent analysts is "psychoanalysis as a subversive discipline." But the substance of his paper is the story of how whatever subversive elements psychoanalysis may contain came to be thoroughly displaced by the bourgeois aspirations and authoritarian inclinations of both the European emigres and the younger Americans who sought to wrest power from them, only to wield it themselves in equally authoritarian ways. Both groups had long since distanced themselves from their earlier leftist and notably undemocratic leftist, pasts. The Leninist, let alone the Stalinist, mind-set is not one adapted to auto-critique however much it may favor critique of *les autres*. This is not the place to review yet again the dismal history of excommunication from or marginalization by the IPA of many of the most creative minds in the history of psychoanalysis, from Adler, Jung, Rank and Ferenczi, to Fromm, Spotnitz, Kohut and Lacan.

This is not to deny the existence in psychoanalysis of voices committed to rational and empirical critique, only to suggest their exceptionality. The work of Morris Eagle (1984, 2011) provides an example of someone whose academic rather than full clinical initiation into the guild no doubt contributed an element of marginality that, combined with his continuing involvement in the university (and his formation at a time when the university itself valued critique) helped to preserve objectivity and a capacity for and willingness to engage more critically with the field than was typical of fully initiated practitioners. Among the latter, the work of Mitchell and Greenberg (1983) clearly aimed in the right direction, although it was seriously hampered both by their relational bias and their undialectical insistence that psychoanalytic theories must adhere to what they saw as either the "drive-structure" or the "relational-structure" models. Their denial of the validity or coherence of what they dismissed as "mixed-model" theories rendered them unable to deal adequately with Kleinian theory and the work of Kernberg that was so heavily influenced by it, for in these approaches "drive" had already been implicitly or explicitly redefined in relational terms.

There is no doubt that, today, in addition to the ideological Freudians, Kleinians, Lacanians, Kohutians and assorted relationalists and intersubjectivists, there exists a broad group of liberal-minded psychoanalysts who seek to be familiar with and to integrate, in practice if not in theory, most of the major current paradigms and to flexibly utilize them as they seem relevant and useful in differing clinical situations. This, in my opinion, is what a responsible psychoanalytic clinician ought to do and how he or she ought to be trained. The popularity of the works of Nancy McWilliams (1994, 2004) suggests that many colleagues may be operating in this non-ideological and pragmatic way. On one level, this is all to the good, but such pragmatic integration calls for the critical evaluation of competing theories and practices to determine which (or which parts of which) merit our continuing attention and which should simply be discarded. Among the latter are, for example, literal versions of Freudian drive theory that see our love and hate as bubbling up from the somatic sources that Freud was honest enough to admit he could not, especially in the case of aggression, identify; and the theory of primary narcissism, undifferentiation or oneness at the beginning, an idea never accepted by Melanie Klein (1952) and now empirically invalidated by infant research (Stern, 1985).

What is psychoanalysis?

In academic circles in the humanities and social sciences psychoanalysis often seems to be understood as a kind of *Weltanschauung* or worldview, like Marxism or existentialism, structuralism or poststructuralism, a conceptual perspective from which various human phenomena may be interpreted. On the other hand, many psychoanalysts themselves, especially those with backgrounds in so-called "mental health," seem to regard it less as *theoria* than as *praxis*, as a mainly clinical discipline. In my view, psychoanalysis at its best involves a dialectical relationship in which theory and practice are mutually determining, theory both informing practice and being re-formed by it. It may well be that, as Fonagy and Target (2003) indicate, psychoanalytic practice is not logically deducible from its theory. But that is because psychoanalysis is not reducible to science in any simple sense. After considerable equivocation on this point, Lacan appears to have concluded that psychoanalysis cannot be considered a science precisely because it remains committed to truth in a manner he considered distinct from modern science. In post-Cartesian science, "Truth was set aside; it became a secondary consideration compared to that of applying to reality a symbolic grid, expressible in numeric terms, and developing the endless set of relations among the elements constituting that symbolic grid" (Fink, 1995a, p. 60). In this view, while in no way to be identified with the religious and philosophical discourses from which modern science separated itself, psychoanalysis is irreducible to science in any ordinary sense: it is a peculiar discipline and *praxis* that desires less the truth *about* a subject than the subject's recognition of the hitherto occluded truth of its desire.

In a review of Frederick Crews's (2017) latest catalogue of Freud's faults and blunders, George Prochnik (2017) points out that, despite what Crews sees as the scientific invalidation of psychoanalysis, he acknowledges that Freud, along with Shakespeare and Jesus, "is destined to remain among us as the most influential of 20th century sages." Herein lies a conundrum: "The creator of a scientifically delegitimized blueprint of the human mind and of a largely discontinued psychotherapeutic discipline retains the cultural capital of history's greatest playwright and the erstwhile Son of God." Neither Crews nor his reviewer offer an explanation for this curious state of affairs. In my view, it is because, like Jesus and Shakespeare, Freud, Klein, Bion, Winnicott and company offer us existential, psychological and moral truths that transcend what empirical science is able to generate or comprehend.

In *Why Freud Survives. He's Been Debunked Again and Again—And Yet We Still Can't Give Him Up*, Louis Menand (2017) writes:

> The principal reason psychoanalysis triumphed over alternative theories and was taken up in fields outside medicine, like literary criticism, is that it presented its findings as inductive. Freudian theory was not a magic-lantern show, an imaginative projection that provided us with powerful metaphors for understanding the human condition. It was not "Paradise Lost"; it was science, a conceptual system wholly derived from clinical experience.
>
> (para. 42)

Yet despite widespread skepticism with respect to its status as science psychoanalysis persists—precisely *because* it provides powerful metaphors for understanding the human condition. In Menand's view:

> As Crews is right to believe, this Freud has long outlived psychoanalysis. For many years, even as writers were discarding the more patently absurd elements of his theory ... they continued to pay homage to Freud's unblinking insight into the human condition. That persona helped Freud to evolve, in the popular imagination, from a scientist into a kind of poet of the mind.
>
> (para. 33)

But having established Freud as a "poet of the mind," Menand proceeds, like the culture at large, to implicitly devalue poetry by confining truth to science, arguing that "... the thing about poets is that they cannot be refuted. No one asks of *Paradise Lost*: But is it true? Freud and his concepts, now converted into metaphors, joined the legion of the undead." But is it really true that no one asks of *Paradise Lost* is it true? Surely it remains a classic of Western literature precisely because, like the words of Jesus and the texts of Shakespeare, people have for generations found it contains existentially important truths and so have preserved it, undead, unlike the lesser poetry it allowed to die? In Western culture, we have for so long equated truth as such with merely one of its manifestations, the type of truth derived from empirical science, that it seems odd to even speak of poetic, let alone moral, truth. But the myths, sacred texts and literature we consider classic are celebrated over lesser forms not merely because they are more aesthetically pleasing but because they are at the same time felt to be *truer* in important ways.

Just as religion fails to colonize the sacred, so science holds no monopoly on truth, its competence being for the most part restricted to knowledge of material and biological objects, lithosphere and biosphere. But human beings are *subjects* as well as objects. Existence (*Existenz*) in the noösphere involves Imaginary and Symbolic transformations of the Real, of raw beta elements by the alpha function ("alphabetization") that, for Bion (1963), generates the conceptions, dreams, myths and metaphors that either live us or, through critical self-reflection, we learn to live and modify in creative ways. All this is not to deny a scientific dimension to psychoanalysis, but only to say it is irreducible to science, just as it is irreducible to poetry, hermeneutics or ethics. It is a peculiar mixture of all these things.

However we conceive the essence of psychoanalysis, hopefully the analyst's approach is informed by her familiarity with a wide range of psychoanalytic theories and models of the mind, with the patient's responses to her interventions influencing her understanding and leading to modifications and innovations in her theory and technique. According to Kant (1781–1787): "Thoughts without content are empty, intuitions without concepts are blind. The understanding can intuit nothing, the senses can think nothing. Only through their unison can knowledge arise." But it is important that we place our theories within the wider context of the experience and intuition, and (let it be said) the wisdom, derived not merely from training and practice but from living (Lomas, 1987). In psychoanalytic circles there is the widespread illusion that virtually anyone, provided the right training, can become a "good enough" analyst, when the truth is that good analysts, if not "born rather than made," are people who have a psychological gift that, if they are lucky, will manage to survive disruption by training and occasionally be enhanced by it. In my view, a major part of that gift is what I call *conscience*, something that is quite distinct from the superego (Carveth, 2013, 2016a, 2016b, and Chapter 2 here), and that no amount of training can provide. Conscience is grounded in the true as distinct from the false self (Winnicott, 1960a). In order to be a true analyst one must be, to some degree, despite our brokenness and fallenness, a true self. As in the case of poetic and moral truth here we are in an area—perhaps a "transitional area" (Winnicott, 1953, 1971a)—beyond the ken of empirical truth and natural science.

The illness metaphor

Whatever scientific and technical dimensions it may possess, psychoanalysis is also, and not peripherally but centrally, an ethical enterprise, valuing life over death, love over hate, kindness over cruelty, gratitude over envy and consciousness over unconsciousness (Carveth, 2013, chapter one). For this reason it cannot be reduced to an exclusively or primarily scientific or technical process, or even to an entirely rational one, since the "oughts" or values that underlie it cannot be derived from any "is" or empirical description. The desire of the properly functioning analyst—that is, the analyst who is not psychopathic or excessively narcissistic—is grounded in conscience, transcending the merely normative superego. Although he works hard to disguise the fact, Freud, like Shakespeare and Jesus, has "the mind of a moralist" (Rieff, 1959).

As Thomas Szasz (1961) pointed out, the value judgments underlying the theory and practice of psychotherapy and psychoanalysis have traditionally been masked by the language of health and illness. Although Freud mostly hides his ethical vision behind a medical façade, in a few places he makes comments that, like parapraxes, momentarily and partially elude the censorship. Yet even when he writes, "… in the last resort we must begin to love in order not to fall ill, and we are bound to fall ill if … we are unable to love" (Freud, 1914, p. 84), love, far from being an end in itself, is reduced to a necessary means: we *must* begin to love if we want to avoid falling ill. In Freud's seemingly utilitarian view, health values are made to appear primary. But if they really were it would make little sense to risk health or life in pursuit of other values—for a woman, for example, to endanger her life and health by choosing to give birth to a child or, more generally, to risk sacrificing one's health and life for another, or out of commitment to a cause. Like many evolutionary psychologists today, neither Freud nor such followers as Heinz Hartmann (1939, 1960) understood that as creatures who, while certainly remaining animals, have significantly transcended our animality through our attainment of symbolic functioning, human beings are no longer exclusively guided by the biological values of life and health, but consider many things more important than mere adaptation and survival. Who was it (Thoreau? Bertrand Russell?) who said: "There are some societies in which the only place a decent person can be is in jail"? At Nuremberg we hung Nazis for following orders we insisted they should have disobeyed even at the cost of certain death.

Instead of acknowledging the values entailed in negative judgments of behavior or experience we often resort instead to the language of illness describing it as "sick" or "mad" rather than "bad." If, as Szasz explains, there is evidence that satisfies the scientific community that certain forms of "mental illness" have an organic cause, then these, by definition, are *physical*, not *mental* illnesses. Their symptoms may be expressed mentally, but if such proof were to exist, then their causes would be known to be physical and, hence, they would be physically-based medical conditions. Szasz argued that the category "mental illness" is in reality reserved for conditions people *want* to believe are illnesses but that cannot be proved to be illnesses. But why do we want to believe these conditions are illnesses? Because we are reluctant to admit we dislike them to such a degree that it seems insufficient to acknowledge the role of our values in a judgment we want to claim as objective. To say I dislike you says something about me as well as you. To say you are sick puts the focus on you more than me and it places your behavior in a category beyond the limit of what I can reasonably be expected to tolerate. Certainly there is objectivity in descriptions of the clusters of behavior and experience we call hysteria, obsession, compulsion, paranoia, narcissism, etc., but in calling these "illnesses" or even "disorders" we obscure the fact that we are devaluing them because they fall short of or violate our values, tastes and ideals.

As Szasz argues, to say a person is mentally ill is comparable to calling an economy sick: one is speaking metaphorically. Since metaphors are frequently literalized we end up confusing metaphorical illness with real illness. "Typhoid fever is a disease. Spring fever is not a disease; it is a figure of speech, a metaphoric disease. All mental diseases are metaphoric diseases, misrepresented as real diseases and mistaken for real diseases" (Szasz, 2004). Since conversion hysteria entails evading painful feelings and psychological or emotional conflicts by converting these into pseudo-physical symptoms based upon unconscious mimicry (as distinct from psychosomatic disease, which is real disease in which emotional factors play a significant role, and from malingering, which is conscious faking of physical illness or dysfunction), then psychiatry is hysterical insofar as it attributes emotional suffering to supposed physical causes in the absence of supporting evidence for its claims. Like other forms of hysteria, psychiatry is highly resistant to a psychoanalytic cure: it resists facing and working through the emotional conflicts at the root of "mental illnesses" insisting, despite the absence of evidence, that they are physically-based conditions.

Freud himself was an hysteric. His famous hysterical fainting episodes provide merely one illustration. Although for a time he tried to conceptualize his persistent symptoms, including depression, as arising from what he called an *actual* as distinct from a *psycho*neurosis, a condition of an essentially somatic order supposedly without psychological meaning, the concept of the *actual* neurosis was dropped by subsequent psychoanalysis because no cases of it were found. This notion of the *actual* neurosis is an early instance of the denial of agency and meaning that is typical of hysterical psychiatry. Freud, however, was eventually able to acknowledge the psychoneurotic basis of a range of symptoms. Consequently, psychoanalysis has often been able to see through hysterical denial, repression and somatization to the motives and meanings underlying the manifest behavior.

Naturally, those who seek to evade the mental pain consequent upon recognizing the implications of Szasz's argument will do so by attempting to undermine or deconstruct the distinction between mental and physical that it rests on. They will argue that this distinction reflects an outmoded mind/body dualism and that, in reality, these categories are inseparable: every psychological state has a physical basis or effects and every physical state has corresponding psychological and emotional manifestations. In this view, human reality is psychophysical and it makes no sense to fall back into a dualism that would separate illness into "physical" on the one hand and "mental" on the other as it is always already both. A truly modern perspective, it is argued, must reject such dualism for all illness (redefined subjectively as suffering) is psychosomatic, manifesting in both the psyche and the soma. If, in this view, there is no mental illness that is only because there is no physical illness either, for illness is always both, i.e., psychosomatic. All suffering, by definition, is now illness. In the past, it was only that portion of human suffering caused by objectively defined organic pathology that fell within the province of medicine, strictly defined. Mental suffering—that is, suffering apparently not arising from objective medical pathology—constituted an ambiguous field that psychology and psychiatry shared with ministers, priests and pastoral counselors, those interested in the "cure of souls," and philosophers concerned with man's "existence" (*Dasein*). But over time psychiatry came to colonize this area essentially through medicalizing definitions of mental suffering as illness.

As clever as this rejection of dualism and broadening of the concept of the psychosomatic may appear, it entails a misuse of the deconstructive method, which properly employed, seeks to undermine not only false distinctions but also regressive fusions, not merely to link what has been separated, but to separate out what has been merged. The reality is that some illnesses are defined not primarily *subjectively*, i.e., in terms of felt discomfort, distress or pain or even in *functional* terms as in the case, for example, of paralyzes of unknown origin, but *objectively* in terms of observable tissue pathology. While in the latter conditions there is often psychological distress as well as physical pathology, the condition is defined and diagnosed by the latter, not the former. While there is no doubt that all illnesses are psychosomatic in the very broad sense that psychological as well as somatic factors play a part, this way of defining the term "psychosomatic" represents a fundamental alteration of its former meaning: an objectively defined medical illness believed to have significant psychological or emotional causes. It is ironic that, today, one is more likely to find recognition of the psychological and emotional basis of hysterical and psychosomatic conditions among real doctors than among psychiatrists. The latter, out of their very desperation to be doctors after all, seek to affirm the non-mental (albeit as yet indemonstrable) organic basis of such conditions, resisting the very idea that they might be the outcome of psycho-emotional factors. Having argued, against Szasz, that mental illness *does* really exist, today the psychiatrist, a supposed expert in mental illnesses, is busy arguing that such illnesses are not really mental but physical (neurological, neuro-chemical, etc.). This deprives psychiatry of its *raison d'être* and the psychiatrist of her role, for she is neither a neurologist nor a pharmacologist.

Where in all this should the psychoanalyst stand? As Szasz recognized, although mental illness is a myth, the psychological and emotional conflict and suffering of human beings is all too real and irreducible to supposed (albeit unproven) organic causes. Due to our relative freedom from biological determination as *les animaux dénaturés* (Vercors, 1952), conflict, anxiety and guilt are unavoidable features of our existence. While it is important to distinguish existential from neurotic anxiety (Kierkegaard, 1843a), authentic guilt from mere "guilt-feelings" (Buber, 1965), and persecutory from reparative guilt (Klein, 1948; Grinberg, 1965), these are all conditions of the human *psyche,* which while requiring the existence of a functioning brain, is no more reducible to its organic foundation than a TV program to the TV set that displays it. Psychoanalysis entails a dialogue through which the analysand's core anxieties, phantasies and conflicts are reviewed, revived and to some extent relived in the transference to the analyst and in which resistances to de-repression may be analyzed and overcome through the medium of full speech and the analyst's empathic understanding, forbearance, containment and tactful confrontation.

In the physical sciences, we have had to learn to bear the principles of uncertainty and complementarity and the unavoidable incompleteness of mathematical systems (Barrett, 1958, chapter two). Knowing one thing always entails not knowing others. We raise one thing into *figure* only by dropping others into *ground*. In psychoanalysis, we are interested in facilitating both conscious reflection about what has hitherto been pre-reflective and promoting growing awareness of what has been dynamically repressed. Yet the knowledge I acquire about myself as other (the self that is other than my specular ego) necessarily excludes both the subject engaged in knowing it and what in me yet remains beyond this expanded self-awareness. Psychoanalysis is inadequately comprehended in terms of other discourses, such as the medical (the analyst is concerned not with the body or the brain, but with the mind), or the educational (the analyst is concerned less with the transmission of knowledge than with its discovery), or the religious (while, like the properly functioning priest, motivated by conscience, the properly functioning analyst does not serve the superego or the Church, though psychoanalytic institutions inevitably blur this distinction).

Ideological vs. critical psychoanalysis

Failing to maintain the dialectic between theory and practice, if some colleagues privilege the latter over the former, often in a pragmatic, eclectic, "anything goes" fashion, others do the reverse. In my experience it is not rare to encounter psychoanalysts so closely identified with their particular paradigm or school of analytic thought that they seem more committed to adhering to their privileged therapeutic ideology, orthodox or heterodox, than to the goal of helping patients. Like the proverbial mathematician who rose at the annual meeting to deliver the toast,—"Here's to pure mathematics, and may it never be of any damn use to anyone!"—such colleagues appear to have forgotten that psychoanalysis is a form of psycho*therapy*. The degree of its helpfulness to the patient at times seems of lesser significance to true believers than the degree to which it adheres to idealized standards of what in their view a true psychoanalytic process should look like. The fact that the operation was conducted with precision can even render insignificant the fact that the patient "died." Even those of us committed to a view of psychoanalysis as helping analysands recognize the discourse of the other (the unconscious) should at the same time be concerned as to whether or not this helps. In some, more or less psychotic, cases something else is indicated, as many analysts, including the later Lacan, have understood.

If, following Beit-Hallahmi (2015; Carveth, 2016d), we regard magical thinking as a defining feature of religion, then the essentially religious character of ideological psychoanalysis has long been evident. Many illustrations of this might be cited, but one of the more concerning instances I have encountered among mainstream psychoanalysts is the suspicion of and prejudice against colleagues who were analyzed by analysts subsequently discredited for boundary violations (with patients other than those who subsequently became analysts and the targets of suspicion). It is as if the sins of the fathers are visited upon the sons who are seen as tainted by the fathers' transgressions. "Like father, like son" seems to be the belief when it comes to the "offspring" of disgraced analysts for whom the stipulation "innocent until proven guilty" appears suspended. Unlike the children of ordinary transgressors, they are denied the benefit of the doubt—unless and until they purify themselves by undergoing another analysis with a not-yet-discredited analyst, an analytic version of purification rituals such as the *mikvah*. In so imagining the power of analysis to do harm when conducted by a subsequently disgraced analyst, these colleagues give evidence of their belief in its omnipotent power to do good—as if good parents cannot produce bad children, or bad parents good ones. As if we *know* a whole lot more about how things work than we do. Ironically, this prejudice suggests those who hold it conceive psychoanalysis as a process in which identification rather than discovery of the unconscious is paramount—an idea they might question in theory if not, apparently, in practice. For Lacan (1973), at least:

> Any conception of analysis that is articulated—innocently or not, God only knows—to defining the end of the analysis as an identification with the analyst, by that very fact makes an admission of its limits. Any analysis that one teaches as having to be terminated by identification with the analyst reveals, by the same token, that its true motive force is elided.
>
> (p. 271)

For the orthodox, only treatment conducted by a member of the IPA at a rate of four (now, thankfully, three) sessions per week with the patient reclining on a couch counts as psychoanalysis. By this definition psychoanalysis is all but disappearing, except in those few places in the world where government-funded health care schemes cover it when provided by analysts who happen to be physicians. Even here, many of the patients enjoying this form of treatment (as I confess I did) are themselves candidates in analytic training being analyzed by medical training analysts. In today's world, even where cost is not an issue, many people are too busy to be able to carve out of their work week sufficient hours to travel back and forth to an analyst's office in order to be in it for four or even three, fifty (or more likely forty-five) minute hours per week. The reality is that most analysts worldwide are seeing their patients once or twice a week, sometimes sitting rather than reclining and, increasingly, meeting via telephone, Skype or FaceTime.

While this fact is a cause of great concern for the orthodox who define psychoanalysis so narrowly, it is less so for those who define it more broadly (e.g., Gorman, 2002, 2008) as talk therapy delivered by a trained analytic therapist with a psychoanalytic intent and guided by psychoanalytic goals and principles—namely, by inviting analysands' free speech and encouraging careful attention to their language, phantasies, transferences, resistances and repetitions (and to the therapist's countertransference), in order to promote the emergence into reflective consciousness of what has hitherto been pre-reflectively and dynamically unconscious. Defined broadly in this way, psychoanalysis can occur at varying frequencies, employing couch or chair or distance technology with individuals, couples or groups. Most training analysts are honest enough to admit that sometimes an analytic process may occur in once weekly treatment, while there is no guarantee it will emerge at four or even five sessions per week. This is not to deny the advantages often derived from more frequent sessions and the use of the couch. While, like candidates in psychoanalytic training, some patients may certainly benefit from and some may require more frequent sessions (as in the case of Mrs. A, discussed at the end of Chapter 2), a great deal can often be accomplished by the talented and experienced therapist at one or two sessions per week, even when delivered by distance technology. This may well be the future of psychoanalysis. Beyond the clinic, I believe its future lies in the continuing development of the new field of critical psychosocial studies. Here scholars, researchers and practitioners from a wide range of disciplinary backgrounds and theoretical paradigms may learn to dialogue and work together, overcoming not only the estrangement between sociology and psychoanalysis (Chancer & Andrews, 2014), but also between the competing paradigms within philosophical, social and psychoanalytic thought.

In the following I offer a number of essays in critique—of Freud, Bion, Winnicott, Lacan, Fromm, Racker, Kohut, Becker, Britton and others. Toward the end of my essay on Racker's concepts of concordant and complementary countertransference, I raise the question as to why it is that Racker's error (associating the concordant countertransference with empathy) has gone largely unnoticed for over half a century in psychoanalysis. I point to an obvious collective resistance to anyone having the temerity to even comment at all critically upon the Emperor's dress, let alone to call him naked. Rigorous and direct critique of established figures has been pathologized in psychoanalytic circles and viewed as a form of oedipal acting-out against authority. In my view, it is so seen by people who have adopted what I, along with Loewald (1979) and Sagan (1988), view as itself a pathological resolution of the Oedipus complex on the part of those who, instead of creatively finding a way to symbolically "kill" the parents and, in sublimated form, to fulfill incestuous desire—that is, to grow up—confuse deference and masochistic submission to authority with maturity. Here fulfillment of the demand for recognition by and identification with the *subject-supposed-to-know* (Lacan, 1967–1968) are confused with emancipation of the drive.

Dialectical deconstruction

Here and there additions and revisions have been made to bring the papers collected here more or less up to date. Nietzsche (1901) distinguished the decadent desire to destroy for the sake of destruction from the healthy desire to clear away and open up a space for creativity. One hopes that out of the negativity of critique something positive may emerge. Perhaps by chipping away at what seems wrong or one-sided some aspect of truth may be glimpsed. I hope what emerges is a vision of a *critical* as distinct from an *ideological* psychoanalysis that far from promoting identification with the competing paradigms brings them into mutual dialogue and critique. In this way, hopefully, the concretized phantasies, constructions, literalized metaphors and contrasts, links and splits that bedevil the thinking of psychoanalysts as much as their analysands may be dialectically deconstructed. The image of the Roman god Janus was chosen for the cover of this book because it suggests (Rothenberg, 1989) the need to bear the tension of the opposites, not privileging one pole over the other, in order to move dialectically beyond them. If the term deconstruction seems excessively negative or unconstructive, this to me is part of its virtue. It is the analysand's business, not the analyst's, to find a way to *be* and then construct a life-and-death in the clearing opened up through deconstruction of the fixations, delusions, illusions, idols and inhibitions that have hitherto kept both the analysand and his or her analyst in thrall. Although in his theory of thinking Bion (1959, 1962a, 1962b) fails to adhere to a truly dialectical perspective in that he privileges linking over separating (see Chapter 9) and conceives thinking as *coupling* (of a preconception with a realization, even a negative realization) and not also as *conflict* leading to a higher-order compromise-formation or synthesis, his overall understanding of psychoanalysis as promoting the progressive evolution of the mind toward emotional truth is congruent with the approach elaborated here.

* * *

Chapter 1 offers a Kleinian critique of Freud's *Civilization and Its Discontents* and deconstructs several of the binary oppositions through which his argument is constructed. When he finally overcame denial and recognized human destructiveness as an equally fundamental part of human nature as sexuality, Freud proceeded to project his earlier naiveté onto the Bible, which unlike his own earlier Enlightenment optimism, had all along conveyed a dark view of human nature, but notably one that recognized our destructiveness as existential instead of falsely naturalizing and projecting it onto the supposed animality in humanity as an instinctual drive. In so attributing human aggression to the id, Freud failed to recognize its roots in superego and ego, in socially internalized pseudo-morality, individual and collective narcissism and technical rationality, and to see that what is prosocial about us arises from our mammalian and primate animality and our identification with our nurturers. Because, unlike Melanie Klein, he did not distinguish persecutory from reparative guilt (superego from conscience), Freud bemoaned the build-up of the former in civilization while failing to recognize our need for much more of the latter. The chapter concludes with a brief discussion of Kenneth Lonergan's recent film *Manchester by the Sea* that movingly depicts both the savagery of the superego and conscientious efforts to counteract it.

Chapter 2 extends the differentiation between conscience and the superego. Freud's decision to fold conscience and the ego-ideal into the superego restricted our attention to conflicts among and within only three of the five major mental structures, obscuring conflicts such as those between the superego and the conscience, the conscience and the ego-ideal, the ego and the ego-ideal and the ego and the conscience. Whereas the superego is an identification with the aggressor turning aggression against the self, the conscience is an identification with the nurturer mediating love and concern for others and the true self. Whereas the superego generates persecutory anxiety and punitive guilt, the conscience generates concern, depressive anxiety (not depression), and the need to make reparation. Although, unlike the superego, the conscience is not sadistic and tyrannical, but loving and forgiving, its "bite" is sharp and its "still small voice" insistent. Roy Schafer's so-called "loving and beloved superego" is, I argue, not really the superego at all but the conscience. It is essential to distinguish guilt grounded in one's own wrongdoing from that induced (*via* projective identification) by people unwilling to acknowledge faults and failings in themselves. Analysts who conflate neutrality vis-à-vis the superego with neutrality vis-à-vis the conscience are in clinical error, for while analysts must refrain from normative judgment they must also carry the conscience in the treatment until such time as their analysands are able to accept this responsibility themselves.

The chapter concludes with a discussion of the case of Mrs. A, in illustration of these points.

Chapter 3 distinguishes illusioning and disillusioning, constructionist and deconstructionist, identifying and disidentifying, gnostic and agnostic elements in the therapeutic process. While ultimately favoring the latter, I argue both are necessary, for in order to analyze we must first provide the conditions that make analysis possible. With more disturbed patients' techniques of emotional attunement, mirroring and joining the resistance may be necessary means to the ultimate end of analysis—provided, that is, the empathically immersed analyst does not succumb to projective counteridentification, "going native" like the proverbial anthropologist and joining the culture instead of studying it, remaining trapped in the Lacanian Imaginary and never making it back to the Symbolic. While more integrated analysands may benefit from a technique conveying "paternal function" and promoting "acceptance of castration," many of the patients (sufferers) who seek our help have come undone and need help, "maternal function," in putting themselves together again, as the later Lacan himself appeared to recognize in his work on the *sinthome*.

Balancing the Freudian and Lacanian bias toward separation ("paternal function") is the bias toward connection ("maternal function") characteristic of self psychology, intersubjective and relational theory to which we turn in Chapter 4. In my view the "identity diffused," unstructured, "narcissistic personality of our time"—the "Tragic Man" whose emergence both Kohut and Marcuse thought rendered the Freudian concept of "Guilty Man" obsolescent—turns out to be guilty after all. For the deficits and defects characterizing the disordered self, do not only stem from inadequate provision, but also involve the self-directed rage consequent upon trauma and deprivation. Whereas the "narcissistic neuroses" had been considered unanalyzable because they do not manifest "object-instinctual" transferences, Kohut usefully described their analyzable "selfobject" transferences. In light of infant research that increasingly called into question the Freudian idea of primary narcissism or undifferentiated states of autism and symbiosis at the beginning (Stern, 1985), Kohut redefined the concept of the selfobject as performing needed functions *for* the self, not incompletely differentiated *from* it. The difference between Kohut's view of the idealizing transference as resumption of a thwarted developmental need and Kernberg's view of it as a defensive reaction to underlying destructive wishes likely arose from work with different patient populations. For Kohut, the therapeutic process involves a "disruption-repair cycle": disruptions due to inevitable empathic failures are repaired by being understood as triggering painful states of fragmentation and depletion in vulnerable selves who may turn to substances or "driven" sexuality or aggression ("disintegration products") in an attempt to hold themselves together. Three patterns of theorizing are distinguished. Self psychology displays elements of monistic and dualistic thinking; intersubjectivity theory is markedly dualistic; while Freudian theory displays both dualistic and dialectical trends. A range of dualisms are dialectically deconstructed. An extensive summary of the argument is presented at the end of the chapter.

Chapter 5 offers both an appreciation and a critique of Lacanian theory. Despite its anal-sadistic obscurantism and related defects, Lacan's work has much to offer. His deliteralization of Freudian discourse and humanization of the unconscious as "neither primordial nor instinctual" is invaluable, as are his distinctions between human desire and organic need and between the phallus and the penis. The Sartrean *néant* becomes Lacan's *manqué à être*, the lack of being that de-stabilizes identity and generates desire. Whatever empirical support Lacan's theory of the mirror stage may or may not enjoy, his vision of the (specular) ego as an Imaginary idol or false self, distinct from the barred subject of the Symbolic opened up through "acceptance of castration" (read "crucifixion") is too important to ignore. While Lacanian theory may seem less a "return to Freud" than a baptizing of him, Lacan's secularized Catholicism is not to be confused with attempts to exploit his concepts in the service of religion, the triumph of which for Lacan would represent the defeat of psychoanalysis. Lacan's phallocentrism and his privileging of absence over presence, the Symbolic over what Kristeva calls the semiotic, are subjected to critique, while his view of human desire as the desire of the other is affirmed. In the earlier, Lacan psychosis is understood as "foreclosure" of the gap opened up between subject and object, while perversion results from failure of oedipalization to establish another, the third, as the object of the mother's desire. The later, Lacan offers a view of psychosis as disconnection of the Borromean rings and the *sinthome* as a means of reconnecting them. A dialectical psychoanalysis transcending both the "metaphysics of presence" and the "metaphysics of absence" and capable of offering "maternal" as well as "paternal" function is affirmed.

Chapter 6 entails a critique of the melancholic existentialism of Ernest Becker and Peter Berger. Like the "metaphysics of absence" that the early Lacan grounded in a theory of primary fragmentation (*le corps morcelé*), these authors relativize all world-views as humanly constructed illusions except their own vision of the Real as chaos and death. For Becker and the "terror management theory" deriving from his work, human beings suffer from an unbearable primary death anxiety irreducible to infantile fears. Society offers illusions of immortality for the denial of death. Dismissing all positive attitudes toward human existence as founded upon denial and illusion, Becker fails to question his own fundamental attitudes of despair and disgust, Similarly, Berger fails to relativize the state of chaos or anomy that he posits as the reality underlying the socially constructed illusions that make life bearable. Ideologies that rationalize depression by grounding it in the alleged reality of chaos and death defend against recognition of its other possible sources, such as unconscious guilt. By "existentializing" mental pain instead of analyzing it, these perspectives rationalize the leap into illusion as the only alternative to despair, thus, precluding the relief that might be attainable through deeper self-knowledge.

In Chapter 7 Heinrich Racker's contribution to our understanding of countertransference is discussed, specifically his distinction between concordant and complementary countertransference. Like Helene Deutsch, Racker was mostly concerned with the complementary countertransference because he identified the concordant with empathy. But concordant countertransference, when it is relatively unconscious, may disturb empathy as much as relatively unconscious complementary countertransference. Both may enhance empathy and understanding when they are relatively conscious and the object of the analyst's self-reflection. Several clinical vignettes are discussed to illustrate this point. If, as I claim, Racker was mistaken in associating the concordant countertransference with empathy, why has this error gone largely unrecognized in our literature for over half a century? The answer, I believe, is an intellectual inhibition due to widespread interpretation of critique of established theories and theorists as Oedipal acting-out and the resulting taboo against it.

Two important themes in Donald Winnicott's work are addressed in Chapter 8: his theory of the role of aggression in the finding of an object and his notion of a core self that must never be found. In the spirit of comparative psychoanalysis I associate the narcissism that characterizes relations with subjective objects with the pathology of the "false self," Heidegger's inauthentic existence and Lacan's Imaginary ego; while relations with objective objects are associated with the "true self," authentic being-in-the-world, and the (barred) subject of the Symbolic. Winnicott's obscure discussion of the role of destruction in the development of object relations is clarified in light of his posthumous writings. His notion of a permanently incommunicado core of the self is traced to an unresolved schizoid element in his character resulting in a sense of reality as persecutory, as in the melancholic existentialism of Becker and Berger and the "metaphysics of absence" of the early Lacan.

Chapter 9 offers a dialectical critique of Neo-Kleinian theory insofar as it has envisaged emotional growth as development beyond the splitting and part-object functioning of the paranoid-schizoid position to the ambivalence and whole-object functioning of the depressive position (Ps→D). In this view, Ps functioning is regarded as primitive in contrast to the maturity of D. But this perspective is itself a manifestation of splitting, viewing Ps as all-bad and D as all-good, failing to recognize Klein's own understanding of splitting as an achievement, the first organization of the mind, however much failure to overcome it is a problem. A dialectical understanding recognizes the good as well as the bad in Ps (including the adaptive necessity of splitting in defending ourselves against predators) and the bad as well as the good in D and seeks to synthesize what is creative and life-enhancing in both. Bion's shift from writing Ps→D to writing Ps↔D only appears to do this. Bion's and Britton's conception of creativity as involving cycles of disintegration followed by reintegration involves a valid recapitulation of contributions by others, but their associations of the paranoid-schizoid position with fragmentation rather than order, and the depressive position with order and with depression, are called into question. Bion's vision of psychopathology as attacks on linking needs to be supplemented by recognition that psychopathology equally entails attacks on de-linking or separating. The claim by the Symingtons that Bion's approach is dialectical is disputed. In a truly dialectical perspective the "feminine" bias of the "linkers" is not replaced by the "masculine" bias of the "splitters," but by a "bisexual" concept of mental evolution through cycles of integration, disintegration and reintegration on higher levels.

Chapter 10 offers an appreciation and critique of the work of Erich Fromm whose contributions are currently undergoing a long overdue revival. Fromm has often been classified as a Neo-Freudian member of the culturistic school of psychoanalysis. But whereas in rejecting the under-socialized model of human nature characterizing Freud's biologistic instinct theory the culturalists succumbed to an over-socialized, socially determinist model, Fromm embraced an existential humanism (with similarities to, yet profound differences from, Sartrean existentialism) offering a dialectical understanding in which human reality is irreducible to nature or culture or their simple interaction. Like Marx, Fromm presents a qualified essentialism distinguishing human nature in general from its various socially and historically conditioned forms. While critical of aspects of Fromm's work, such as his resort to the naturalistic fallacy, exaggeration of humanity's break with nature, sociological relativization of the Oedipus complex, and anthropocentrism, his critique of the authoritarian superego is endorsed, as is his clear understanding of the ethical foundations of psychoanalysis and the role of humane values in clinical practice.

In my "Postscript," I summarize the main themes of this work. We need to reverse Freud's decision to merge conscience and ego-ideal into the superego and recognize the important distinction between the merely normative and often immoral superego grounded in identification with the aggressor, and the conscience grounded in our mammalian and primate heritage and early identification with the nurturer. Not only has the role of conscience been obscured, but so has the very nature of psychoanalysis as a "value-infused" rather than a "value-free" enterprise. Our confusion with respect to values has had destructive consequences for our theory, our practice and our institutional life. Rightly seeking not to be "superego-ish" with patients, we have not clearly understood it is our responsibility to carry the conscience in the treatment until such time as the patients under our care are able to assume this responsibility themselves. From the beginning, unconscionably authoritarian, hierarchical, secretive and exclusionary practices have characterized our organizations. Due to our confusion of conscience with mere rule-following driven by castration anxiety (superego) we have precluded its adequate assessment in applicants for analytic training and promotion to training analyst status. In addition to promoting comparative psychoanalysis whereby the concepts central to different paradigms are compared and contrasted, my work is both a plea for and an exercise in dialectical thinking. In identifying the binary oppositions in play in our own and our analysands' discourses and exposing the privileging of one pole over another, we aim to advance toward the ultimately incompletely achievable synthesis that it is our responsibility to seek even while recognizing its ultimate unattainability.

Chapter 1

Civilization and Its Discontents
A Kleinian re-view

As early as his 1908 essay on *"Civilized" Sexual Morality and Modern Nervous Illness,* Freud was preoccupied with what he saw as the conflict between socialization pressures and our sexuality and aggression. But whereas in this early essay he places the term "civilized" in quotation marks to indicate ironic distance and goes on to offer a critique of an excessively repressive civilization, some two decades later, in *Civilization and Its Discontents,* the aging Freud (1930) has pretty much switched sides. Now civilization is a "thin veneer" protecting us from our own and others' barbarous drives. While a few people of exceptional strength of character may be able to inhibit their antisocial drives without deceiving themselves about them, and a few may have the talent to redirect or "sublimate" them in prosocial directions, the majority are forced to resort to repression, setting up the inevitable disguised return of the repressed in neurosis, the price of civilized order.

Civilization, Freud concluded, requires inhibition, especially of what he had come to view as our innate aggressive drive, which though exacerbated by frustration was, for him, ultimately a biologically-given, asocial or antisocial element of our human nature:

> men are not gentle creatures who want to be loved, and who at the most can defend themselves if they are attacked; they are, on the contrary, creatures among whose instinctual endowments is to be reckoned a powerful share of aggressiveness.
>
> (p. 111)

To support his view he quotes the Roman playwright Titus Maccius Plautus: *Homo homini lupus est*—man is a wolf to man. But this comparison is deeply unfair … to the wolves, a highly prosocial species that, to my knowledge, has never been guilty of designing death camps, or dropping atomic bombs on civilian populations, or videotaping the rape, torture and murder of their victims for future enjoyment of their humiliation and pain. Freud's thinking often transcends common sense, but here he succumbs to it, projecting the perverse destructiveness unique to humans onto animals, claiming all this "reveals man as a savage beast to whom consideration towards his own kind is something alien" (p. 111).

In the face of the devastation of Europe brought about by the First World War, together with the masochistic self-destructiveness he had come to recognize in so many patients, Freud (1920) finally overcame his longstanding resistance to acknowledging aggression as an equally fundamental part of human nature as sexuality and announced his final dual-drive theory of *Eros* and *Thanatos*. He then proceeded to misattribute (project) the naive optimism he had earlier shared with Enlightenment thought onto the Bible:

> Why have we ourselves needed such a long time before we decided to recognize an aggressive instinct? ... We should probably have met with little resistance if we had wanted to ascribe an instinct with such an aim to animals. But to include it in the human constitution appears sacrilegious; it contradicts too many religious presumptions and social conventions. No, man must be naturally good or at least good-natured. If he occasionally shows himself brutal, violent or cruel, these are only passing disturbances of his emotional life, for the most part provoked, or perhaps only the consequences of the inexpedient social regulations which he has hitherto imposed on himself.
> (Freud, 1933, p. 103)

In this passage, Freud seems entirely unaware of the fact that the optimism of his own earlier thought that he now mocks belongs not to the Bible, but to elements of Enlightenment thought and the social sciences stemming from it. It was his own loyalty to the anti-religious Enlightenment and his estrangement from the Bible (and the father who beseeched him to return to it) that prevented him from overcoming his own naiveté until the First World War and his own clinical experience finally made him see what the Bible had recognized all along. In its vision of human beings as fallen, perverse and broken sinners, even after salvation or redemption, the Bible is far more congruent with Freud's late, much darker view of human nature than he was ever prepared to acknowledge. Unlike Freud, however, the Bible does not naturalize or biologize human destructiveness, instead recognizing it as a misuse of our uniquely human freedom and self-awareness—that is, it maintains an essentially existentialist, rather than a biologically and/or environmentally determinist view (Fromm, 1941, 1973; Herberg, 1957; Niebuhr, 1957).

Naturally, I am in no way disputing the fact of the human aggressiveness, destructiveness and sadism to which Freud calls our attention, only his characterization of it as bestial or animalistic. Like Freud, we commonly project onto animals the dark, uniquely human traits we do not wish to acknowledge in ourselves. In *The Uniqueness of Man*, the distinguished biologist Sir Julian Huxley (1943) argued that now that the battle waged on behalf of Darwin by his grandfather, Thomas Henry Huxley, had been won, we could afford to turn our attention to what a unique and truly bizarre kind of animal we are, both biologically and psychologically. It is my experience that, today, any mention of this line of thought, any stress on the discontinuity between humanity and the rest of nature, any emphasis upon our uniquely symbolic consciousness, is likely to bring down on one's head a chorus of criticism of the supposed arrogant anthropocentrism entailed in any such claim and its blindness toward humanity's ecological destructiveness. Such critics generally fail to realize they themselves are now making the case for "the uniqueness of man": the uniquely destructive consequences for both human beings and their ecosystems that follow from our relative freedom from the instinctual controls and biological determinants governing the behavior of other species.

We seem reluctant to recognize the uniqueness of our destructiveness. We like to think of it as "inhuman" when, regrettably, it is one of the things most human about us. We engage in massive projection of this uniquely human destructiveness on to animals that, unlike us, mostly fight and kill to survive and protect their young, not to impose their favored abstract ideologies upon one another, nor to amass great wealth while impoverishing others, nor to enjoy sadistic pleasure. The latter requires the uniquely human capacity for empathy, by which I do not mean sympathy, but the purely cognitive capacity for what George Mead (1934) called "taking the role of the other"—imagining oneself in the other's shoes, as it were. Without this capacity the sadist would be unable to enjoy the other's pain or humiliation, or the con man to find the words needed to manipulate his mark. Empathy and sympathy are two quite different things. Empathy informs me you are in pain; sympathy enables me to care and wish to help. A student will occasionally counter the idea of sadism as a uniquely human trait, protesting: "My cat is sadistic! Look at how it tortures and toys with the mouse it captured!" I point out that if you take away the mouse and substitute a crumpled bit of paper, the cat will do the same thing. It enjoys batting around the mouse or the ball of paper, but not because it attributes suffering to either. Sadism is a human capacity we prefer to think of as "inhuman."

Look at our everyday language.

"He's a real animal!"
"She's a parasite."
"He's a leech."
"She's a bitch."
"He's a snake in the grass."
"She's a bloodsucker."
"His behavior was beastly."
"She's a cow."
"He's a dirty dog."
"She's a vulture."
"He's a total rat."
"She's a vixen."
"He's a pig."
"She's a Black Widow."
"He's a cockroach."

Then there are the famous human "monsters" we "bestialize":

"Julius Streicher: the Beast of Franconia."
"Ilse Koch: the Beast (Witch, Bitch) of Buchenwald."
"Clifford Olsen: the Beast of British Columbia."
"Ilsa: She-Wolf of the SS."

Recent research on the moral behavior of animals (De Wall, 1997, 2009) tends to indicate that, for the most part, they are not "beastly," at least not in the ways humans often are. Only human beings capable of empathy can invent diabolical forms of torment.

As Erikson (1950) pointed out, Freud offers us a "centaur model of man" that conceives our fundamental conflict as between mind and body, culture and nature, the uniquely human vs. the animal in man. While body, nature and animal are conceived as the source of our antisocial inclinations (id), reason (ego) and culture (superego) are viewed as prosocial. Freud viewed human sexuality and aggression as arising from biological, somatic sources, by which he did not mean the brain, but bodily zones. He resorted to a biological rather than a psychological or existential conception of human passion. It is true he chose not to use the German term *instinkt* referring to animal instinct, but the term *triebe* referring to human drives, which differ from animal instincts in being far more open to learning and social influences in their aims and objects, which can be displaced, reversed, etc., and are to a considerable extent acquired rather than biologically fixed or pre-programmed. It is true that the conception of Freud as a biologically reductionist instinct theorist was made worse by James Strachey's mistranslation of *triebe* as instinct instead of drive. But in *Instincts and Their Vicissitudes*, Freud (1915a) writes:

> If now we apply ourselves to considering mental life from a *biological* point of view, an "instinct" appears to us as a concept on the frontier between the mental and the somatic, as the psychical representative of the stimuli originating from within the organism and reaching the mind, as a measure of the demand made upon the mind for work in consequence of its connection with the body.
> (pp. 121–122)

He insists the *triebe* arise from *somatic* sources—despite his admission that he could never specify the somatic source of the aggressive drive.

The result is Freud's (1923) mind/body dualism in which, adapting Plato's metaphor, reason (ego) is the human rider attempting to guide the beast (appetite, id) upon which it is precariously perched:

> The functional importance of the ego is manifested in the fact that normally control over the approaches to motility devolves upon it. Thus in its relation to the id it is like a man on horseback, who has to hold in check the superior strength of the horse; with this difference, that the rider tries to do so with his own strength while the ego uses

borrowed forces. The analogy may be carried a little further. Often a rider, if he is not to be parted from his horse, is obliged to guide it where it wants to go; so in the same way the ego is in the habit of transforming the id's will into action as if it were its own.

(p. 24)

While the image is vivid and evocative of our profound sense of conflict, it is ultimately misleading. For our sexual and aggressive passions do not in fact "bubble up" from our animal bodies but "trickle down" from our uniquely human minds. Whereas for Freud friendship and a host of other social goods are transformations of sexuality, we know clinically that sexuality may itself at times be a transformation of something else; it may be driven by aggression, for example, or a need to ward off depression or an unbearable state of fragmentation of the self.

Freud (1920) began to recognize the inadequacy of his drive theory when, after the devastation of the First World War, he finally (implicitly if not explicitly) broke with Darwin and re-situated psychoanalytic theory on the basis of a new Greek dualism that echoed the work of his pre-Socratic precursor Empedocles for whom all of reality reflects the struggle between *philia* (love) and *neikos* (strife). The fact that Freud chose to give capitalized Greek names to his two new forces, *Eros* and *Thanatos*, is an indication that he was moving far beyond his earlier biological reductionism, subsuming the earlier sexual drive in a far wider "principle" of life, integration and connectedness, while counterposing this to the utterly un-Darwinian notion of a "drive" toward death. While biological reductionism was not transcended, for he insisted the death drive had an organic foundation, his thinking was clearly tending in a more psychological, philosophical and existential direction.

This is not the place to trace Freud's own and his followers' struggles to interpret in shifting ways the meaning of *Thanatos*, nor to explore the pessimistic consequences for social theory entailed in his biologizing of human passion. Instead, some three decades ago, both I myself (Carveth, 1984a) and Eli Sagan (1988) raised a psychoanalytic question: What latent content, what unconscious phantasy, may lie behind the manifest content of Freud's sociological theory? Since Freud himself was not loath to psychoanalyze philosophy, it would be unfair to privilege psychoanalytic theory and forebear from the psychoanalysis of psychoanalysis. Beneath the narrative of a frustrating civilization, one demanding instinctual renunciation and engendering resentment and discontent, do we detect the presence of the projected castrating father-imago and, possibly beneath that, the preoedipal mother, both our first nurturer and first tyrant and oppressor? Is *Civilization and Its Discontents* more a projection of an almost universal castration phantasy than a contribution to social theory? Certainly most sociologists, having a profound sense of what society gives us rather than what it is imagined to take away, have for the most part not been inclined to accept this aspect of Freud's thinking.

In recent decades it has become clear that in blaming the alleged animal in man and valorizing reason and culture, Freud got it backward: that much or most of the evil humans do—their racism, sexism, heterosexism, classism, etc.—is learned or acquired from culture (superego), while our prosocial inclinations appear to have a biological basis. In associating the id with our allegedly natural destructiveness we have been blinded to the loving, caring and sympathetic inclinations grounded in the innate, unlearned attachment systems we share with other primates. At the same time, through a series of ingenious experiments, recent infant research shows that children as young as three months of age distinguish right from wrong, good from bad, and prefer the former (Bloom, 2010, 2013). This is not evidence of an entirely "innate" morality, for even three-month-old infants have had considerable opportunity to identify with the loving nurturance of their caretakers. However it does demonstrate that the roots of conscience arise in early attachment, long before the internalizations of cultural ideology at five or six years of age that Freud described as forming the superego. It is high time that psychoanalysts deconstruct the false equations of the id with immoral nature (when much of what is truly moral in us stems from innate attachment tendencies and early identifications with the nurturer), and the superego with moral nurture (when a great deal of our immorality is culturally acquired).

Today it is the fashion among liberal-minded psychoanalysts to advance the wishful illusion that due to his support for free clinics (Danto, 2005) and some degree of income redistribution grounded in his experience of poverty as a child (Freud, 1933, Lecture 35), Freud was at the very least a liberal, if not a social democrat (Richards, 2016). Anyone interested in scholarly objectivity, however, will be forced to take note of such contrary facts as the inscription he wrote in presenting one of his books to Mussolini: "Benito Mussolini with the respectful greetings of an old man who recognizes in the ruler the cultural hero" (Roazen, 2005, p. 33). In its stress upon the dangerously regressive and irrational proclivities of groups, Freud's (1921) *Group Psychology and the Analysis of the Ego*, like the works of LeBon, Tarde and others, contributes to the literature on "mob psychology" produced by bourgeois thinkers fearful of the power of the masses to make revolution, as they had in 1789 and again in 1917. Given the central emphasis in his group psychology on the need for strong leadership to prevent "regression," his obliviousness to groups organized instead by democratically instituted charters of rights and responsibilities, his disparaging remarks about the proletariat as lazy, stupid and oversexed, his view of America, including its democracy, as "a mistake; a gigantic mistake" (Jones, 1955, p. 67), and his organization of the IPA along authoritarian, top-down lines with secret committees dedicated to the preservation of the faith, and so on, Freud's gesture of respect toward the Great Leader becomes intelligible. His view of the superego as the source of law and order and a bulwark against barbarism formed a central element of his increasingly reactionary sociopolitical vision—a perspective that may well have inclined readers such as Henry Kissinger (Pound, 2014) to view Western or, more accurately, American power as the superego defending civilization against the unruly, primitive id forces threatening from the East. Despite the importance Lacan gives to *le-nom-du-père*, he was quick to recognize the cultural conformism of the adaptationist Freudian ego psychology dominant in America for decades.

The valorization of the superego as the preserver of law and order never sat well with Freud's clinical insight into its destructiveness and its central role in psychopathology. The superego, he explained, is formed by repressing aggression and turning it back against the ego through the process Anna Freud (1936) described as "identification with the aggressor." Instead of attacking hated others, we identify with them and aggress against or punish ourselves. It is easy to forget that suicides are self-murderers. Among Freud's greatest and enduring contributions is his discovery of the unconscious need for punishment in a wide range of conditions that, on the surface, appear to have nothing whatever to do with moral issues—with wrongdoing, sin, guilt, the need to be punished or to punish oneself. In the first century CE, the Roman Stoic Philosopher Lucius Annaeus Seneca (n.d.), "Seneca the Younger," wrote: "Let wickedness escape as it may at the bar, it never fails of doing justice upon itself, for every guilty person is his own hangman." In his classic text, *Man Against Himself,* Karl Menninger (1938) describes in thorough detail how the operations of the unconscious hanging judge, the superego, underlie not only depression, masochism and suicide, but a whole range of "guilt-substitutes"—self-sabotaging, self-limiting and self-tormenting conditions. Freud (1916) called attention to the "fear of success" (underlying procrastination and the tendency to "clutch defeat from the jaws of victory"); "those wrecked by success" (I think of all those graduate students who having finally completed and successfully defended their dissertations immediately fall into what I think of as a "post-Ph.D." depression analogous to the post-partum depression suffered by many women after successfully delivering a baby); and the "criminal from a sense of guilt" whose guilt rather than following the crime precedes it, a crime unconsciously committed in order to get caught and punished—so the "perp" leaves clues, returns to the scene, etc. The unconscious need for punishment at the hands of the tyrannical superego is also at work in a host of hysterical and psychosomatic conditions that bring pain and torment upon the self.

Having cited Adorno, for whom "The history of philosophy is the history of forgetting," Jacoby (1975) claims "what was known to Freud, half-remembered by the Neo-Freudians, is unknown to their successors" due to a process of *social amnesia* in which "society remembers less and less, faster and faster" and "the sign of the times is thought that has succumbed to fashion" (p. 1). In psychiatry, psychology and psychoanalysis we have experienced some five decades of forgetting of the central importance of guilt in human experience. The reason for this is not hard to find. As cultural historian Christopher Lasch (1979) explained, since the 1960s we have been living in the "culture of narcissism" created by advanced consumer capitalism, a culture characterized by what Herbert Marcuse (1964) called "repressive de-sublimation" in which self-indulgent consumption rather than self-regulation is encouraged, a culture hostile to rules, regulators and whistle-blowers (just ask Edward Snowden). If, as the old saying has it, the superego is soluble in alcohol, in narcissism it appears it may be liquidated altogether. But this is merely an appearance. A narcissist's unawareness of—that is, his refusal to face—his guilt doesn't mean he doesn't have any, only that he works hard to keep it unconscious. But the repressed returns in a myriad of disguised self-sabotaging and self-tormenting ways.

As probing as are his insights into unconscious guilt, Freud's analysis of this phenomenon is flawed by his failure to distinguish the two fundamentally different types of guilt subsequently differentiated by Melanie Klein and her co-workers (Klein, 1948; Grinberg, 1964): the punitive or *persecutory* guilt inflicted by both Freud's post-oedipal and Klein's pregenital superego on the one hand, and on the other the *reparative* guilt that stems from what I recognize as a conscience quite distinct from the superego. As I elaborate in Chapter 2, Freud's (1923) merging of both conscience and the ego-ideal into the superego is regrettable: whereas the superego is about punishment fueled by aggression—mostly turned on the self, though often self-righteously displaced onto scapegoats—conscience is about caring, both for others and one's true self, caring fueled by attachment and love. Whereas persecutory or punitive guilt is generated by the superego, reparative guilt is generated by conscience. The superego wants to beat, the conscience to heal. If I injure someone and while he bleeds I self-flagellate, that is punitive guilt; but if I put down my cat-o'-nine tails and reach for my first-aid kit and start bandaging, that is reparative guilt. Those naive psychologists who think guilt is something we need to rid ourselves of have only persecutory guilt in mind. But a good deal of our confusion in this area is due to the pseudo-moral superego's need to masquerade as the conscience. In order to unmask this impostor we need only heed the following advice: "By their fruits ye shall know them" (Matthew 7:20). The fruits of the superego are humiliation and pain, while those of conscience are forgiveness and reparative love.

Freud himself was not alert to this distinction and failed to see that while we need less persecutory guilt in civilization we need a great deal more reparative guilt. In other words, we need less superego and more conscience. Whereas the conscience is grounded in our primate heritage, our innate attachment tendencies and capacities, and in our earliest nurturing experiences and identifications, the superego, as Klein understood, is grounded in pregenital introjection of the persecutory part-object (the so-called bad breast), together with later turning of aggression away from the oedipal rivals back against the ego, to which is then added internalization of (often immoral) cultural values via the parents' superegos. Despite his clinical awareness of its sadism, Freud's association of the superego with prosocial constraints on our antisocial inclinations has made it difficult for us to keep its destructiveness clearly in mind, including the antisocial ideologies (the racism, sexism, heterosexism, classism, etc.) we internalize in socialization (which, in this respect, might well be thought of as "antisocial-ization").

It is worth noting in this connection that the terrorists responsible for the 2001 attacks on the World Trade Center were superego-driven ideologues more than id-driven psychopaths—not unlike the Nazi doctors most of whom, as Robert Lifton (1986) discovered, were racist ideologues, no more psychopathic than Truman and those who dropped atom bombs on Hiroshima and Nagasaki without giving the Japanese a prior opportunity to observe a test, or the so-called "counter-terrorists" currently waging our terroristic "war on terror." One reason why in *The Still Small Voice* (Carveth, 2013) I recommended distinguishing the superego from conscience is that while the superego plays a central role in the cycle of violence wherein the formerly terrorized come to terrorize others, the conscience represents our only hope of transcending it. A second concerns the fact that by folding ego-ideal and conscience into the superego, psychoanalytic structural theory lost the opportunity to carefully study each of the fifteen types of inter- and intra-systemic conflict among and within the five agencies of the mind: id, ego, superego, ego-ideal and conscience (see Chapter 2). While claiming to be "*the* psychology of the innermost mental processes of man in conflict" (Kris, 1938, p. 140), the failure to differentiate between the superego and conscience has effectively excluded a significant part of the field of mental conflict from the purview of Freud and his followers.

Neurotic sufferers are self-tormentors, even when their self-torture has its roots in trauma and the more or less unconscious rage arising from it. Victims of abuse usually end up as abusers, directing their unconscious rage at themselves and often enough also at others. Male violence against women is, in my view, often grounded in deep unconscious resentment and rage toward our first nurturer, first frustrator and first dominator—still today, most often the mother. In the all-too-present historical cycle of violence we witness victimized people unconsciously imposing their own victimization upon others and in this way bringing further victimization upon themselves. Wilfred Bion (1957) writes of the "bizarre objects" created when the bad object is attacked and its fragments proliferate into a multitude of bad objects—as in those narratives and films (e.g., *The Sorcerer's Apprentice*) in which when you chop off the monster's head it immediately grows five more. In seeking to destroy terrorism we create many more terrorists, not least by becoming terrorists ourselves.

In order to understand how victims come to victimize themselves and others the concept of the superego is essential. Trauma generates rage that for a variety of reasons is turned on the self in the form of the superego. As we have seen, the superego is formed through identification with the aggressors; instead of retaliating against them I identify with them and turn my aggression against myself. Later, as a defense against self-victimization, I may identify with my persecutory superego and victimize (scapegoat) others in my place. Through projection these others come to embody my own aggression, a projection aided by evidence of *their* aggression, including that which mine has provoked in them. In this way the cycle of violence is perpetuated.

It is essential for victims to recognize the aggressor in themselves and to seek to disarm and make peace with the enemy inside, rather than continuing to project, provoke and find it in the other and thus, perpetuate rather than breach the vicious cycle. While Freud was right to point out the neurotic consequences of the build-up of punitive guilt due to the repression of aggression and its turning against the self (superego), he failed to understand that authentic morality (conscience) is not something we learn from society, but something that derives from our primate heritage and our earliest experiences of life-giving nurturance, experiences that elicit hope and gratitude and kindle our need to nurture others. While we are certainly in need of the inhibiting, punishing and nay-saying "paternal function," we are even more fundamentally in need of the life-affirming "maternal function." Conscience not only calls us to reject the immoral superego and the false societal values comprising it; it requires us to recognize that "the enemy is us." As G.K. Chesterton (1927) put the point:

> No man's really any good till he knows how bad he is, or might be; till he's realized how much right he has to all this talk about "criminals," as if they were apes in a forest ten thousand miles away; till he's got rid of all the dirty self-deception of talking about low types and deficient skills; ... till his only hope is somehow or other to have captured one criminal, and kept him safe and sane under his own hat.
> (p. 466)

But in addition to the persecutory guilt resulting from my turning of my reactive aggression on myself, there is that which is *induced* in me by others who narcissistically refuse to bear it themselves. While it is important to recognize and overcome the inner sadist instead of projecting it outwards onto others, it is equally crucial to discern how much of the guilt I experience is really *mine*, and how much has been induced or projected into me by others. Some of the guilt and inferiority that cripples people is not necessarily grounded in their own aggression, but results from projective identification or induction by hostile others. There appear to be several types of "identification with the aggressor," one formed through my retaliatory aggression toward the aggressor (which makes me an aggressor too), another through my compliant identification with the aggressor's devaluing and dehumanizing images of me. The hostile superego thrives upon my own aggression turned inwards, plus the poisonous messages about me that I have incorporated from others. Recognizing, sorting out and working through these dynamics instead of projecting the poison outwards onto enemies is a painful yet liberating experience that sometimes happens (on the individual level) in the psychoanalytic process. In Kleinian terms this marks advance from the paranoid-schizoid to the reparative position.

Whereas for Freud the central human problem is the conflict *between* mind and body, the uniquely human and the animal in man—that is, between a socialized ego-superego and a primitive, ultimately animal id—for Melanie Klein the conflict is one *within* the human mind and heart between our love and our hate, our constructive and our destructive inclinations. In transcending Freud's centaur model of man, Klein was following out the implications of Freud's own thinking more consistently than he himself managed to do. It was, after all, Freud himself who in 1920 altered his earlier psycho-biological theory of drives into his final dualistic drive theory of *Eros* vs. *Thanatos*, the life drive vs. the death drive. Klein's achievement was that while manifestly adhering to Freud's concepts she came to treat the life and death drives as, to all intents and purposes, entirely psychological and emotional motives or passions of love on the one hand and hate on the other. In other words, whereas Freud himself was never able to entirely transcend *material* in favor of *immaterial* or *psychic reality*, Melanie Klein managed to do so, transcending psycho-biology in favor of psychoanalytic psychology. If the past century has shown us anything, it is the involvement of human reason (ego) and human ideals and ideologies (superego) in the perpetration of evil. The problem is not the animal in man; it is the conflict in our hearts and minds between our love and our hate, between our employment of our uniquely human capacities for reason, idealism and empathy in the service of nurturance or of sadistic aggression and revenge.

Over time, many analysands develop sufficient trust in (and respect for) their analysts so that the latter are able to confront them in ways that are not experienced as moralistic reproaches, or that cause them to attack themselves, but that instead quicken and enliven their conscience. Safán-Gerard (1998) has provided a rich illustration of this type of work (Carveth, 2016c). Freud discovered the role of the transference in therapy. Subsequent analysts elaborated the role of empathy, "holding" and "containing" in the healing process. Through therapeutic provision of illusion ("maternal function") patients can be helped to achieve developmental milestones previously unattained, to advance beyond the narcissistic, paranoid-schizoid position to the depressive/reparative position where they can begin to tolerate therapeutic disillusion and deconstruction ("paternal function"), to gain some critical distance from core phantasies and transferences, to develop the capacity for concern, and then to work through the neurotic symptoms and inhibitions accompanying this advance.

But it is quite another matter to achieve such progress on the collective level. For here the sort of intense, tried and true bond between therapist and patient that provides the context in which such healing can occur is largely absent. As Alford (2001) explained, in small groups where face-to-face contact occurs one can encounter and be affected by the other, whereas in larger, more anonymous groups such feedback is unavailable or apt to be processed very differently. Alford points out how in large groups personal identity is less supported and anxiety generated. For these and other reasons it is hard for people to find in large group settings the kind of responsiveness that facilitates personal growth and, as a result, regression rather than progression all too frequently occurs. The trouble with abstract substitutes for the therapist, such as a loving and forgiving God for believers, or a trusted theory of history providing political guidance, is that such abstractions are precisely that—abstractions—rather than living, breathing others with the heart and the conscience to confront. Such abstract others are not really "other" and can as easily support destructiveness as personal growth. They can easily come to represent not the conscience, but the superego, which in any case, frequently seeks to masquerade as and even usurp the role of conscience, even though it is driven by hate rather than love.

Feeling that my trusted therapist is fundamentally on my side sometimes allows me (eventually) to tolerate him being "other," thinking differently, even confronting my darkness. An abstract other, such as God or a prized theory of the laws of historical development, are as likely to feed my madness as to help me overcome it. Occasionally an admired and trusted leader may earn sufficient authority to appeal to conscience and persuade people to forebear from and harness their destructiveness. But one who does so risks becoming its target and being crucified in the process.

As both Fromm and Levinas (1961) understood, it is through the face-to-face encounter with a concrete other that the wall of narcissistic self-enclosure may sometimes be breached creating an authentic opening to the other. Whereas for Sartre (1943) the look of the other objectifies me and transcends my transcendence causing my world to "hemorrhage" and "bleed" toward him or her (pp. 349–352), for Levinas the face of the other, while equally disrupting my narcissistic equilibrium, calls me, not to a "battle to the death of consciousnesses" (Sartre, 1943, p. 65), but to my infinite responsibility toward the other. In marked contrast to Sartre (1944) for whom "hell is other people," Erich Fromm, as Burston (1991) points out, "resembles Martin Buber in thinking that relationships based on reciprocal validation and individuated fellowship are not only possible but in fact prerequisite to the experience of authentic selfhood" (p. 92). While, for Sartre, at least under conditions of bad faith, human relations fail to transcend sado-masochistic, paranoid-schizoid dynamics, both Fromm and Levinas describe the move toward, caring for and commitment to the other characteristic of the reparative position. This is the goal of any genuinely healing psychotherapy, a goal that may only be approached through authentic, "I-Thou" (Buber, 1937), person-to-person encounter, a form of meeting that may only take place in a sacred space beyond all theory and technique—a space that in light of Sagan's (2001) reassertion of the *secular sacred* must not be allowed to be colonized by religion.

In *Manchester by the Sea* (2016) writer and director Kenneth Lonergan movingly depicts both the savagery of the superego and efforts on the part of conscience to counteract it. After his wife has called an end to a raucous, alcohol and cocaine enhanced party with his buddies, Lee puts a log on the fire, then walks out to buy more beer, apparently neglecting to replace the fire screen. He returns to find the house in flames. While his wife survives his three children are burned to death. Lee is blamed both by himself and his wife. Astonished that upon investigation the police are not charging him (one officer even kindly pointing out that, like millions of other people, he has made a tragic mistake), Lee seizes one of their weapons in a thwarted attempt to kill himself. His subsequent existence is one of barely contained, mostly self-directed rage, depression and self-punishment. His ex-wife has managed, to some extent at least, to move on. But haunted by guilt over the savagery of her past judgment and cruel reproach of Lee and by conscientious concern about the damage she sees him doing to himself, Randi finally confronts and tries to reach him with love and forgiveness. But he can't accept it, later explaining to the bereaved nephew he feels unable to parent: "I just can't beat it!"— that is, the life sentence inflicted by the savage superego. Fortunately, with the help of conscience and those who, like Randi and the concerned police officer, are capable of compassion and forgiveness, some of us, sometimes, can.

Chapter 2

Expanding structural theory
Id, ego, superego, ego-ideal and conscience

The last thing a narcissist wants to face is his guilt. At the very time when the "culture of narcissism" created by consumer capitalism was producing "the narcissistic personality of our time" (Lasch, 1979)—a character embodied for us today in Donald Trump—psychoanalysts, like the narcissists they were studying, were in flight from the dynamics of guilt, self-punishment and the superego. By the late 1950s, Sandler (1960) had already noticed that in the indexing of cases at the Hampstead clinic there was a "tendency to veer away from the conceptualization of material in superego terms"; he was wondering why "therapists have preferred to sort their clinical material in terms of object relationships, ego activities and the transference, rather than in terms of the participation of the superego" (p. 129). Two decades later, Arlow (1982) observed that "[S]uperego function has been shunted to one side by the current preoccupation with the persistence of the regressive reactivation of archaic idealizations" (p. 230) and that "[T]he concept superego itself rarely appears as the central topic of a clinical or theoretical contribution" (p. 229). Würmser (1998) referred to the superego as the "sleeping giant" of contemporary psychoanalysis.

While the giant slept, having been anesthetized in society at large and in the psychoanalytic thinking it spawned, Friedrich von Hayek, Ayn Rand, Thatcher, Reagan, Milton Friedman, Alan Greenspan and a host of others laid the foundations for the dismantlement of the social state. With avid assistance from the "banksters" and "fraudsters" of Wall Street and "the City," neoliberals prepared the ground for the economic crisis of 2007–2008. It was no accident that the flight from guilt in psychoanalytic thought coincided with the shift from productive industrial to consumer capitalism and the rise of neoliberalism or free-market fundamentalism. *Ironically, the psychoanalytic preoccupation in the 1970s and 1980s with narcissistic characters incapable of bearing guilt coincided with a flight from guilt in psychoanalysis itself.* In several streams of psychoanalytic thought the central role of guilt-evasion in pathological narcissism was obscured—an instance of what Russell Jacoby (1975) referred to as the "social amnesia" in which "society remembers less and less faster and faster" and in which "the sign of the times is thought that has succumbed to fashion" (p. 1).

More recently, the emergence of the Occupy movement and whistle-blowers such as Assange, Manning and Snowdon coincided with a series of psychoanalytic books and articles with titles such as: *You Ought To! A Psychoanalytic Study of the Superego and Conscience* (Barnett, 2007); *Guilt and Its Vicissitudes: Psychoanalytic Reflections on Morality* (Hughes, 2008); *The Quest for Conscience and the Birth of the Mind* (Reiner, 2009); *The Still Small Voice: Psychoanalytic Reflections on Guilt and Conscience* (Carveth, 2013); "Reflections on the absence of morality in psychoanalytic theory" (Frattaroli, 2013); and *Guilt: Origins, Manifestations, and Management* (Akhtar, 2013). But if this "comeback" in psychoanalytic thought reflected any shift in the wider culture, it was too little and too late. What Rangell (1980) described three and a half decades ago (in *The Mind of Watergate*) as the "syndrome of the compromise of integrity" led not only to the 2008 crisis of neoliberal capitalism but also, as in earlier such crises, to the emergence less than a decade later of "21st century fascism," a project that, as Robinson (May 11, 2011) predicted, "does not—and need not—distinguish between the truth and the lie."

At the same time as psychoanalysts turned away from the dynamics of guilt and self-punishment many lost interest in or repudiated structural theory, often complaining of the reification of structural concepts. But, in my view, this rationale is really a rationalization of the retreat from psychoanalysis as, in the words of Ernst Kris (1938), "*the* psychology of the innermost mental processes of man in conflict" (p. 140). Most psychoanalysts have understood that the concept of mental "structure"—like that of "social structure"—is a metaphor and that psychoanalysis, like all physical and social sciences, proceeds through the use of metaphors of this sort. So the danger of reification is not really the issue; the view of psychopathology as conflict and of the mind itself as conflict is what is really being resisted here. If Karl Marx is the conflict theorist of society, Sigmund Freud is the conflict theorist of the mind. Although in many ways I have followed the Kleinian development of Freudian thought, I remain steadfastly Freudian in my adherence to the structural theory as an illuminating conceptualization of the mind in conflict. It is because I find structural theory so valuable that I want to expand it to include the conscience and the ego-ideal, the two structures that in *The Ego and the Id* Freud (1923) subsumed into the superego.

The concept of the ego-ideal as the "heir to primary narcissism" (Freud, 1914), the projection into the future of infantile omnipotence and perfectionism, is useful and worth reinstating as a separate mental structure and function. It enables us to conceive of self-esteem regulation as comparison of one's real ego with one's ego-ideal, generating states of inflation and deflation depending on the relative distance between them. But the ego-ideal is confined to the field of narcissism, for in such assessments one's attention is entirely on oneself, not the other. Conscience, on the other hand, is grounded in object love, the "capacity for concern" (Winnicott, 1963a) not merely for the self but for the *other*. While the ego-ideal enables me to feel good or bad about myself by advancing toward or falling away from my ideals, occasionally I actually manage to get my mind off myself, my progress or regress and glimpse the reality of others and even, sometimes, to care about *them*, not just about *me*. In this light there are three dimensions of self-esteem regulation. In addition to measuring myself in relation to my ideals, I assess myself in terms of what I owe to others (conscience) and how well or poorly I conform to internalized rules or standards (superego).

Freud's decision made it difficult for us to recognize the differences between the superego, the ego-ideal and the conscience and, more importantly, to study the conflicts among them—such as, for example, the "moral injury" suffered by soldiers who in obedience to the superego did unconscionable things for which they cannot forgive themselves. In explaining the superego as internalized culture (in addition to id aggression turned back against the self), Freud largely neglected to point out that it will therefore be the repository of the culture's racism, sexism, heterosexism, authoritarianism, materialism, etc.—that is, that it will pressure the individual to act in accord with values that while *normative* may well be *immoral* by the standards of conscience. I published a paper by the title *The Immoral Superego* (Carveth, 2015a) precisely to drive home this point. It was the Scottish psychoanalyst Ronald Laing (1967, p. 98) who pointed out that in a squadron of airplanes one plane might be *out of formation*, but the squadron itself may be *off course*—which means that the one plane that is out of formation might actually be *on course*. A person conforming to his superego might be in conflict with his conscience; and a person might be called by conscience to defy her superego.

Conscience

Most dictionaries define conscience as an inner faculty or voice that distinguishes right from wrong and generates guilt when we choose the latter. Prior to widespread secularization in the West, conscience was considered a manifestation of the divine in an otherwise "fallen" human nature. Moral conflict was depicted as a battle between the divine and the demonic, Christ and Old Adam, with conscience pulling toward the former and away from the latter. With the Enlightenment and the rise of secular social science, conscience came to be seen as a social product, a manifestation in the individual psyche of social norms (folkways, mores and laws) internalized in socialization. Now individual moral conflict was associated with tensions among the different elements of the psyche, much as Plato (380 BCE) had conceived it as conflict among the three elements of the soul-appetite, reason and spirit. In *The Ego and the Id*, Freud (1923) adapted Plato's model, renaming appetite *id*, reason *ego* and spirit *superego*. At the same time, regrettably, Freud chose to make conscience a superego function, viewing it as a representative of the culture formed through the child's internalization of the parental superegos. Moral conflict now entailed either *inter-systemic* conflict among superego, ego and id or *intra-systemic* conflict within the superego between incompatible internalized norms deriving from socialization into conflicting cultures, subcultures, or incompatible parental value-systems (as in so-called "schismatic" families).

Transcending the normative

In identifying conscience with the superego, Freud made it a social product, an embodiment of the normative, rather than a moral force capable of conflicting with and morally challenging the social norms. Just as in relativistic social science a society could only be judged immoral from the standpoint of another society's equally relative morality, for psychoanalysis the superego could only be judged immoral by another superego representing the conflicting values of a different culture or subculture. Conflict between internalized norms and some other, non-internalized source of conscience—between a societal voice and a voice that in some manner transcends the merely societal and is capable of judging it—became difficult to posit in a purely secular context, a world without God, although adherents of various forms of humanism attempted to do so by positing universal human rights and needs. For Hegel (1820–1829) and for Fromm (1951), Sophocles' *Antigone* embodies the conflict between authority, Creon's refusal to bury an enemy of the state, and a humanistic ethic grounded in a profound sense of what we owe to those with whom we are in relationship, Antigone's conscience-driven obligation to bury her brother.

The secular sacred

While the idea of an ethic grounded in something more fundamental than the socially constructed laws of men has usually been associated with the sacred laws of God, today a purely secular social science and psychoanalysis can conceive the still small voice of conscience in entirely non-religious, non-supernatural terms, as emanating from the innate, unlearned attachment systems (Bowlby, 1969–1980) we share with our primate cousins. We are social by design, not through the imposition of sociality upon an allegedly asocial or antisocial nature. We come into the world designed to attach to the primary caretakers upon whose nurturance we depend for survival and development and with whom we form early identifications. Recent research (De Waal, 1997, 2011) has demonstrated the biological roots of moral behavior in animals and infant research (Bloom, 2013) has shown a preference for right (helpful) over wrong (harmful) in infants as young as three months of age. In addition to whatever biological basis exists for this behavior, by three months infants have already had plenty of opportunity to identify with their nurturers, to know what it is to receive love and feel the need to return it.

The superego

In addition to allowing conscience to be subsumed by the superego, Freud never fully reconciled his differing views of the superego itself. Over time, in his clinical writings, he came increasingly to emphasize its harshness and cruelty and its central role in psychopathology as the inner sadistic tormentor resulting from turning of aggression back on the self, thus, generating depression, masochism, the fear of success, being wrecked by success, self-sabotage ("clutching defeat from the jaws of victory"), becoming a "criminal from a sense of guilt" and other self-harming and self-limiting behaviors. Yet, in his sociological writings he could still view the superego as the positive force that preserves the thin veneer of civilization by preventing the barbarous id from running amok.

While it is true that the superego can redirect aggression away from others and back against the self, some analysts became so focused on its prosocial benefits as Law that they lost sight of the fact that sometimes the Law is (or can become) racist, anti-Semitic, genocidal, and of the superego's central role in suicide and such *suicide-substitutes* (Menninger, 1938) as depression, moral masochism, psychosomatic and hysterical suffering, etc. Like a trapped animal that chews off its leg to save its life, people try to placate the murderous superego by unwittingly sacrificing their careers, their sexuality, their marriages, their health.... Alternatively, they may defensively identify with the attacking superego, making others its target, sometimes inflicting irreparable harm in an orgy of sadistic scapegoating. Heinrich Racker (1957) described situations in which the patient places the analyst "in the situation of the dependent and incriminated ego" and develops what he called a "mania for reproaching" (p. 141). We commonly see self-righteous moralists exonerating themselves by projecting all wrongdoing onto the others and glorying in cruelly castigating, punishing or exterminating them.

In *Civilization and Its Discontents* Freud (1930) described the build-up of guilt and self-punishment resulting from the need to preserve civilized order by repressing aggression, which then, via the superego, is retroflected upon the self. But he did not recognize Melanie Klein's (1948; Grinberg, 1964) crucial distinction between punitive or persecutory guilt and "depressive" or reparative guilt, and therefore, he failed to see that while it is true that we need less of the former, we need a great deal *more* of the latter—that is, less superego and more conscience. Paradoxically, people sometimes prefer to experience shame (and other injuries inflicted by the superego) to reconciling with conscience, experiencing contrition and making reparation. In other words, superego torment often functions as a resistance or a defense against the narcissistic injury entailed in hearing the voice of conscience, acknowledging guilt and regret and seeking to make reparation.

As Bion (1962a, 1962b) understood, ultimately the analytic task involves leading people to the point where they can begin to understand that their early decision to base their lives on the avoidance of pain has only led to more pain. While some are able to reverse that early decision and face necessary pain as the only way to escape the unnecessary additional pain they bring on themselves, others are simply unwilling or unable to bear the narcissistic wound entailed in acknowledging guilt. I think this is due to an inability to overcome paranoid-schizoid splitting and achieve ambivalence. If one cannot at the same time remember one's goodness, then any admission of badness is totalized and feels like a shameful revelation that one is a poisonously all-bad creature—a view of the self that makes not only guilt, but life itself unbearable.

The ego

If psychoanalysts have at times lost sight of the destructiveness of the superego, the same can be said for the reality-testing ego. If it is not informed or in some sense enveloped by an intact conscience, the ego pursues a purely instrumental rationality, one that can be pressed in the service of psychopathy. This kind of instrumental rationality is essential to the creation and mass manufacture of the killing machines employed in the service of superego ideologies. Associating the superego with morality and the ego with reason, psychoanalysts have found the roots of both antisocial sexuality and aggression in the id drives that Freud (1915a) insisted arose from somatic sources. Civilization, he concluded, requires inhibition, especially of what he had come to view as our innate aggressive drive, which though exacerbated by frustration was, for him, ultimately a biologically-given, asocial or antisocial element of our human nature. In projecting our uniquely human viciousness onto animals and the alleged animal in ourselves we appear to have got it backward. Only human beings, capable of empathy, are able to invent diabolical forms of torture. The evidence suggests that our prosocial tendencies are grounded in the innate attachment systems we share with our primate cousins and in early identifications with nurturing others, while our destructiveness appears grounded in our uniquely human symbolic functions (both ego and superego) that often lead us to care more for abstractions, ideologies and ourselves than for others or even life itself.

Expanding structural theory 49

But what about the so-called "loving and beloved superego of Freud's structural theory," the topic of Roy Schafer's influential (1960) paper by that title? While many of its readers overlooked what Schafer himself was honest enough to admit—that this loving superego was not Freud's but Schafer's—for me, what Schafer is describing is not the superego at all but what I distinguish as the conscience and what Melanie Klein identified as the internal whole good object in which conscience is grounded and with which it is identified.

Fifteen conflicts

Along with the ego-ideal and the conscience, Freud (1923) merged the function of self-observation into the superego. While self-observation does not require a separate structure, being a self-reflexive ego function that variously involves looking at oneself from the standpoint of the superego, the ego-ideal and the conscience, I believe it makes sense to expand psychoanalytic structural theory to include the conflicts *within* as well as *among* the five mental structures: id, ego, superego, ego-ideal and conscience. I say *within* as well as *among* because we need to look at *intra*-systemic as well as *inter*-systemic conflicts—e.g., the conflicts within the id between libido and aggression, our love and our hate; within the ego between conflicting identifications (with so-called "masculine" or "feminine" figures, for example); within the superego between opposing internalized value-systems (say, between one's ethic of non-violence and one's patriotism, or in immigrant families between old-world and new-world values); within the ego-ideal (say, between ideals of truthfulness and kindness); and within the conscience (say, between conflicting attachments and loyalties).

In addition to conflicts *within* each of the five structures there are the conflicts *between* them:

ID vs. id, ego, superego, ego-ideal, conscience
EGO vs. ego, id, superego, ego-ideal, conscience
SUPEREGO vs. superego, id, ego, ego-ideal, conscience
EGO-IDEAL vs. ego-ideal, id, ego, superego, conscience
CONSCIENCE vs. conscience, id, ego, superego, ego-ideal

When we remove the overlapping categories and the five *intra-systemic* conflicts, ten *inter-systemic* conflicts remain, some of which have been difficult for us to think about and study due to Freud's merging of five structures into three. According to the so-called Sapir-Whorf hypothesis (Calhoun, 2002), if we see and then label, we also label and then see. Even in light of criticism of strong versions of this hypothesis it remains the case that, to some degree at least, having labels enhances our capacity to see while not having them makes it more difficult. In *Nineteen Eighty-Four*, a book of startling relevance in our "post-truth" era of "alternative facts," Orwell (1949) describes how the Ministry of Truth strives to remove from the language terms (personal identity, self-expression, free will) that might facilitate "thought-crime" and undermine Big Brother's project of total control. It is for such reasons that I feel folding conscience and ego-ideal into the superego was a mistake and separating them out enhances our thinking in this field.

i *Id vs. Ego*: we are familiar with these.
ii *Id vs. Superego*: and familiar with these.
iii *Id vs. Ego-Ideal*: in addition to conflicting with internalized rules, my drives may conflict with and constitute a threat to my ideal self-image. My rage might threaten my ideal of equanimity and balance; and my sexual impulses might threaten my ideals of propriety, normality and gender.
iv *Id vs. Conscience*: in addition to conflicting with internalized rules and ideals, my drives may conflict with and constitute a threat to my attachments, my significant others. My aggression might harm them; and my sexuality might lead to betrayal and loss.
v *Ego vs. Superego*: reason may conflict with internalized rules; it may seem irrational to adhere to what may appear outmoded or inappropriate rules and standards. (For example, many feel this is the case vis-à-vis IPA training requirements today.) Rational calculation of self-interest may well conflict with superego requirements. Military indoctrination tells me I should follow orders, but doing so may threaten my death. Some feel adherence to outmoded IPA standards may be the death of psychoanalysis.
vi *Ego vs. Ego-Ideal*: my ego-ideal as a loyal and patriotic soldier may conflict with my rational recognition that this is likely to get me killed.
vii *Ego vs. Conscience*: while my ego tells me what is rational my conscience tells me what is right (not merely what is normative).

The ego is about reality-testing; it is governed by the reality principle. I'm sure Edward Snowdon's rational ego told him he was crazy to blow the whistle, but his conscience prevailed over both rational calculations and his merely conventional morality—the pseudo-morality of the superego.

viii *Superego vs. Ego-Ideal*: Normative standards may conflict with one's ideals. In the medieval Church it was normative to sell "indulgences," but Martin Luther believed this practice represented a corruption of core Christian ideals. Having nailed his *Ninety-Five Theses* to the door of All Saints' Church in Wittenburg in 1517, called before the "Diet of Worms" in 1521 he is famously reputed to have said, "Here I stand; I can do no other. God help me!" Under the banner of the superego, for many years psychoanalytic institutes refused training to homosexuals, though most of us now condemn this as heteronormative, prejudicial and in conflict with our ideals of fairness and equality.

ix *Superego vs. Conscience*: Eli Sagan (1988) used Mark Twain's (1885) *The Adventures of Huckleberry Finn* to illustrate conflict between superego and conscience: Huck's racist superego demands he turn his runaway slave companion Jim in to the authorities while his conscience requires him to protect the friend he loves. After an agonizing mental struggle, Huck tears up the letter informing on Jim, deciding he will go to hell rather than betray his friend. Huck's superego is racist because he was raised in a racist culture and internalized the racism forming his parents' superegos. The superego will pressure the individual to act in accord with values that while *normative* may well be *immoral* by the standards of conscience.

People who hear and seek to follow their conscience often find themselves in conflict with their society and the superego embodying its commands. Often they feel called to conscientiously object and sometimes to defy their superegos and their societies in the name of conscience. The recent film *Hacksaw Ridge* (2016) tells the story of Desmond Doss, the first conscientious objector to be awarded the American Medal of Honor for service above and beyond the call of duty while refusing to bear arms as a medic during the battle of Okinawa. Abraham felt called by God to sacrifice Isaac. How could he be sure the voice he heard was God's or that he was the Abraham being summoned? While Kierkegaard

(1843a) celebrates him as a "knight of faith" capable of "the religious suspension of the ethical," I would have preferred Abraham to have had enough conscience to engage in what I think of as "the ethical suspension of the religious" and, like Antigone, to defy the superego/authority in favor of attachment and love.

x *Conscience vs. Ego-Ideal*: my ideal to be a loyal member of my society, group, organization or family may seriously conflict with conscience if it judges the behavior of my society or group to be immoral. I'm sure Edward Snowdon wanted to be a loyal American and I'm sure he was socialized to see that as keeping state secrets. But his conscience called him to be a whistleblower because he came to view the state as behaving immorally, unconscionably.

The truth seems to be that people who develop a strong conscience represent a threat to organizations of all types because they do not consider the interests of the organization as of first importance. Their loyalty is to what is true and what is right, whereas many organizations come to consider the interests of the organization, of the group, as taking precedence over truth, justice and goodness. We need only think in this connection of the bishops who covered up for priests who were sexual predators or, closer to home, senior members of psychoanalytic societies who sometimes did the same for boundary-violating or incompetent colleagues.

In this connection, I recall a patient, a talented accountant, who having worked privately for years, took an important job as a chief financial officer of a large company. On welcoming him, the president explained that: "here, the company comes first." My patient, a life-long evangelical Christian, replied: "With all due respect, sir, for me God comes first, my family second, and the company third." He was shortly back in private practice. I'm sometimes tempted to ask analytic colleagues: "What comes first for you, psychoanalysis or the IPA?" Some, I expect, might respond: "Well, aren't they one and the same?"

The capacity for concern

Whereas the superego conforms to the talion law, eye for an eye, returning hate for hate, the conscience conforms to a similar law of reciprocity, returning love and nurturance for love received. Anyone who has achieved bowel control and language has been loved, however inadequately—we *know* this and we know we are obliged to give love back. This is the core of conscience, the ethic of love and responsibility, what Winnicott (1963a) called the capacity for concern for the *other*—a capacity we acquire as we begin to transcend Klein's narcissistic, paranoid-schizoid position and move into the reparative position. This is a transformation that in *On Narcissism*, Freud (1914) had already, albeit briefly, described as from narcissism to object love, writing that "in the last resort we must begin to love in order not to fall ill, and we are bound to fall ill if, in consequence of frustration, we are unable to love" (p. 85). This is the fundamental transition that the French-Jewish philosopher Emmanuel Levinas (1961) would later describe as entailing the disruption of our narcissistic self-enclosure through the shocking encounter with the face of the other and the recognition of our infinite obligation to respond.

This is a more fundamental part of our being-in-the-world than the societal and parental values and ideologies we internalize in socialization. Without doubt, sometimes internalized rules are congruent with and reinforce conscience. But very often they fly in the face of it. Conscience extends far beyond the merely normative and therefore, cannot be subsumed by the superego. Very often we adhere scrupulously to rules, but if "our hearts aren't in it" we may be dismayed when (speaking metaphorically) St. Peter bars us entry for this reason. Sometimes our hearts require us to violate the rules. In so associating the conscience with the heart, with object love and identification with nurturers, there is no implication that, unlike the often harsh superego, the conscience is necessarily soft and lax, incapable of making itself heard or exercising pressure on wrongdoers. Far from it. Although not loud, harsh and intimidating, as the authoritarian superego (Fromm's [1947] authoritarian conscience) generally is, the bite of conscience (Fromm's humanistic conscience) is insistent and in the long run difficult to resist. But its disapproval, like that of a good parent, is not attacking or devaluing, but sad, concerned and ever hopeful of a turning. The strength and courage required to be a conscientious objector should not be minimized.

Just as it transcends the merely normative, so also conscience transcends the merely rational, precluding the ego, like the superego, from functioning as a conscience. In many situations it seems rational to be immoral and highly irrational to choose the good. The ego-ideal cannot serve as a conscience, since in measuring my real ego against my ideal my focus is entirely on me, not the other. The ego-ideal is a narcissistic structure reflecting self-concern, something quite distinct from the capacity for concern for the other. If, for example, I seek to be a good parent so that I can see myself and be seen as such, this is quite distinct from the good parenting that flows from genuine love of one's child who can certainly tell the difference. *The attempt to care in order to live up to an ideal of caring is not the same thing as caring. It is a performance, not the real thing.*

Beyond reason

While the rational ego can tell us what *is* or what is likely to be, it cannot tell us what *ought* to be. Since the eighteenth century work of the philosopher David Hume we have understood that reason cannot deduce an *ought* from an *is*; that science is *descriptive* not *prescriptive*. Like other long-standing philosophical axioms (such as the distinction between analytic and synthetic propositions, matters of definition and matters of fact) the fact/value distinction and the naturalistic fallacy (the idea that the ethical can be grounded in the natural) have been subjected to critique by both "pre-modernists" seeking to revive an ancient concept of an "objective reason" supposedly capable of the intellectual apprehension of the form of the good (Horkheimer, 1947), and by "post-modernists" seeking to deconstruct the "fact/value" and "analytic/synthetic" *dichotomies,* but as it turns out, without being able to de-stabilize these crucial *distinctions.* While Putnam's (2002) title, *The Collapse of the Fact/Value Dichotomy*, is dramatic and appears radically challenging, the actual substance of his argument concerns only the collapse of an impossibly exaggerated or "sharp" version of the fact/value distinction. It is quite true that the preferences for logic over illogic and facts over illusions themselves entail value judgment. But to acknowledge this in no way gets around the fact that reason (and the ego that deploys it) is impotent to tell us which ends or consequences we *should* prefer, or even to authorize our preference for clear over muddled thinking. My preference for intellectual coherence, like my preference for pleasure over pain, cannot be objectively validated. If we attempt to do so by pointing to consequences we inevitably arrive at an ultimate value judgment (usually the preference for life over death) the entirely subjective rather than objective basis of which cannot be evaded. On examination, it becomes evident that the deconstruction and complication of the *dichotomy* fails to undermine Hume's fundamental *distinction*.

Without authorization

Ultimately the value directions informing conscience come from the id: either from Freud's *Eros* (Erich Fromm's *biophilia*), which values love and life, or Freud's *Thanatos* (Fromm's *necrophilia*), which values hate and death. No one can authorize—rationally or empirically justify—the fundamental value choice between what Freud (1930) called these "immortal adversaries." Clearly, what I am calling conscience is governed ultimately by *Eros*. There are those who choose differently, opting for Fromm's *necrophilia* and what we might call a *Thanatic* superego.

Ultimate value choices are inevitable, unavoidable, but in my view nothing beyond ourselves requires us to choose one way or another, neither God nor history, nor nature nor one's instincts or feelings. We "choose" and in so doing reveal who we are. In *Existentialism Is a Humanism*, Sartre (1946) tells the story of a student, the son of an aging and dependent mother who lost her other son in the war against Hitler and is estranged from her collaborationist husband. Should he go and fight or stay and care for her? Reason cannot provide the answer; there are persuasive arguments on both sides. He could seek priestly advice, but there are collaborationist priests, priests of the resistance, and fence-sitters: he is deciding what advice to receive in choosing who to go to for it. He cannot simply consult his instincts or feelings as they conflict; which should he follow?

For Jean-Jacques Rousseau (1754) our ethics derive not from reason, but from feeling. He saw ethics as grounded in "pity" or fellow-feeling. But while some people feel pity or sympathy and choose to help, others are pitiless and choose either to remain indifferent or to hurt. It does no good to say those who are pitiless, indifferent or cruel are "sick," for this medical metaphor is merely a mask for moral judgment, a spurious attempt to naturalize what are ethical choices. In the psychoanalytic view our feelings are ultimately anchored in the drives, in *Eros* and *Thanatos*, libido and aggression, our love and our hate. But the fact that our value choices *originate* in our love and hate and their various combinations does not at all specify which of the drives *should* predominate. The fact that the superego is grounded in hate while the conscience is grounded in love in no way determines which agency is to be preferred. Some prefer love over hate, others the reverse. Some people are more lovers than haters, while others are more haters than lovers. This suggests that our fundamental preferences, for love or hate, life or death, are deeply rooted in character structure and that while perhaps not entirely determined by environmental and biological conditions are certainly irreducible to "choice" in any simple sense of that term, as Sartre himself came to recognize.

No other *Weltanschauung*? Really?

Freud (1933) argued that psychoanalysis has no other *Weltanschauung* than that of science itself and is only interested in "submission to the truth and rejection of illusions" (p. 182). While acknowledging that in practical life the making of *ultimate* value judgments is unavoidable, these are left to the liberty and responsibility of the individual. In this view, psychoanalysis is committed only to a *penultimate* "ethic of honesty" (Rieff, 1959, chapter nine), restricting itself to helping analysands transcend self-deception. But the idea that psychoanalysis has no ethic other than that of honesty is not honest. At best it is an illusion, hopefully without a future. For, like it or not, "Where id was there ego shall be" (Freud, 1933, p. 79) is a moral imperative requiring far more than replacing illusion with truth: it enjoins us to transcend impulsive action and, instead, develop ego strength, prudence, discretion and self-mastery. Developing ego where id was "is a work of culture—not unlike the draining of the *Zuider Zee*" (p. 80); sublimation of primitive drive is encouraged. But overcoming our illusions, developing self-control, sublimating our drives—this is still not enough. In addition, we must transcend narcissism in favor of object love, we must bind *Thanatos* with *Eros*, and we must overcome the harsh, primitive superego that is a "pure culture of the death instinct" (Freud, 1923, p. 52). In these and other ways, the Freudian ethic far exceeds the demand for self-knowledge. Psychoanalytic therapy, however much it has tried to disguise the fact, has always implicitly chosen, advocated and practiced an ethic it refuses to preach, an ethic in which love is better than hate; life is better than death; kindness is better than cruelty; gratitude is better than envy; etc. I share and do my best to practice these values, but I cannot claim they are authorized by God or by the deified Reason with which many have sought to replace him.

Conscience: a training requirement

In my view a central aim of psychoanalysis and analytic therapy is to emancipate conscience from its domination by both the superego and the ego, by both internalized pseudo-morality and by instrumental reason. And the single most important requirement for training and practice as a psychotherapist is to have a well-developed and functioning conscience, not merely a sophisticated ego (many psychopaths have that), nor merely a well-socialized, normative superego (for well-socialized and superego-driven people often behave unconscionably). Lifton's (1986) studies of the Nazi doctors revealed they were, for the most part, not psychopaths, but racist ideologues. Although psychopathic leaders, such as Stalin, certainly contribute disproportionately, the greater part of human destructiveness is not committed by psychopathic personalities, but by superego-driven, hardworking, loyal "do-gooders" who commit evil in the name of what their organizations and ideologies define as good.

Since the ego-ideal is a narcissistic structure in which I focus on myself, not the other and my rational ego can bring reason to bear on questions of value, but it cannot generate them or authorize value choices, it is necessary to posit conscience as the ethical center of the personality, grounded in our mammalian and primate sociality, our attachments and our identifications with our nurturers. Recently Frattaroli (2013) has written incisively about "the absence of morality in psychoanalytic theory and practice" and of Freud's (1905c) moral obtuseness with respect to, if not collusion with, the sexual abuse of Dora—a case study that, to our shame, is still not taught (in most psychoanalytic institutes) as what it is: an example of psychoanalysis at its worst. Only if we can acknowledge our own guilt-evasion, study the conflicts within and among the five structures, and re-orient ourselves on a conscientious basis can psychoanalysis hope to realize its emancipatory potential for our patients, our societies and our world. Analysts have recognized the importance of careful self-observation and monitoring of our countertransference in maintaining responsible clinical work (Coen, 2013), but such self-monitoring is only fruitful when it is informed and guided by a well-developed conscience, not merely by rules enforced by a castrating and intimidating superego. To take but one example: while well-socialized and superego-driven analysts will refrain from sexually exploiting patients out of a fear of being caught, and others will do so out of a narcissistic need to uphold their ideal self-images, conscientious therapists will do so out of genuine concern for their patients' welfare.

Real and induced guilt

In dealing with guilt we must distinguish that for which we are truly responsible from guilt-feelings induced in us through projective identification by others who are too narcissistic to own up to their own hurtful acts and impulses and to bear the resulting guilt themselves. The inferiority feelings of oppressed people are often attributed, both by themselves and others, to their own defects or shortcomings when in reality such feelings result from relentless projective identification on the part of their oppressors. Freud (1923, p. 50, n. 1; Fernando, 2000) described people who suffer from so-called "borrowed" guilt, a term that, as Paola Leon (2015) has pointed out can be quite misleading as they never asked to borrow it and the last thing its donors want is for it to be given back. Certainly there are those who employ Fairbairn's (1952) "moral defense" and take on the guilt of others in order to preserve needed object ties, but in so doing they are usually yielding to guilt-induction by narcissists unwilling to bear such guilt themselves. Aside from such induced guilt, a great deal of the pain and symptomatology from which our patients suffer arises from guilt-evasion—from their inability and/or refusal to bear the pain of reparative guilt. When patients complain about feeling "guilty" and yet carry on with behavior that is harmful to themselves or others, they need help discerning how much of such persecutory guilt and shame results from trauma and induction and how much arises from ongoing evasion of reparative guilt. For the only escape from pseudo-guilt is through reconciliation with conscience and the move into contrition and reparation. While for the narcissistic ego this is a painful process, it offers the only avenue of escape from the persecutory superego.

Non-judgmental yet conscientious

As Karl Stern (1975) pointed out, "one of the oldest traditions in medicine, even outside psychiatry, and even before Christianity.... In ancient

Chinese and Greek medicine ... one of the natural rights of the patient was not to be morally judged by the physician" (p. 71). Beyond such medical and professional requirements, a range of religious traditions provide different versions of the command to "Judge not." Experienced therapists know that if the patient encounters moral judgment on the part of the therapist the therapy will fail, either because the outraged patient will leave or because he or she will derive masochistic gratification in submitting to judgment and punishment by an external superego in the form of the therapist. But does establishing such a non-judgmental atmosphere mean one necessarily becomes blind, deaf and dumb when it comes to moral issues—that like the three wise monkeys one "sees no evil, hears no evil and speaks no evil"? Does good therapeutic technique involve "turning a blind eye" to the ethical dimensions of the patient's behavior and problems? On the contrary, Stern argued the most effective therapeutic situation is one where patients have "a complete sense of non-condemnation" by therapists who have "something in their personalities that gives the patient a sense of the primacy of charity and acceptance," who do not preach, but who at the same time convey to their patients "an awareness that the therapist ... believes in moral values" (p. 73). Here is where the distinction between superego and conscience becomes crucially important. Patients have a right to expect acceptance and exemption from superego judgment by their therapists, but whether they know it consciously or not, they need the therapist to have a conscience and to be able to hear its "still small voice," for the entire therapy depends upon their receiving the help they need in order to begin to be able to hear it themselves.

Therapists who confuse neutrality vis-à-vis the superego with neutrality vis-à-vis the conscience are in clinical error. As Susan Buechler (2016) has recently pointed out in an essay entitled: *Choosing Life: Fromm's Clinical Values*:

> Some analysts try to prove they have no vision of health. They just follow the patient's lead, expressing no values of their own. To me, this is the postmodern edition of the classical analyst's neutrality. On the contrary, I think we can't function without the inspiration that conviction can lend us. Passionate desires for our patients can center us and imbue our work with stamina and courage.... But my main argument when analysts profess they are not motivated by their own

values is that I don't believe it is true. How we understand health shapes what we focus on, remember, and comment on, whether we know it or not. There is no such thing as value-free treatment.

(p. 2)

Most psychoanalysts value love and life over hate and death. It is only by helping our patients reconcile with their loving conscience that we strengthen them vis-à-vis their superego's sadism—liberating them, not from the analyst's moralism, but their own. Despite revealing the power of self-deception and wishful illusion, Freud (1927) wrote: "The voice of the intellect is a soft one, but it does not rest till it has gained a hearing" (p. 52). Regrettably, like the voice of reason, the still small voice of conscience frequently goes unheard owing to a range of defenses against it.

In recent years, we have heard a great deal about our responsibility to offer patients essential analytic "holding" and positive, de-toxifying "containment" in a non-judgmental "atmosphere of safety"—i.e., an atmosphere free of superego moralizing—but very little about the need to find tactful, respectful and therapeutically effective ways to confront and evoke conscience in guilt-evading patients. Safán-Gerard (1998) has offered an illuminating account of her attempts to do just this with a narcissistic man whose exploitativeness she initially failed to confront out of a fear of being superego-ish and toward whom in reaction she then became scolding while punishing herself for this by allowing him to accrue a debt. When she finally came to recognize all this she shifted gears, reestablished proper boundaries and instead of addressing his exploitativeness and guilt-evasion began to point out to him those instances when he managed to show some genuine concern, remorse or regret, small steps toward the depressive position. In this way Safán-Gerard refrained from normative judgment of his promiscuous, selfish and at the same time self-sabotaging behavior, while drawing his attention to the fact that the latter served as punishment for what on some level he felt was wrong and pointing to those moments when he was capable of registering some genuine feeling of concern or regret. In this way, while avoiding the superego she at the same time carried the conscience in the treatment, thus, assisting him to take small steps toward carrying it himself.

Technical implications

In his "Foreword" to August Aichhorn's (1935) *Wayward Youth*, Freud writes that Aichhorn's method of working with delinquents "had its source in a warm sympathy ... and was rightly guided by his intuitive understanding of their psychic needs" (p. vi.). In addition to his personal warmth, Aichhorn's success appears to have been due to his evolution of a technique that circumvented resistance and facilitated the development of a working alliance by joining and mirroring the rebellious, anti-authority attitudes of his charges. It is significant that Aichhorn was Heinz Kohut's first analyst and the man who inspired both Kohut's (1971, 1978) and Hyman Spotnitz's (1969) innovative work with narcissistic patients. Kohut's technique of mirroring and empathic attunement entails a moderate version of techniques of mirroring and "joining the resistance" (rather than confronting it) evolved by Spotnitz and his colleagues for use with highly narcissistic patients with whom standard analytic interpretive technique is often ineffective or counterproductive. The use of "joining" in work with "thin-skinned narcissists" (Britton, 2004) might be described in Kohutian terms as working through an "alter-ego" or "twinship" type of selfobject transference. *Gorillas in the Mist* (1988) portrays the work of primatologist Dian Fossey with mountain gorillas in Rwanda. Originally an occupational therapist who had worked with autistic children, Fossey got closer than any scientist before to gorillas in the wild by employing a mirroring technique. She mimicked them: when they snorted, she snorted; when they growled, she growled, etc.

It is difficult to address guilt-evasion in narcissistic patients without inviting their projection of the superego, which conveniently gets them out from under its internal pressure by placing it outside in the analyst. Seeking to avoid this, in addressing the callous and promiscuous acting-out of such a patient, one might, for example, smilingly ask him as he saunters into one's office: "So, how many girls did you manage to degrade last night?" The "boys will be boys" smile would offset the superego attack while the word "degrade" would indicate one has a conscience. In work with such patients, it is wise to preface one's interventions by reminding them one is aware of the trauma and emotional pain that drives them; that is, to situate their acting-out in this context and to display sympathy with them around this, if not with the destructive behavior it generates—in other words, to let them see that one regards them as victims as well as victimizers. At the same time one needs to help them see the myriad ways they punish themselves for what they themselves clearly on some level regard as wrongdoing. Beyond this, like Safán-Gerard (1998), one needs to focus on the moments when they express shame, guilt and remorse for the damage they have done to others and themselves. Frequently they acknowledge they have to be drunk or otherwise drugged to act-out in ways they know are wrong. Often their manic triumph through such action rather quickly gives way to self-disgust and the behavior stops without anyone having to tell them to stop it.

Case vignette: no rest for the wicked

After the crisis that prompted her to leave her marriage to a verbally abusive man had been resolved and Mrs. A was proceeding with her new life and a new relationship, she dropped back to once weekly, then bi-monthly and eventually monthly meetings by telephone. But when, after her highly conflictual divorce was finalized and she was preparing to remarry, her ex-husband's cancer came out of remission and he soon died, she began to suffer from anxiety, panic attacks, insomnia, gastro-intestinal pain and depression. It became evident that she had a quasi-delusion that she had killed her ex-husband by leaving him and that he was tormenting her from beyond the grave. None of the sleeping aids, anti-depressants and supplements prescribed by her family doctor, her psychiatrist and her naturopath was of any use. As her situation worsened, I told her she would either find her way onto my couch three times a week so we could resolve this psychologically or she would likely wind up hospitalized and on heavy anti-psychotic medication.

My directness about this has to be understood in the context of her stubborn resistance to psychological understanding. Although she had never terminated the psychotherapy altogether, whenever she felt better she would lower the frequency of her sessions and be willing to attend only by phone. Throughout our work she had expressed considerable skepticism about psychology. As a girl she had been interested in science and technology; at university she studied physics and mathematics and had no interest in such "soft" fields as literature, the humanities and social sciences. Her skepticism about psychological interpretation was evident when we discussed the dream she had the night before beginning the three times per week analysis on the couch. She was attempting to ascend in a strange old, coin-operated elevator, but had no coins. When I suggested she might feel a little rueful that this old-fashioned elevator-analysis was going to cost her some considerable "coin," she laughed uproariously. When I asked what was so funny, she chuckled and said: "Come on, Don, that's pretty far-fetched!" Oddly, despite her commitment to "hard" science and her skepticism regarding psychology, Mrs. A subscribed to some very "kooky" New Age beliefs in the field of cosmology and a credulous readiness to patronize various alternative health care practitioners and make use of their highly questionable theories and practices and to consume the various supplements they recommended for the range of largely hypochondriacal, hysterical and psychosomatic problems from which she suffered. In other words, the magical, omnipotent thinking underlying her idea that she had somehow murdered her ex-husband and was being persecuted for this crime was also evident here.

For some time, we focused on the quasi-delusion—*quasi* because, intellectually at least, despite speculations about immune systems, etc., Mrs. A knew it was scientifically doubtful that her decision to separate from her husband had caused his terminal illness. Her grown children remarked that their father had done nothing to reorganize his life after the separation. We discussed how in the context of the verbal and emotional abuse she had tolerated from him for years the idea that she had killed him was, no doubt, grounded in the anger and death-wishes she had done her best to repress. Gradually, with the intensification of the analytic process other elements of the case began to emerge—such as her life-long asthma, her claustrophobia and her hypochondria. The latter seemed based in an early, hostile identification with her mother who spent much of her time in bed suffering from depression and various hypochondriacal complaints.

Mrs. A had no memory of her early years so I instructed her to carefully interview her eight-year elder sister about this. It turned out that the patient was kept for several years in a crib under a slanted gable ceiling beside the mother's bed. Her sister would come home for lunch to find the mother still in bed in the dark, smelly room with the baby in need of a change. She reported being struck by how passive and unmoving the baby was—until she perceived the straps holding her down. This early neglect and enforced inhibition of activity and aggression is, I believe, the basis of the patient's reactive hyperactivity, hatred of passivity and claustrophobia. Her father was relatively absent, busy with work and, as she learned years later, with at least one or more ongoing affairs. Both in her childhood and in her marriage, Mrs. A had a lot to be angry about, but her anger had been both repressed and displaced outwards onto others, including her children who had had an irritable and at times explosive mother (as had their mother, my patient).

More and more Mrs. A's disidentification with the helpless infant she had been and her defensive hyperactivity, impatience, irritability, anger and need for control came into view. She and her ex-husband had self-righteously divided the world into "winners" and "losers" and had contempt for the latter as part of a right-wing sociopolitical ideology that had distinctly racist elements. She had utter contempt for "layabouts" and "welfare bums"; she had great difficulty hiding her anger and contempt when a supposed expert, a nurse-practitioner who spoke only broken English, "took forever" to examine her in a manner that, to Mrs. A, revealed utter incompetence. When telemarketers called she would scream at them and abruptly hang up. It turned out that in primary and secondary school she always managed to be at the head of the class and deeply resented and envied kids who despite not working as hard or achieving as much success as she did were nevertheless, rewarded by their parents in ways she was not. Road rage was a big problem: she became very annoyed in traffic and inclined to scream and flip the finger at drivers who enraged her in one way or another. One man became so angry at this that he chased her for miles until she escaped by turning into a police station. If her plane was delayed on the tarmac, Mrs. A's claustrophobia would emerge to the point where she was close to having a panic attack. It seemed as her anxiety and anger at being "trapped" rose so did her fear she might provoke airline security into throwing her off the plane. In this context, her resistance to being on my couch three times per week was understandable. She experienced me, like traffic or asthmatic congestion, as her binding, suffocating, persecutory mother. The "layabouts," "bums" and "freeloaders" represented her "useless" mother. Here we have a clue to the psychoanalysis of right-wing ideology, which at least in the case of Mrs. A, clearly involved a transference of both the hated, helpless self and the "useless," binding early mother-imagos onto the "losers" she held in such contempt.

The split-off anger arising from early trauma that had for years been discharged upon others through her irritable, at times explosive, entitled, self-righteous, judgmental and controlling behavior and attitudes was now also turned against herself as punishment. Until we discovered her preverbal trauma and began to discuss its implications it had received "zero process" (Fernando, 2009). After some months of intensive analytic work on all this, Mrs. A underwent a minor medical procedure that required her to remain lying down on a gurney for some time afterwards. She began to feel anxious and trapped, but was now more able to calm herself, recognizing that the rails on each side resembled the bars of a crib. Despite her desperation to find technical solutions to her problems, "quick fixes" of one sort or another, Mrs. A gradually came to understand her delusion of persecution, her fear of going to hell for killing her husband, as a projection into the future of a mental catastrophe, an emotional breakdown that had already occurred (Winnicott, 1965). Unearthing the preverbal history of hellish immobilization and understanding how it motivated her reactive hyperactivity, anger and need for control enabled Mrs. A to begin to resolve her resistance to personality changes yielding positive self-esteem, strengthening her conscience at the expense of her savage superego.

Chapter 3

Is there a future in disillusion?

In his 1953 review of John Bowlby's *Maternal Care and Mental Health*, Winnicott (1989) writes:

> I think Bowlby has omitted reference to the change-over from a relationship to a subjective object to a relationship to an object that is objectively perceived.... This disillusionment process belongs to health, and it is not possible to refer to an infant's loss of object without referring to the stage of disillusionment, and to the positive or negative factors in the early stages of this process which depend on the capacity of the mother to give the baby the illusion without which disillusionment makes no sense.
>
> (p. 429)

While both illusioning and disillusioning, constructionist and deconstructionist, elements are necessary in any optimally functioning analytic therapy, in contemporary psychoanalysis we may have become so focused on the responsibility that we, like mothers, have to provide illusion, that we are in danger of forgetting that we also share her responsibility to disillusion for, as Winnicott reminds us: "In terms of the earlier stages of the individual's integration ... the mother (in particular) plays her role as the one who disillusions her infant" (p. 145).

In associating the disillusioning aspects of psychoanalysis with deconstruction, I am employing this term, as in other of my writings (Carveth, 1984b, 1987), in a broad sense to refer to a critical approach that seeks in regard to any text, including that jointly created by analysand and analyst, to expose its latent or background assumptions, the various identities and oppositions out of which it is composed, the way it privileges one pole of a binary opposition over another rather than moving dialectically toward an ultimately incompletely attainable higher-order synthesis, its hidden contradictions, the disguised return of the repressed within it, and so on. In other words, although cognizant of the work of Derrida (1976) and others in the post-structuralist tradition, my use of deconstruction is sufficiently general as to make it virtually synonymous with what I see as the essence of psychoanalytic thinking in the first place. Despite Freud's mysterious turning away from his early enthusiasm for Brentano and his later disparagement of philosophy (Brook 2015), psychoanalysis has in my view, at its best, always entailed a process of dialectical deconstruction.

Analytic vs. non-analytic psychotherapy

In the concluding paragraph of their Preface to *Freud and Beyond*, Mitchell and Black (1995) write:

> The story is sometimes told that in the last years of his life one of the most important innovators in post-Freudian psychoanalysis had taken to bringing a gun with him when he presented his work at more traditional institutes. He would place it on the lectern without comment and proceed to read his paper. Invariably someone would ask about the gun, and he would say, in a pleasant voice, that the gun was for use on the first person who, rather than addressing the ideas he was presenting, asked instead whether they were "really psychoanalysis."
> (p. xxiii)

Whereas Mitchell and Black appear to approve of this analyst's oddly aggressive and intimidating appeal for tolerance, allow me to register my disapproval through a partial identification with the aggressor. Only partial because although having learned from experience I may well steel myself, I do not arm myself before presenting to psychoanalytic colleagues. But if I did decide to pack a gun, it would be for use on the first person who suggested that raising this question, whether this or that theoretical or technical approach is "really psychoanalysis," is somehow illegitimate or intellectually out of court. For it is a peculiar type of intellectual tolerance that is based on a prohibition backed by intimidation against raising certain questions, especially questions concerning the fundamental nature and defining features of our discipline and practice.

When many years ago I was asked to teach a course on termination to the fourth-year candidates at my institute, my initial reaction was, to be honest, less than enthusiastic. The topic and its associations with finitude, separation, terminal illness and death held little appeal. But as I surveyed the literature in the area in preparation for the course, I discovered that it raises all the most difficult, because they are the most fundamental and therefore, the most suppressed and evaded, questions in our field. For how are we to know when our work is more or less complete unless we know what it is that we are working at? How are we to know when it is time to terminate unless we know what goals we set out to accomplish? How can we tell whether or not the patient is "cured," or even whether an analytic process has taken place, unless we have some idea as to the defining features of the latter and, further, some notion as to how to distinguish an analytic cure from one brought about by suggestion, conversion, transference, support or Paxil?

So here we are, faced with the terrible, fundamental issues. How is analytic therapy distinguished from non-analytic therapy? What are the goals of psychoanalysis? How does it work? What is it about the therapeutic relationship and dialogue that contributes to or detracts from the achievement of genuinely psychoanalytic aims? Unless we have some answers to such questions, however tentative and approximate, we are in no position to be able to answer such practical questions as whether analytic progress is or is not being made; whether the analysis is helping or harming; whether the patient is or is not ready for termination; or whether what is taking place is really psychoanalysis or some other form of more or less useful psychotherapy. The fact that ideological psychoanalysts, orthodox or heterodox, seek to impose in an authoritarian manner their particular definitions of psychoanalysis is reason to decry ideology and authoritarianism in psychoanalysis, but not to seek to ban fundamental questions and conflicts in regard to its essential nature and definition.

Illusioning or disillusioning?

Certainly both Sigmund Freud and Melanie Klein gave pretty clear answers to these questions. They viewed psychoanalysis and analytic, insight-oriented, dynamic or uncovering psychotherapy as treatments for emotional disorder. And they viewed functional emotional disorders as conditions in which the patient's relationship to reality, his or her reality-testing, is, to a greater or lesser extent, impaired. Both Freud and Klein viewed neurotics and psychotics, their followers subsequently included borderline personalities as well, as captured or "possessed" by a range of positive or negative illusions or phantasies, which distort their relationship to the things, events and people around them. Patients were viewed as, to varying degrees, estranged from reality due to the operation of a wide range of distorting psychological processes such as repression, reaction-formation, displacement, transference, denial, projection and projective identification, to mention but a few of such defensive processes.

Since psychopathology was viewed as a condition in which one suffers from illusions and delusions, therapy was conceived as disillusioning, that is, as helping patients to fight free of their distorting transferences, projections, pathological identifications and irrational beliefs. Since pathology was seen as mistaking phantasies or feelings for facts, therapy aimed at enhancing reality-testing by helping patients become acquainted with their phantasies and feelings and their potentially distorting effects. In all this, there was no denial of the fact that therapists too have illusions and confuse reality and phantasy. Freud referred to the therapist's distorting transference as countertransference and the Kleinians came to include under this rubric the emotional effects induced in the analyst by the analysand's projective identifications as well. The traditional psychoanalytic insistence that analysts themselves undergo analysis as a precondition of practice is based on this recognition.

In these respects, Freud and Klein and their followers were operating, broadly speaking, as Enlightenment rationalists. But theirs was a chastened rationalism, tempered by romanticism's recognition of the irrational depths of human nature. But, however qualified in this respect, it was a rationalism determined to subject the irrational to a rational inquiry that, through knowing it, would disarm, or at the very least sublimate or redirect it, and bring it, for Freud (1933) at least, under an overall "dictatorship of reason" (p. 170). By definition, this was expected to be a reasonable dictatorship, reasonable enough to give the passions and the unconscious their due. But do we know of many reasonable dictatorships? While the goal of an integration of reason and emotion, Apollo and Dionysus, is laudable, over time Freud shifted away from a view of the unconscious as ordered by the laws of the primary process that he discovered—which, being orderly, might well be a source of both vitality and creativity—toward an increasingly dark view of the id as "a chaos, a cauldron of seething excitations" (Freud, 1933, p. 73), a kind of witches' brew, or a swamp that, like the Zuider Zee, needed to be drained for the sake of civilization (p. 80). For the late Freud, rather than being a potential source of creativity, the unconscious constituted a barbarous threat to the thin veneer of civilization. For many Freudians, analysis became more a matter of seeking rational mastery over, rather than integration of, emotion and the unconscious.

Freud, Klein and their followers were disillusionists; practitioners of what Nietzsche called the art of mistrust. Along with Marx and Nietzsche himself, they belonged to the Western tradition of suspicion (Remmling, 1967) whose adherents sought emancipation from the idols of the age by unmasking the false consciousness and dominant ideologies that are the collective equivalent of the personal illusions and delusions, the wishful thinking, transferences and projections that distort the neurotic individual's relation to reality. In a wider sense, such disillusionism belongs to what in various spiritual traditions is known as the *via negativa* or negative path wherein salvation or enlightenment is achieved less by direct discovery and affirmation of the truth than by seeing through the veil of Maya, the pseudo-truths that we mistake for it; less through knowledge (*gnosis*) of the one true faith than by transcending the counterfeit creeds that stand in the way of any genuine salvation; and less by direct discovery of the true self than by fighting free of the false selves that are its masquerades. For Simone Weil (n.d.): "It is not up to us to believe in God, but only not to grant our love to false gods."

The disillusionist spirit is captured nicely in the title of Erich Fromm's (1962) *Beyond the Chains of Illusion: My Encounter with Marx and Freud*. The notion of liberation as breaking the chains of illusion fits nicely with the saying: "And you shall know the truth; and the truth shall make you free," which sounds as if it might have been penned by Marx or Freud, but is actually attributed to Jesus (John 8:32). Understood in the Hebraic sense as a truth of the heart and not merely in the Hellenistic sense as a truth of the intellect, I think it is congruent with Wilfred Bion's conception of truth as the essential nutriment of the mind. According to the Symingtons (1996):

> O is the truth which can be known through the medium of science, religion or art. Different facets of O are known through these

different media. When O emerges in the psychoanalytic process, contact is made with that ultimate reality which illuminates the sciences, religion and art. Bion made contact with O through the medium of psychoanalysis, but his ultimate concern was with O and not the vehicle through which it was approached. His concern went deep into the sinews of existence.

(p. 181)

And, like Freud himself, Bion had a deep sense of the profound resistances in both the individual and, even more so, in the group to the emergence of such truth.

For workers in the tradition of suspicion therapeutic progress is judged in terms of advancing disillusionment. Are our patients succeeding in progressively overcoming their resistances, fighting free of their illusions (their transferences, projections, pathological identifications, false and distorting beliefs), and improving their capacities for reality-testing, for distinguishing phantasy from fact, past from present, inner from outer, the Imaginary from the Real, or are they not? The relative success or failure of the treatment and the timing of its termination are judged by these criteria, among others.

While for some all this may sound obvious and more or less taken-for-granted, for others the model I've just presented will sound alien and perhaps offensive. Those who have this reaction may wish to raise a host of objections to what they regard as the arrogance, authoritarianism, positivism, scientism, intellectualism, phallogocentrism, etc., of this perspective. For many today, the disillusionist perspective is not only regarded as outmoded, a relic of the past, but as morally suspect, best consigned to the dustbin of history along with the Eurocentrism, racism, patriarchal sexism, heterosexism and homophobia with which it is thought, I believe incorrectly, to be inextricably associated.

For many psychoanalysts a very different model of emotional disorder, therapy and cure became dominant. It is a model in which patients or clients are not so much seen as suffering from illusions that need to be transcended and conflicts that need to be understood, resolved or transformed, as from psychological deficits that need filling-in and from arrested development that needs to be resumed. It is important to recognize that both the therapies of construction and of deconstruction, of identification and disidentification, recognize the role of trauma, abuse and deprivation, among other factors, in the genesis of emotional disorders. In my opinion, it is simply incorrect to reduce the difference between the therapies of faith and the therapies of doubt to that between perspectives favoring nurture and those emphasizing nature in the genesis of psychopathology, or to identify the disillusionist approach with a now outmoded drive theory that evades recognition or underplays the significance of environmental factors in pathogenesis. In referring to drive theory as outmoded I refer to its literalistic form in which the *triebe* are defined by aim, object, pressure and source, the latter being held to be a somatic organ or zone (Freud, 1915a). In a broader, more psychological and less reductively biologistic form, as a theory of libidinal and aggressive *motives* and of oral, anal, phallic and oedipal *meanings* (freed from their alleged somatic sources, without of course denying the grounding of mind in brain) it remains significant.

While certainly acknowledging environmental factors, in the deconstructionist approach trauma, abuse and deprivation are seen as generating anxiety, rage, guilt, conflicts, defenses, transferences and projections in need of analysis. In contrast, in the constructionist or synthetic (as distinct from analytic) therapies, such factors are viewed as generating psychological defects, deficits and arrests that require the therapist's provision of the psychological and emotional nutriment of which the patient is thought to have been deprived and hence lacks, and provision of a climate in which arrested development may be resumed, this time in the presence of and under the benign influence of the therapist.

In this latter framework, what is considered therapeutically essential is not the therapist's provision of insight or self-knowledge leading to self-mastery. Rather it is the provision of corrective emotional experiences (Alexander & French, 1946) of holding (Winnicott, 1960b, 1962) and positive containment (Bion, 1962b), empathic understanding, affect attunement, selfobject responses to mirroring and idealizing needs, and optimal responsiveness (Bacal, 1985) as distinct from optimal frustration (Kohut, 1978), opportunities to internalize a good object (Klein, 1959) and to form positive identifications and the transmuting internalization (Kohut, 1978) of such experiences by the patient that is held to be curative. Under the conditions of safety, understanding and positive responsiveness provided by the therapist, the structural defects and deficits resulting from trauma, deprivation and arrested development are thought to be filled-in and new, healthier structures based on positive internalization and identification with the empathic and optimally responsive therapist are thought to be developed.

In this perspective, therapy is less a matter of removing pathogenic presences (anxieties, phantasies, illusions, transferences, projections, etc.) than of filling-in or compensating for pathogenic absences (the deficits and arrests resulting from environmental failure in childhood). Essentially, the damage done by parental deficiency, deprivation, impingement or outright abuse is to be corrected through internalization of the therapist's goodness. However much it may be denied, this alternative model is clearly one of therapy as a kind of reparative reparenting.

Without digressing into an historical account of how this shift in the conception of pathology and cure came about, suffice it to say that although the displacement of the insight/mastery model by the corrective emotional experience or reparenting model is most evident in such approaches as those of Guntrip (1971) and Kohut (1978) and their followers in relational psychoanalysis and self psychology, it has its roots both in ego psychology and certain aspects of Winnicott's (1960b, 1962) wonderfully inconsistent theorizing (the Kleinian and even Freudian elements were never disavowed despite the increasing privileging of illusion over disillusion and the gradual shift to a model of provision rather than analysis).

Although Freud himself took the fateful step of introducing the metaphor of structure into his psychology, he himself never allowed the notions of structural defect and deficit to displace his fundamental conception of pathology as rooted in conflict, phantasy and distortion and, hence, of the cure as conflict-resolution, reality-testing and mourning. But following the extension of Freud's structural thinking by Hartmann (1939) and the latter's introduction of an adaptive point of view emphasizing the importance in development of an "average expectable environment" (Winnicott's "facilitating environment"), pathology came increasingly to be conceptualized as structural defect, deficit and developmental arrest arising from environmental failure. Anna Freud's early insistence against the Kleinians that the child's ego is too weak to sustain analysis without a prior period of education and support (Edgcumbe, 2000) contributed to the legitimation of therapeutic approaches that were more supportive than analytic. As a result of these and other developments many analysts began to shift their understanding of the therapeutic process, away from conflict-resolution through insight, reality-testing, mastery and mourning toward a model emphasizing the therapeutic provision of corrective emotional experiences in which defects and deficits are filled-in through transmuting internalization and identification, and in which developmental arrests are overcome through the resumption of normal development in the context of and under the benign influence of the therapist *in loco parentis.*

It is not my wish either to polarize these models or to too easily set aside their fundamental and real differences by leaping to the dialectical logic of *both/and* rather than *either/or*. I believe that therapeutic provision is necessary, but insufficient, to bring about therapeutic disillusionment. In order for the latter to occur, a therapeutic or working alliance entailing an atmosphere of safety and trust, including confidence in the therapist's reliability, empathy, affective sensitivity and respect, must first have been established. In addition, any therapy that enables the patient to arrive at genuine insight and self-knowledge must in itself be regarded as a type of corrective emotional experience. But I believe that, today, the conditions or means to the end of therapeutic disillusionment—including the necessary and strategic provision of illusion in the earlier phases of work with more disturbed patients—have in some quarters become ends in themselves.

Via negativa

In his provocative essay, *Truth Therapy/Lie Therapy*, Langs (1980) argued that all the various criteria by which we might distinguish different types of talk therapy—supportive vs. analytic or dynamic; expressive vs. uncovering; empathic vs. interpretive; intrapsychic vs. interpersonal; one-body vs. two-body; etc.—pale in significance in relation to the more fundamental distinction between therapies that are fundamentally directed toward uncovering, facing and working through maddening memories, phantasies, wishes and feelings ("truth therapy") and those that seek to help by shoring up defenses against such disturbing contents ("lie therapy").

Although he acknowledged a role for lie therapy and recognized its helpfulness in certain contexts, Langs sought to clarify the status of psychoanalysis as a truth therapy, as Freud himself certainly conceived it. If I am uncomfortable with the notion of "truth therapy," this is certainly not because in the spirit of postmodern epistemological relativism I wish, like Pilate, to ask: "What is truth?" and wash my hands, but because, although truth exists, it is very hard to come by. Making its attainment the goal of therapy, smacks to me, of hubris. So I prefer the *via negativa* in which therapy is less a matter of arriving at the truth than of clearing the path toward it by removing a whole host of pseudo-truths, illusions or delusions that pass for it and that block the way to its progressive approximation.

That last phrase is reminiscent of Popper (1972) and I recognize a parallel between what I'm saying here about analysis and what he said about science—namely that it is less a matter of verification than of falsification, less a matter of achieving absolute knowledge of the truth, than of progressively approximating an ultimately incompletely knowable reality through a never-ending process of eliminating errors and illusions. With this in mind, I propose that we substitute for the distinction made by Langs (*Truth Therapy/Lie Therapy*) that between therapies, on the one hand, that in the long run seek to deconstruct and disillusion and those, on the other, that are content to construct or illusion. Whereas the disillusionist seeks ultimately to negate, falsify, debunk, deconstruct and invalidate various beliefs or phantasies considered pathogenic, the illusionist, engaging in a very willing suspension of disbelief, seeks to, at the very least, acknowledge the plausibility of, if not to affirm, confirm or validate, various constructions deemed to be of therapeutic benefit to the patient (and not merely as a temporary means to the long-term goal of disillusion). Whereas the constructionist seeks to inspire a new or a renewed faith by affirming the patient's narratives and metaphors, the deconstructionist raises doubt with respect to every narrative, most especially in regard to those taken so literally and held so unquestioningly that their status as metaphors or perspectives, as more or less plausible constructions, has been lost sight of altogether.

The goal of deconstruction is not the destruction of meaning, but only the revelation of particular meanings as more or less plausible approaches to and approximations of the truth, not the truth in and of itself. But while the goal of deconstruction is not the invalidation of belief as such, the entirely negative connotation in therapeutic circles of the term invalidation may cause us to forget how soothing, reassuring and liberating it was when, as children, our significant others did us the favor of invalidating our nightmare fears. Such invalidation is, I feel, an essential element of therapeutic work, especially with psychotic and near-psychotic patients.

I hope one day to write a paper entitled: "On Optimal Invalidation in the Therapeutic Process" to complement Bacal's (1985) emphasis upon "optimal responsiveness." Of course, Bacal might respond that sometimes the optimal response is invalidation! Although such an admission is gratifying up to a point, it at the same time arouses skepticism regarding a theory so infinitely expandable as to be able to say this.

Ogden (1986) nicely captures the spirit of the deconstructionist attitude toward clinical psychoanalysis:

> It is necessary that both the analytic discourse between analysts and the analytic dialogue between analyst and analysand serve as "containers" for the experience of confusion and not knowing. If all is going well in the analytic process, the analysand will inevitably complain that he understands even less at present than he did at the beginning of the analysis. (More accurately he understands less than he thought he knew at the outset of the analysis, and he is learning to tolerate not knowing.)
>
> (p. 2)

Here, of course, the sort of "knowing" and "belief" that must be therapeutically surpassed refers to what may otherwise be described as dogma, ideology or reification, or as an alienated or undialectical consciousness (characteristic of what Klein called the paranoid-schizoid position). It concerns the human proclivity to take one's stories and oneself entirely seriously, thus, succumbing to what Nietzsche called the "spirit of solemnity" characteristic of those whom Jean-Paul Sartre called *les salauds* (a difficult term to translate, although perhaps the "stuffed shirts" will suffice).

Parenthetically, it should be emphasized that if, for the disillusionist, it is important not to believe in anything, it is even more important not to believe in nothing. That is, if one opts for the deconstructionist approach it must be carried out consistently, to the point at which one becomes disillusioned even with one's disillusionment. Nihilism is still an "ism," a belief system, as much in need of deconstruction as any other. As Eliot (1950) says, "Disillusion can become itself an illusion if we rest in it" (p. 136). In other words, deconstruction as a therapeutic method is not just about dismantling the manic defense against depression; it is about dismantling (i.e., analyzing and resolving) the underlying depression as well.

Gnostic or agnostic?

In 1927, Freud, the great disillusionist, published *The Future of An Illusion*, which raised the question of the survival of religion in the age of science. Although in the 1960s and 1970s many social scientists confidently embraced the "secularization hypothesis," the idea that religion was in decline and would continue to be (Berger, 1967), by the late 1980s confidence in this hypothesis had been shaken. In the former Soviet Union there was a renewal of Orthodoxy; in both North and South America evangelical Christianity was on the rise and gaining in political influence; in the Islamic world secularization had made few inroads whatsoever. But the data Beit-Hallahmi (2015) reviews supports the secularization hypothesis: "It is clear that humanity is investing much less in religious activities today compared to 1000 years ago, 500 years ago, 100 years ago, or 50 years ago" (p. 206). In major surveys, "the number of individuals who identify as having no religion ... has been growing worldwide" (p. 207).

For Reiff (1966), the very decline of conventional religion led to "the triumph of the therapeutic." Like other secular ideologies, "antitheologies," or "surrogate faiths" that attempt to fill the vacuum and palliate the "nostalgia for the absolute" (Steiner, 1974) arising from the "death" (Nietzsche, 1882, section 125; 1886, section 343) or "eclipse" (Buber, 1952) of God in Western culture, the new ideologies of psychotherapy, however manifestly irreligious, have nevertheless, frequently functioned as its surrogate. At times such therapeutic "substitute faiths" have threatened to displace the tradition of suspicion that challenged religion. Operating through inspiration, identification and conversion (the transference cure), they have enjoyed increasing influence, at least among that portion of the population still interested in a *psyche* irreducible to somatic (neurochemical) processes. The anti-foundationalism and radical cultural relativism of postmodern theory casts as much doubt on the existence of truth as it does on the existence of God. In this context, critical reason (as distinct from merely instrumental or technical rationality) is itself called into question. If truth can no longer be distinguished from error or illusion, what point is there to critique? In this context, psychoanalysis, the form of psychotherapy traditionally most allied to the Enlightenment spirit of critique is itself in danger of being eclipsed, in psychiatry by biological reductionism and in the field of psychotherapy by fundamentally irrationalist, romantic and revisionist therapeutic religions, some of which nevertheless insist upon their right to advertise themselves in the therapeutic marketplace under the psychoanalytic "logo" even while having long abandoned any genuinely psychoanalytic *logos*.

I find it useful to think of the conflicting therapeutic strategies of today less in terms of truth and lie than of agnostic vs. gnostic therapy, the therapies of Enlightenment through disillusion wrought through doubt and the deconstruction of belief, vs. essentially religious or ideological therapies offering salvific belief ("saving knowledge" or *gnosis*) or a renewal of faith. Here, of course, I am employing the terms religion and faith both in the conventional sense of the dogmas and practices of churches, synagogues, mosques and temples and also with reference to a psychological or spiritual healing, a "cure of souls" or a "restoration of the self" achieved, not through the arts of suspicion and disillusion, but through a renewal of faith or belief—in some Other, or others, or in one's "self"—through connecting or reconnecting to some community of belief or milieu of "selfobject responsiveness."

I do not wish to leave the impression that I think of all religion and mysticism and spirituality as illusioning. That is one, perhaps the dominant, type of religiosity. There is another disillusioning or antinomian type of religion. Here we have, for example, the so-called "Death of God" theology (Vahanian, 1957; Altizer, 1970) that welcomes the collapse of the old faith for it is seen as idolatrous in any case. In so-called "religionless Christianity" (Bonhoeffer, 1953) for example, it is held that atheism as loss of faith in the pseudo-god of superstition is an essential precondition of development toward a mature faith, for the old deity was merely an idol in any case, a graven image that stood in the way of recognition and worship of the living God. Such antinomian forms of spirituality are profoundly disillusioning, but not in the service of positivism or atheism, but out of loyalty to what Tillich (1952) called "the God above God." On the other hand, those who, with Freud (1927, 1930), reject the "demythologizing" (Bultmann, 1958) or "As If" (Vaihinger, 1911) strategies of interpretation as attempts to deny one's atheism by manipulating the meaning of words will conclude that Tillich's "God beyond God" is merely another version of what Pascal (1669) condemned as "the god of the philosophers" as distinct from "the God of Abraham, Isaac and Jacob." In this light, Tillich's disillusionism, like that of Bonhoeffer, has fallen short. Decades earlier, in *Civilization and Its Discontents*, Freud (1930) wrote:

> It is ... humiliating to discover how large a number of people living to-day, who cannot but see that this religion is not tenable, nevertheless try to defend it piece by piece in a series of pitiful rearguard actions. One would like to mix among the ranks of the believers in order to meet these philosophers, who think they can rescue the God of religion by replacing him by an impersonal, shadowy and abstract principle, and to address them with the warning words: "Thou shalt not take the name of the Lord thy God in vain!"
>
> (p. 73)

Like Epstein (1995), I believe disillusionist psychoanalysis shares with certain Buddhist traditions a common commitment to the *via negativa* in which systematic deconstruction and disidentification promote a condition of non-attachment to every idolatrous image of the self and others. Here again, let us recall Ogden's (1986) belief that:

> If all is going well in the analytic process, the analysand will inevitably complain that he understands even less at present than ... he thought he knew at the outset of the analysis, and he is learning to tolerate not knowing.
>
> (p. 2)

I think this parallel becomes most evident in a certain version of Lacanian psychoanalysis that seeks (or at least is supposed to seek) to systematically dismantle the Imaginary specular "ego" (composed of all the images, representations and narratives that compose the self as idol) in favor of the emergence of the living "subject" that I think in some ways parallels Winnicott's (1960a) "going-on-being" understood, not reductively as referring exclusively to our psychosomatic existence, but existentially with reference to our ex-istence as symbolling and self-reflexive human subjects.

It is not my purpose here to go into the intricacies and obscurities of Lacanian psychoanalysis, religionless Christianity, Zen Buddhism or existentialism, so let me attempt to clarify the fundamental distinction I wish to emphasize—that between gnostic or constructionist therapies that operate primarily through processes of identification, and agnostic or deconstructionist ones that operate primarily through processes of disidentification. This, of course, is an analytical distinction, which means that in reality any therapy is likely to be a mixture containing both identifying and disidentifying elements in varying proportions. Certainly agnostic, deconstructionist or disidentifying therapy depends for its existence and effectiveness upon the presence in the therapy of gnostic, constructionist and identifying elements. For any therapy to work, there must exist a working or therapeutic alliance, an atmosphere of safety, some degree of basic trust or faith in the therapist and the process, and some considerable degree of shared belief or "knowledge" of what therapy is, what the respective roles of therapist and patient are, what goals they are working together toward, and so on. All this implies a degree of co-construction of the therapeutic space and process and an inevitable element of mutual identification. Beyond this, in work with more seriously disturbed patients, the provision of therapeutic illusion may be necessary for a considerable time before therapeutic disillusion becomes a possibility. For if, as Eliot (1944) writes, "human kind cannot bear very much reality" (p. 8), then such patients can, initially at least, bear even less.

But while I would suggest that deconstructionist or disidentifying therapy requires a background of constructionist and identifying elements, these are necessary, but insufficient to qualify the therapy as deconstructionist. For a therapy to constitute itself as agnostic (a therapy of doubt) as distinct from gnostic (a therapy of belief), it must move beyond this background of identification toward the disillusionist task. Like Winnicott's mother, it must move beyond the phase of providing illusion toward that of providing a corrective emotional experience of therapeutic disillusion and disidentification. Nothing less is "good enough." From a deconstructionist point of view, the problem with constructionist therapies is that they mistake the necessary conditions of analysis for analysis itself. The following table is an attempt to characterize the two approaches I've been describing along a number of different dimensions.

In a workshop following presentation of an early version of this chapter a participant noted that I seemed to identify with and privilege the agnostic over the gnostic approach. She wondered whether this identification required disidentification and whether my privileging of disillusion over illusion was not itself a kind of ideology or idolatry in need of deconstruction. I agreed she had a point. But I went on to add that in helping me recognize, deconstruct and disidentify from my bias, she had

Table 3.1 Illusioning and disillusioning

Faith	Doubt
Gnostic	Agnostic
Belief	Unbelief
Constructionist	Deconstructionist
Identifying	Disidentifying
Inspiration (synthetic)	Interpretation (analytic)
Empathic inquiry (Cs, Pcs)	Insight (Ucs)
Empathy as an end in itself	Empathy as a means to promote insight
Validating experience and the truth content in distortions and delusions	Invalidating distortions, overcoming self-deception, enhanced reality-testing
Pathology as defect, deficit and arrest	Pathology as conflict and distortion
Pathogenic absences	Pathogenic presences
Work within the metaphor or phantasy	Work outside the metaphor or phantasy
Therapy as provision	Therapy as analysis
Treat the child within	Deconstruct the phantasy of a child within
Help patients to integrate their multiple selves	Promote disidentification from the phantasy of being multiple
Repair developmental deficits through transmuting internalization of the empathic analyst	Promote disidentification from the phantasy of deficit and defectiveness
Help patients resume arrested development toward adulthood through a process of reparenting by the therapist *in loco parentis*	Promote recognition by patients that they are adults and their therapists are their more or less competent employees
Imaginary	Symbolic

at the same time validated the disidentification model. She was practicing it herself and encouraging me to do the same and for this I thanked her. Keeping in mind this higher-order commitment to disillusion, I have subsequently attempted to place greater emphasis upon the necessary provision of illusion "without which disillusionment makes no sense" (Winnicott, 1989, p. 429).

Melting frozen metaphors

As a result of experiences both on and behind the couch, I early came to the conclusion that, among other factors in the therapeutic action of psychoanalysis, the insight and mastery to be obtained through the deliteralization, deconstruction or dereification of literalized, reified, concretized, "dead" or "frozen" metaphors (and contrasts, splits or binary oppositions) are central to the psychoanalytic cure (Carveth, 1984b). The distinction between live and dead metaphor respectively overlaps to some degree Bion's (1962b) distinction between alpha and beta elements (the former have undergone "alpha-betization"), which itself resembles Segal's (1957) distinction between symbolic representation and symbolic equation, which in turn parallels Klein's (1946) distinction between the depressive/reparative and paranoid-schizoid positions. Whereas on the level of the depressive position the distinction between the metaphorical and the literal is maintained and each form of conceptualization and communication is employed in its proper domain, on the paranoid-schizoid level the distinction is blurred or lost altogether and the subject treats the metaphorical as the literal and *vice versa*. When the metaphor refers to the object, literalization turns analogy into identity and, as a result, a multi-dimensional view of the object is lost by a mind that, in this way, becomes one-dimensional; when it refers to the self, it effects a one-dimensional equation of the self with some concept or image—the paradigm case being the infant's misidentification of itself with its mirror-image in the mirror phase (Lacan, 1977, chapter one).

Through such experiences as helping A to see that the oral defense of his doctoral dissertation might not, in actuality, entail submission to a gang-rape and that the members of his examining committee might actually wish him well, or assisting B to understand that her lacking a penis was not equivalent to her *being* a "lack," or promoting C's recognition that employing his penis in sexual intercourse was not equivalent to the launching of a cruise missile, I came to understand that a significant portion of the emancipatory potential of psychoanalysis lies in its power to "resurrect" or bring "dead" metaphors back to "life." This process of turning identities back into analogies, of restoring the mental gap or space between a metaphorical concept and its object that enables us to remember that while a woman may in some ways be *similar* to a castrated man she is not one, or that while a man's wife may in certain respects *resemble* a vampire she may not literally be out for his blood, is I believe a central ingredient of both psychoanalytic insight and the analytic cure.

Clinical Vignette: In the latter example, Mr. B had been speaking of his wife as a vampire for weeks while I, of course, had been assuming that he, a highly intelligent and articulate man, was intentionally and self-consciously speaking figuratively. Gradually, however, the pervasiveness and concrete quality of his metaphor began to dawn on me and I ventured to say: "Of course, she is not a vampire." His response was immediate and loud—"But she is!"—and he proceeded to review for me yet again the many ways in which her behavior so eminently qualified her for this description. But when, allowing that his wife might well *resemble* a vampire in some respects, I nevertheless insisted that she was not literally a monster, he saw the point and was both startled and momentarily confused. However close to psychosis he undoubtedly was at times, to his credit he proceeded not only to disengage from this particular "dead" metaphor, but also to review and achieve some critical distance from a range of other metaphors that in concretized form had been controlling his thought and action. Although it in no way constituted integration and working through of the projected oral hate and envy underlying his "dead" metaphor, the fact remains that the psychic differentiation and integration entailed in its deliteralization (i.e., the progression from primary to secondary process thought or from the paranoid-schizoid to the depressive position), however incomplete and temporary, helped my patient to disengage from his battle to the death with his wife and enabled him to let go and walk away before either of them were, quite literally, killed.

In employing the terminology of "dead" and "live" with respect to metaphor we must avoid the false and unintended association of the former with states of relative emotional "deadness" and the latter with more "lively" states. In reality, "dead" or concretized metaphor, like paranoid-schizoid processes in general, can lead to states of great emotional intensity, while "live" metaphor, like depressive position phenomena in general, may be productive of more muted or modulated, even at times "deadened," emotional states. For example, if, as in the "dead" metaphor, life is a jungle, then daily existence becomes a very intense matter of life or death.

Despite training in the method of free association and familiarity with the primary process mechanisms of condensation and displacement that Lacan (1977), following Roman Jakobson (Jakobson & Halle, 1956), recognized as metaphor and metonymy respectively, it would seem that many analysts still fail to appreciate that psychic reality, as a system of concretized and absolute (primary process) or abstract and relative (secondary process) associations of one thing with another, is a system of metaphors, "dead" or "alive." This fact is evident in the reactions of some colleagues to criticism of the work of therapists whose technique appears to confirm rather than to question the "dead" metaphors central to their patients' pathology. It used to be not at all rare, for example, for therapists who worked with patients suffering from so-called "multiple personality disorder" or "dissociative identity disorder" to implicitly or explicitly affirm rather than question the patient's identification of the self with one or more figurative sub-personalities. Instead of helping patients deliteralize the concretized metaphors that dominated them and to see they were not literally "possessed" by various "alter-egos," but that it was only *as if* they were, and proceeding to analyze the psychological meanings, functions and origins of this concretized phantasy or fiction, such therapists operated from within the metaphor rather than calling the metaphor itself into question.

But while some therapists working with so-called "multiple personality disorder" took their patients' convictions of multiplicity at face value, others argued that in order in the long run to help the patient achieve an integrated identity it was necessary in the short-run to "make contact with" and at least appear to accept the "reality" of his or her multiple selves. Although it certainly runs the risk of being experienced as patronizing and even dishonest, I have little doubt that in the hands of experienced and skilled clinicians who employ it judiciously, self-consciously and with full awareness of its tactical aim the technique of strategically "joining" the patient's concretized metaphor as a means of liberating him from it can be effective in promoting emotional growth

(Lindner, 1950). But the self-conscious use of techniques of "joining," "taking the side of the resistance" and "paradigmatic intervention" associated with the school of Modern Psychoanalysis (Spotnitz, 1969; Marshall, 1982; Margolis, 1994)—techniques that, as Marshall (1998) pointed out, in some ways parallel self-psychological techniques of "mirroring" and "empathic immersion"—is to be clearly distinguished from the sort of well-intentioned, but excessive open-mindedness bordering on credulity that constitutes a major countertransference resistance to analysis. Ordinarily, in work with a patient who feels haunted, the analyst need not turn his sessions into séances, let alone share his belief in ghosts.

But there is little doubt that a strictly rational, interpretive technique that may be "good enough" in work with neurotic analysands is often ineffective in work with narcissistic, borderline and psychotic patients and in the face of various therapeutic impasses. In work with patients incapable, at least in earlier stages of therapy, of working on more rational levels, or in the face of various intractable narcissistic resistances, joining and mirroring techniques may sometimes be effectively employed as short-term means to the ultimate end of rational self-understanding. I find it ironic when analytic colleagues otherwise inclined to entirely reject the use of non-interpretive techniques as unanalytic, even when deliberately and strategically employed by experienced clinicians in work with patients unreachable by unmodified analytic technique and consciously adopted as a temporary means, a parameter (Eissler, 1953), to the ultimate end of rational self-understanding, themselves "join" their patients' phantasies in ways that more closely approximate a *folie-à-deux* than a considered technical means to a psychoanalytic end.

When some years ago I pointed out to colleagues working with so-called "multiple personality disorder," and who reported asking to speak to this or that "alter," that in doing so they were literalizing rather than deliteralizing or deconstructing the patient's concretized metaphor, I sometimes encountered the response that, for these patients, multiple personality is "no mere metaphor, it is their *psychic reality*!" While, to some, this may sound plausible, empathic, even wise, my own response was to insist that, on the contrary, metaphor is never "mere." The failure to understand that psychic reality *is* metaphor (and contrast) and that we are either controlled by our concretized metaphors (and oppositions or splits) or purchase some degree of freedom and self-control through deliteralizing or "resurrecting" them betrays either a surprising confusion as to the nature of analytic work or a degree of comfort with the model of analysis as conversion, inspiration and identification that I personally still find startling when I encounter it in analytically trained colleagues. What is at stake is the distinctiveness of psychoanalytic technique as an essentially rational modality of psychotherapy as opposed to non-rational, shamanistic techniques of all types, which however helpful they may be in various ways, bear little resemblance to the "truth therapy" (Langs, 1980) initiated by Freud.

Like social anthropologists studying alien belief systems, analysts of all schools are vulnerable to the danger of "going native" and being recruited by the belief system they were initially aiming to analyze. In this connection I recall anthropologist Laura Bohannan's gripping account (Bowen, 1964) of her struggle to retain some critical distance from the belief in witchcraft, so central to the culture she was studying, by returning to her hut each evening and reading Shakespeare. For example, in working psychotherapeutically with cases of so-called "environmental illness," instead of retaining sufficient critical distance from the patient's belief system to be able to appreciate the strong possibility that it may at its core manifest an essentially paranoid process underlying manifestly psychosomatic or hysterical symptoms, the analyst may develop an induced countertransference identification with the patient's belief system to the point of actually coming to share his or her illusion or delusion—a condition Grinberg (1962, 1979) refers to as "projective counteridentification." Analysts committed to the self-psychological and so-called intersubjectivist technique of "sustained empathic immersion" (Stolorow, Brandchaft, & Atwood, 1987) in the patient's subjective world may be particularly vulnerable to this countertransference problem—that is, to being unconsciously induced to extend their "willing suspension of disbelief" to at least a partial acceptance of and identification and collusion with the patient's phantasy system. People convinced they have been abducted by aliens have at times obtained treatment by "alien abduction therapists"; in some cases of so-called "environmental illness" self-diagnosed patients attribute the causes of their symptoms to a toxic environment and, in the absence of supporting scientific evidence, some practitioners agree. Various degrees of credulity toward and collusion with the phantasies and concretized metaphors underlying such "conditions" as "multiple personality disorder," "environmental illness," "multiple chemical sensitivity," "chronic fatigue syndrome," "fibromyalgia" and the like (Showalter, 1997; Carveth & Carveth, 2003), occur in a general medical context that is at best ambiguous with regard to their status and in a psychoanalytic subculture that, in its strong emphasis upon open-mindedness and empathic immersion and its aversion toward older therapeutic ideals of neutrality and objectivity, would seem to invite such countertransference resistance and its enactment.

There is no doubt that attempting to treat such paranoid conditions through confrontation and interpretation of their underlying projective dynamics is unlikely to succeed, at least until a strong therapeutic alliance has been achieved such that the patient's profound anxieties and consequent resistances have been significantly alleviated. Building such an alliance is in such cases the major part of the therapeutic task. Accomplishing it may require years of psychotherapeutic "holding" and positive "containment" before analysis through interpretation becomes possible. But during this period of therapeutic forbearance from confrontation and interpretation, the analyst need not succumb to projective counteridentification, managing instead to operate more like anthropologist Laura Bohannan, both empathizing with and yet struggling to retain critical detachment from the patient's illusion or delusion, perhaps self-consciously and strategically joining it at times, all the while inwardly maintaining a critical awareness of the essentially paranoid nature of the patient's condition. If such "joining" were tactical rather than credulous or ambiguous, the treatment might either be considered a psychotherapy devoted to building the conditions in which a psychoanalysis might eventually be possible or, alternatively, as an analysis in a very early stage in which a parameter is being employed. Although Heinz Kohut's techniques of mirroring and empathic attunement may well have been derived from his analyst, August Aichhorn (1935), the originator of the technique of self-conscious and tactical joining, the latter was more fully developed by Hyman Spotnitz (1969) and his colleagues in Modern Psychoanalysis than in self psychology (Marshall, 1998).

Therapeutic iconoclasm

> Iconoclasm n. breaking of images (lit. or fig. ...); iconoclast n. breaker of images, esp. one who took part in movement in 8th–9th c.

against use of images in religious worship in churches of the East, or Puritan of 16th–17th c.; (fig.) one who attacks cherished beliefs ...
(Sykes, 1982, p. 494)

An *iconoclastic* (breaking of the images) technique that, employing tactics of deliteralization, deconstruction, disillusion and disidentification, seeks to liberate Lacan's (1977) "subject" from the "ego," or Mead's (1934) "I" from the "me," or Winnicott's (1960a) "true self" from the "false self" may, at first, appear exceptional. But I suspect many analysts who may never have given much thought to these issues nevertheless do practice an essentially iconoclastic technique without recognizing it as such. I refer here to therapists for whom the analytic attitude is one of empathic interest in, but skeptical questioning of, every mental production of the patient without exception.

This analytic attitude may be grounded theoretically in different ways for different analysts. The Freudian ego psychologist may, with Brenner (1982), regard everything in the mind as a "compromise-formation" and, hence, as not in any way to be taken literally, but as requiring analysis. But for this to amount to an iconoclastic technique, it must be applied not merely to those of the patient's stories and images that are considered to be pathological, or outmoded, or based on transference or projection, and so on, but to all the patient's stories without exception. In other words, it must not be a matter of deconstructing scenarios considered to be neurotic repetitions in favor of the affirmation of stories considered to be more realistic, healthy or adaptive. In the iconoclastic approach, even the latter are considered to be narrative constructs.

Similarly, many therapists working in the Kleinian tradition may have been unselfconsciously practicing an iconoclastic technique. Without announcing the fact, Klein essentially transformed Freud's drive/defense or instinct/control model into a view of the mind as a phantasy system: as a kind of inner theater in which phantasies of loving and hating, destroying and repairing, taking parts of others into ourselves and putting parts of ourselves into others constitute the dramatic action. Properly understood, for example, Klein's concept of projective identification is not a mental mechanism in the sense of Freudian mechanisms of defense. Rather, it is a phantasy of putting parts of the self into others. Being aware, in this way, that the mind is composed of phantasy, many Kleinians are protected from the danger of reifying such phantasies and treating them as literal facts. This is not to say that such phantasies are not taken seriously. Rather, they are taken seriously as phantasies, for it is understood that our phantasies constitute the tissue of our minds and the basis of our actions. But by systematically viewing all mental contents as phantasy, such contents are systematically deconstructed and, perhaps without the therapist being aware of what she is doing, the patient is being helped to disidentify from each and every phantasy/construction and not merely from those judged to be outmoded, unrealistic or maladaptive. Over time, such systematic disidentification may lead to the relative decentering of the (specular) ego. With the gradual disappearance of the ego from center stage, the *subject*, hitherto "upstaged" or relegated to the wings, may begin to make an appearance. Here the *subject* refers not to anything like a knowable "true self," for in the iconoclastic perspective any self we know is not the true self, merely another idol in need of analytic deconstruction and disidentification. But if such work should prove productive then, freed from domination by all "self-knowledge"—by all the idols, icons and imaginings of the ego—the resurrected *subject* could, like Lazarus, resume its *going-on-being*.

I believe this is how, as therapists, we ought to be working. By this standard, I believe we fail a good deal of the time. The problem is that we are perpetually seduced into believing—that is, into taking quite literally, concretizing or reifying—a good deal of what our patients tell us about themselves. And, of course, in saying this, I do not mean to suggest we should disbelieve our patients, for often they are telling the truth. If, in keeping with an iconoclastic analytic attitude, we insist that our patients' stories, like our own, are constructions, this in no way implies that they are false or untrue. Our stories differ widely in regard to their degree of plausibility. Some are certainly more plausible than others. Some appear utterly implausible. But all are stories, narrative constructions shaping our experience. Once we have entered the domain of symbolic functioning—I am employing this term in a wide sense that includes the registers of both the Lacanian Imaginary and the Symbolic—we have no direct or symbolically unmediated mental access to the Real, apprehending it only through what Bion (1962b, 1963) called the "contact/barrier" achieved by "alpha function." Being induced to uncritically *believe* is quite distinct from the tactical *joining* of the patient's phantasy as a short-run means to the end of disillusionment in circumstances where the patient has not yet developed or has temporarily lost sufficient observing ego to work on more rational levels.

Our experience of any reality is a construction and reality may be construed or symbolized in a variety of ways, some of which are more plausible than others. In emphasizing this point, an iconoclastic technique seeks to open up for the patient a certain critical distance between himself as a critically questioning *subject* and his "ego" regarded as the sum-total of his experiences—that is, of the stories he tells himself about himself. But to insist that there is no experience apart from the constructions or interpretations that constitute it entails no necessary denial of empirical or historical reality. It is merely to insist that although "the facts" can, in a bald sense, often be known, such facts only *signify*—i.e., acquire meaning—through the conceptual structures with which we represent them to ourselves and others. Our experience is never direct or unmediated, but always already the product of interpretation. But contrary to a radical, postmodern epistemological relativism, this in no way implies that facts do not exist, are not discoverable or are irrelevant.

Clinical vignette

Mrs. C knew that her uncle initiated sexual activities with her when she was twelve. There was a good deal of evidence suggesting that something similar had previously occurred with her father, but there were no conscious memories supporting this; it remained an open question in her treatment. But even if such activities with the father had been confirmed, the issue would have been the same as in the case of those involving the uncle, which were indubitable: namely, what stories had Mrs. C elaborated, consciously and unconsciously, to lend meaning to these events? How had these events entered her experience or been taken up by her personal myth (Kris, 1956)? What *Weltanschauung* had she constructed and what experiential world had she devised to endow these events with specific meaning? In other words, how had these events shaped her experience and formed her ego or self?

At the outset of her work with me, Mrs. C was very resistant to the notion that what had transpired with her uncle (and possibly with her father) could be construed as "sexual abuse." This was a reading of the facts that she rejected. She denied that she was in any sense a "victim" and was more inclined to blame herself for what had transpired, even though she knew she had tried to avoid her uncle and that he was the initiator of these activities. Still, she blamed herself for not reporting what was happening to her mother or grandmother. And she was inclined to believe that she must have derived various sorts of pleasure and satisfaction from these events in addition to the distress they caused her. Over time, Mrs. C became more willing to acknowledge some validity to the reading of what had occurred as "childhood sexual abuse" and to accept that, in certain respects and to some degree, she may have been a "victim" and not merely a guilty agent. This greater flexibility of interpretation constituted therapeutic progress in my view.

Theory or ideology?

Some colleagues (illusioning) tend to take seriously the patient's phantasies (e.g., that he contains a helpless child, or suffers from a fragmentation-prone or defective self, or has multiple selves, or that she suffers from environmental illness, or was abused by her father and not just by her uncle in the absence of any memories or supporting evidence of the fact, or was abducted by aliens). Others (disillusioning) seek not to confirm, reify or work within such literalized metaphors, phantasies or belief systems, but rather to deliteralize or deconstruct and promote the patient's disillusionment with and disidentification from them—except when the analyst self-consciously decides to employ a tactic of joining or entering into the patient's phantasy system as a means to the end of helping him out of it (Lindner, 1950).

How easily in psychoanalytic work, without realizing it, we regress from an iconoclastic into an idolatrous, reifying or literalizing technique and from productively triangulated work on the level of the Symbolic to Imaginary dyadic enmeshment and identification. Even otherwise iconoclastic therapists are sometimes inclined to stop analyzing when they feel they have encountered "rock bottom." For Freud (1937), such bedrock was constituted by castration anxiety in the male and penis envy in the female. Few analysts today are inclined to regard such phenomena as unsusceptible to further analysis. Today we are more likely to make this mistake when, having analyzed all the defensive self-images, we feel we have bottomed out, as it were, in an abyss of psychotic emptiness or confusion: a primordial deficiency in the patient's self-structure. This is where our courage as analysts is put to the test. If we can persist with our iconoclastic or deconstructive method, this final myth of primordial chaos and deficiency may itself be exposed as yet another fiction of the "ego" serving a range of defensive functions. It is notable that Lacan himself appears to have been captured by an Imaginary reification of the phantasy of "lack" that prevented him from recognizing that *manqué-à-être* is no more to be privileged than its binary opposite, *plenitude*, or, for that matter, any other signifier.

Psychoanalytic theorists and therapists, not just our patients, fall into the type of literalization I have been describing. Regrettably, the history of psychoanalysis—like human history in general—is, to a considerable degree, a history of reification, ideology and idolatry. One of the benefits of the state of paradigm dispute that has prevailed in psychoanalysis for the past several decades is to make it more difficult (but by no means impossible) for psychoanalysts to continue to hold their theories in an ideological or idolatrous fashion. Paradigm dispute encourages comparative psychoanalysis and facilitates the development of multi-paradigm training programs and the emergence of an ever larger cohort of practitioners who refuse to identify exclusively with any one of the currently available models and who insist upon familiarizing themselves with and utilizing elements of each in a flexible and non-idolatrous fashion, recognizing the concepts composing them as metaphors more or less useful in particular clinical contexts.

Although he gave it the subtitle: *A Synthesis For Clinical Work*, Pine's (1990) *Drive, Ego, Object and Self* offered no real synthesis but only a pragmatic (and politically useful) clinical pluralism. Several years later, Pine (1995) wrote a paper with the title: *One Psychoanalysis Composed of Many*. It seems that Pine himself had become dissatisfied with the sort of pluralism that foregoes attempts at critical integration in favor of the sort of pseudo-tolerance that accepts the existence of multiple perspectives, as long as they each retain their integrity and are in significant ways kept separate from one another (like the meat and dairy products in Orthodox Judaism). Such non-integrative and uncritical pluralism recognizes the existence and affirms the legitimacy of Freudian, Kleinian, Kohutian and other perspectives and even suggests that while one patient might best be understood from within one such framework, another might better be approached from another. But it does not encourage the sort of critical thinking, comparing and contrasting, and winnowing that would lead one to attempt to separate the wheat from the chaff in each perspective, to eliminate the chaff and collect the wheat, and to practice from the standpoint of the resulting open and evolving synthesis.

Attempting to think and to practice in the latter way myself, I find I am sometimes taken to task for borrowing from, overlapping and not clearly fitting into any one of the current theoretical/clinical pigeonholes that characterize our field. There appears to be a latent norm operating to the effect that one should not mention the paranoid-schizoid position (let alone Ps) unless one is a Kleinian; one should not discuss "lack," the phallus or the Imaginary, the Symbolic and the Real, unless one is a Lacanian; nor mention the selfobject transferences unless one is a Kohutian. Such an attitude is, of course, essentially unintelligent, but it does offer a certain satisfaction to minds that need the security of working within one coherent system, or that operate more in terms of flags, emblems and badges of identity than of critical reason.

After several years of discussion in the Curriculum Committee of the Toronto Institute of Psychoanalysis regarding tensions and problems that had emerged in several classes of candidates, it finally became evident that these difficulties were intensified by certain types of instructors and instruction and alleviated by others. In a paper reporting her research in this regard, Levene (1996), who had herself been a candidate in one of the classes concerned, wrote:

> In summary, the results suggest that although the level of class conflict may have multiple determinants, the nature of the teaching model employed—that is, a discrete metapsychological model (either classical, ego psychology, object relations or self psychology, but not more than one preferred perspective) versus a comparative model (a model that suggests there are multiple ways to understand clinical phenomena)—may influence the level of class conflict.
>
> (p. 338)

I believe the difference between what Levene calls the comparative and discrete pedagogical approaches echoes the distinction between iconoclastic (deconstructionist) and non-iconoclastic (constructionist) psychoanalytic techniques. Whereas in the latter, usually without fully realizing it, the analyst joins the patient in the creation and reification of various constructions of his or her past and present identity—as opposed to assisting the patient in the discovery and deconstruction of such constructions and in disidentification from them—so, in the teaching situation, the educator may either seek to communicate the validity of constructions regarded as the truth (the discrete approach), or seek to convey such constructions as metaphors, more or less useful for various purposes and in various contexts, thus, preserving a degree of critical distance and disidentification from them (the comparative approach). In Kleinian terms, this is the distinction between analytic or pedagogical work on the level of Ps or D, between interpretations or theories operating on the level of "symbolic equation" or "symbolic representation" (Segal, 1957).

If in the iconoclastic view psychopathology entails reification and literalization and, hence, the (ultimate) goal of treatment is deliteralization, dereification or deconstruction, then it is ironic that in so many psychoanalytic training settings teaching is not infrequently carried on in a non-iconoclastic manner that reflects the very psychopathology, the literalization or concretization of metaphorical perspectives that we seek to cure. There is even a sense in which non-iconoclastic teaching practices reflect oedipal psychopathology: for in losing any sense of the gap, space or boundary between our theoretical models and the domains they seek to map, there is a loss or denial of triangulation. Instead of the triad composed of the model, the domain, and the "contact/barrier" (Bion, 1962b) linking and separating the two, there is a regression from the oedipal triangle and both the differentiation and integration characteristic of the Symbolic into the splitting and merging, the defusion and confusion, characteristic of the preoedipal dyad and of the Imaginary.

It is for this reason that, in my view, any insistence that proper psychoanalytic technique be purely iconoclastic or disillusioning itself reflects a concretized association and, hence, a regression from a higher-level form of iconoclasm. In the latter, there is recognition of both constructionist and deconstructionist elements in the analytic process. Whereas Grotstein (1996) wished to associate the former with psychotherapy and the latter with psychoanalysis—even while admitting that psychoanalysis inevitably contains psychotherapeutic elements—I believe that in any form of psychotherapy devoted to insight, including psychoanalysis, constructionist elements necessarily coexist with and even establish the necessary conditions (as working or therapeutic alliance, holding environment, conditions of safety and trust, empathic and affective attunement, and so on) under which the deconstructionist element of the therapeutic process may occur. But this is in no way to deny that there are forms of psychotherapy, some of which even insist upon misrepresenting themselves as psychoanalytic, in which constructionist, illusioning and identifying elements have virtually displaced deconstruction, disillusion and disidentification altogether.

If through analytic deconstruction and disidentification we succeed in becoming relatively disillusioned and, eventually, disillusioned even with our disillusionment, we may reach a state in which we no longer believe (in the idolatrous sense) in anything—and certainly not in nothing. It seems that far from needing to possess a firm (specular) ego in order to function in this world, we function far better as subjects liberated from such "possession." If we interpret Freud's and Hartmann's structural ego as the hypothetical apparatus mediating, like the brain itself, the functioning of the subject, then we may say that this (structural) ego functions far better when freed from interference by the "self" (specular ego, self-image or self-representation). For such acts as shooting the arrow, arranging the flowers, falling asleep, getting an erection, having an orgasm, riding a bicycle, freely associating, listening with freely hovering attention (Freud) or without memory or desire (Bion), etc., are quite distinct from and even incompatible with, the act of watching ourselves do or attempt to do these things (Herrigel, 1953; Epstein, 1995)—however essential such watching may be in first acquiring certain skills, in disrupting unwanted habits and, more generally, in self-monitoring, self-correcting and self-controlling activity.

In an important sense, it is not that our most disturbed patients, those in the psychotic and borderline spectrum, have insufficient ego strength or an insufficiently cohesive self. In a certain sense, they suffer from a (specular) ego or self that is far too strong and cohesive (albeit in the rigidity of its fusions and splits) and that exercises a kind of totalitarian control over their lives. Of course, in another sense, they have insufficient (structural) ego strength to be able to deconstruct and disidentify from the (specular or representational) ego or to enjoy a sufficient sense of the gap between themselves as egos and themselves as subjects to at least be able, on occasion, to laugh at themselves.

A higher rationality

While the model of therapy as deconstruction, disillusion and insight through interpretation works well with neurotics organized predominantly on the level of the so-called depressive (Klein, 1959) or historical (Ogden, 1986) position (D), patients suffering from preverbal or preoedipal fixations and organized predominantly on the paranoid-schizoid level (Ps) are highly resistant to it. While it may be the case that such patients require a kind of "ego-building" to facilitate a developmental shift from Ps→D, thereby promoting the emergence of a subject capable of self-reflection and thus, rendering them accessible to ordinary analysis, it is by no means clear that such preparatory work must take the form of a constructionist, illusioning or identifying approach. An alternative to both ordinary interpretive work and ego (self) enhancement through inspiration and identification is ego-strengthening through the resolution of intractable resistances that renders analytic progress through insight, reality-testing, mastery and mourning possible.

In answer to the question posed in the title, I believe there is indeed a future in disillusion. Truth therapy need not always be abandoned in favor of support, inspiration and identification in work with more primitive personalities. What is essential to recognize is that such patients are both terrified and (unconsciously) enraged. They have far too much anxiety to be able very easily to call themselves into question, and far too much basic mistrust (and paranoid anxiety due to projected aggression) to be able to cooperate with the therapist in a working alliance of the sort that generally emerges fairly readily with neurotics. Although they do not free associate or bring interpretable material in the usual ways, through their very resistances they convey to us their own maddening emotional life. By means of emotional induction or projective identification they evoke in us feeling-states of a highly distressing sort that are difficult for us to tolerate.

I employ the term "tolerate" here in order to distinguish positive Bionian containment, in which the analyst "contains" the patient's "poison" in order to "detoxify" or "metabolize" it through "alpha function" and return it in digestible discursive or nondiscursive symbolic forms, from the negative containment in which patients dump their madness (undigested or undigestible "beta elements") into us, giving them relief by driving us crazy, or in which we contain negatively, in the sense of destroying and then evacuating or re-projecting what has been projected into us. While we should certainly avoid overly identifying with the feelings and roles patients pressure us to feel and even enact, we do need to tolerate such induced feelings—i.e., contain them in the positive Bionian sense.

To do this, it is essential that we attempt to distinguish the *subjective* countertransference arising from our personal issues and conflicts from the *objective* countertransference representing the feelings of our analysands that have been evoked or induced in us as they attempt to make us suffer what they suffer—positively, out of a desire to communicate and, negatively, out of sadism. If we can recognize this, we will not take what is happening too personally and, as a result, we may be able to tolerate the induced feelings, to feel compassion for our patients (we know how they feel!), to hold and manage the therapeutic frame, to appreciate and not merely oppose the resistances, even to join them on occasion, and to interpret in a way that our analysands can hear as truthful and begin to use to get a bit outside of and begin to disidentify from their enclosed or foreclosed psychic realities. In these ways, we may be able to assist such patients to tolerate rather than evacuate the psychic pain their pathology has served to evade, to put it into discursive or nondiscursive symbolic forms, to learn to think about it and to begin to learn from experience. What is essential is not that patients put everything into words, but that they put everything into symbolic forms; in my view speech should not be privileged over art, music, dance, mime, liturgy and other nondiscursive symbolic forms (Langer, 1951).

As a part of such containment, it may be necessary at times for the analyst to strategically refrain from calling the patient's psychic reality into question, while maintaining an inner reserve and a determination to confront, question, clarify and interpret once a therapeutic alliance, sufficient observing ego and an object-instinctual as distinct from a narcissistic transference (i.e., a whole-object *vs.* a part-object and part-self transference) have developed. Such toleration by the analyst of the analysand's inability to bear any difference or triangulation of the therapeutic space is not necessarily to surrender the rational goals of analysis, but merely to adhere to a "higher rationality" capable of distinguishing a battle from the war. Yet some patients operating in the paranoid-schizoid position cannot even tolerate the analyst practicing "silent interpretation," thinking but forbearing from sharing one's thoughts with the patient. Britton (1989) describes such a patient screaming at him to, "Stop that fucking thinking!" (p. 88).

Can rationality and self-reflection be achieved by non-rational and non-reflective means? How else could they conceivably be achieved? How are rationality and the capacity for self-reflection developed in children? Do they not at least to some extent come to accept the reality principle and to call themselves into question out of love for us? Is it not our positive containment and holding, in addition to our instruction, boundary-setting and boundary-maintenance that enable them to do this? Surely Winnicott (1989) is correct when he emphasizes the mother's responsibility "to give the baby the illusion without which disillusionment makes no sense" (p. 429) and to view analysis as a process in which, *for a time*, the analyst, like the parents, refrains from asking whether the object is inner or outer, invented or found, constructed or discovered, an act of forbearance (but not of forgetting or blurring these distinctions) that assists the analysand to undergo a crucial *transition* from relations with subjective objects to relations with objects objectively perceived. Unfortunately, it is my impression that these questions are often insufficiently struggled with by those who have abandoned Freud's Enlightenment ideals in favor of some pragmatic version of the cure through suggestion, conversion and transference, the therapeutic or gnostic religions of illusion and identification, from which he always sought to distinguish an authentically emancipatory and disillusionist psychoanalysis.

Chapter 4

Self psychology and the intersubjective perspective
A dialectical critique

As early as the 1950s, psychoanalysts began to report significant changes in the forms of psychopathology they were observing. According to Erikson (1950):

> The patient of today suffers most under the problem of what he should believe in and who he should—or, indeed, might—be or become; while the patient of early psychoanalysis suffered most under inhibitions which prevented him from being what and who he thought he knew he was.
>
> (p. 279)

In contrast to the intrapsychic or neurotic conflicts of the relatively structured personality are what Erikson described as "identity diffusion," the fragmentation and emptiness Kohut (1978) saw as characteristic of the "Tragic Man" replacing the "Guilty Man" of an earlier era. According to Lasch (1979), in the "culture of narcissism" produced by postwar consumer as distinct from industrial capitalism, indulgence and release rather than inhibition and repression are encouraged and the result is "the narcissistic personality of our time."

In *The Obsolescence of the Freudian Concept of Man*, Marcuse (1970) argued Freud had been right, but was now wrong because the social reality had changed, no longer producing what Riesman (1950)—who as Burston (1991) points out was for a time an analysand of Erich Fromm's—called an "inner-directed," but only an "other-directed" type—i.e., what Fromm (1947) described as a "marketing" character. For Marcuse, due to socio-historical changes in the structure of the nuclear family in post-industrial societies "the 'individual' as the embodiment of id, ego, and superego has become obsolescent in the social reality"

(p. 44) and a new personality type has emerged whose ego-identity is diffuse and shifting due to its lack of inner support from internalized values and ideals. In this situation, the "mediation between the self and the other gives way to immediate identification" while "the ego shrinks to such an extent that it seems no longer capable of sustaining itself, as a self, in distinction from id and superego" (p. 47). In these circumstances, the inner-directed character gives way to an other-directed personality oriented less by the "gyroscope" constituted by internalized values and goals than by a wish to achieve a positive self-image in the mirror constituted by significant others and by a radar-like sensitivity to their expectations and responses.

While recognizing the reality of these manifest differences, in my view, on deeper levels "Tragic Man" is guilty. The narcissism, fragmentation, emptiness and other manifest symptoms of the disordered self, however much they reflect early environmental failure, turn out on analysis to be grounded in conflicts with which we have long been familiar. The fragmented self is in my view ultimately produced by a fragmenting, sadistic superego, itself fed by the rage stemming from preoedipal and oedipal trauma and frustration, as well as by the largely unconscious, primitive, persecutory guilt that inevitably arises from such reactive aggression. The defects, deficits, fragmentation and emptiness characteristic of the disordered self are not the simple, direct result of inadequate provision, but rather, the consequence of a devastating attack by an annihilating superego fueled by rage in reaction to trauma. While self psychology lost sight of the self-destructive dynamics mediating between the original trauma and the resulting fragmentation, Kohut's contributions are helpful in the earlier stages of work with narcissistic patients in establishing a working alliance and in understanding the kinds of transferences they produce at the outset.

Because of the very instability of their sense of self and self-esteem such patients are very self-involved, preoccupied either with their inadequacy, depression and lostness or their compensatory grandiosity. In either case they do not tend to develop the object-instinctual transferences (directing feelings of love and hate toward the analyst) characteristic of neurotic patients that Freud believed were necessary if the patient was to be analyzable (since he regarded analysis precisely as the analysis of object-instinctual transference). For Freud, the "narcissistic neuroses" were unanalyzable and several generations of classical analysts, struggling with boredom and irritation as such patients droned on and on about how great or useless they were while showing little interest in their analysts, tended to agree. Heinz Kohut's enduringly valuable contribution was to show such patients do develop transferences and can therefore, be analyzed after all, but these are transferences of a very different type: "selfobject" rather than object-instinctual transferences.

At the outset Kohut printed the term "self-object" with a hyphen and defined it as an object incompletely differentiated from the self. In keeping with this he described a "merger" transference and considered the analyst's countertransference boredom and sleepiness as due to the patient's disinterest in him or her as a separate self. But Kohut soon became aware of the growing impact of infant research that was challenging the Freudian concept of primary narcissism or oceanic oneness at the beginning—a concept long rejected by Klein and her followers. While many mainstream followers of Freud, Mahler and others did their best for years to deny the evidence contradicting their cherished myth of gradual differentiation or separation-individuation out of primordial oneness, they were finally forced to sacrifice the notions of primary narcissism and autistic and symbiotic phases (if not phantasies). As indicated previously, this in my view not only vindicated Klein, but demonstrated that psychoanalytic theory can at times and in some areas yield to empirical evidence, thus, refuting the charge by Popper and others that it in no way qualifies as a science on the grounds that its propositions are unfalsifiable, There is no doubt that some of its propositions *are* empirically unfalsifiable—its foundational value judgments, for example. But that does not mean that *all* of its propositions are immune from empirical testing. In Chapter 10, I argue against Erich Fromm's sociological relativism with respect to the Oedipus complex, which he views as an authority conflict under patriarchy, that there is ethnographic evidence suggesting that, in a slightly modified form (as a narcissistic more than a reductively sexual project), it is universal after all.

Recognizing early on the import of the infant research, Kohut quickly dropped the merger transference and the hyphen and redefined the "selfobject" as an object not incompletely differentiated *from*, but rather performing needed functions *for* the self. He proceeded to list these functions, the first of which is mirroring, normally provided by the mother, the mirroring selfobject. In cases of inadequate mirroring the incipient self sometimes has another opportunity to achieve cohesion through idealization of and identification with the calmness and strength of the father, the idealized selfobject. Later self psychologists added the "alterego" selfobject that provides a kind of "twinship"; an "adversarial" selfobject providing firmness and boundary-maintenance; even an abstract selfobject such as God or an image of future appreciation by posterity that sustains the self in the face of current degradation or neglect. Now patients with disordered selves as a result of inadequate mirroring (mirror-hungry personalities), or insufficient opportunity to idealize (idealizing personalities), and others could be understood as forming selfobject transferences in an attempt to renew thwarted development and repair a fragmentation-prone self.

I think it is now widely recognized that at least a part of the difference in the understanding of narcissistic personalities offered by Kohut (1971) and Kernberg (1975) respectively, had to do with the different patient populations they were treating. Whereas for Kernberg, idealization often amounted to a need to build the analyst up as a defense against a profound unconscious wish to tear him down and destroy him, a dynamic that certainly exists, especially among patients organized on the borderline level, Kohut saw idealization more as a need to resume with the analyst a normal childhood developmental need that was thwarted leading to premature and traumatic disillusionment. Both of these dynamics occur, but with very different types of patients. Here accurate diagnosis is essential to prevent disruptive misunderstanding.

Kohut conceived of the cure as taking place through a "disruption-repair" cycle; at times the analyst's empathic and affect attunement would inevitably fail, the patient would be disrupted, experience fragmentation, and perhaps resort to a "disintegration product"—turning to driven sexuality or substances, for example, in a desperate attempt to hold together in the face of painful states of fragmentation. I think the concept of the "disintegration product" is one of Kohut's most interesting and currently neglected ideas: behavior mistakenly understood in classical theory as manifestations of sexual or aggressive drives could now be understood as driven by a desperate need to hold a fragmenting self together in the face of narcissistic injury and mental pain—that is, as the defensive *use* of sex or aggression in the service not of drive gratification per se, but of self-preservation. Here we may see a certain parallel between Kohut and the later Lacan. Both are concerned with fragmentation or the coming apart of things that should be linked (the self, the

Borromean rings) and the use of various phenomena (disintegration products, the *sinthome*) in attempting a kind of reintegration.

I consider the psychology of the self (Kohut, 1959, 1971, 1972, 1978, 1979, 1984) and the intersubjective perspective (Atwood & Stolorow, 1984a, 1984b; Stolorow, Brandchaft, & Atwood, 1987; Stolorow & Atwood, 1992), clinically valuable, especially in the understanding and resolution of therapeutic impasses in work with more difficult patients, but find significant epistemological and other problems in both. I maintain a distinction between self psychology (or selfobject theory) and the intersubjective approach in light of claims by the authors of the latter that, although widely regarded as an offshoot of the former, their perspective has independent roots in phenomenology and personology and subsumes and transcends self psychology.

Kohut's method of argument, like Freud's, may be regarded as "dialectical" in the sense in which, deriving from the Greek *dialektos* meaning "discourse" and *dialektike* meaning "debate" (Sykes, 1982), dialectic refers to reasoned argument as such. But, beyond this very general usage, the concept is associated with the dialectical logic of Kant, Hegel and Fichte in which thought is held to evolve through the clash of opposites. Although Hegel (1807; Singer, 1983) himself seldom employed this formula, dialectical logic entails the idea of a thesis giving rise to an antithesis that negates it and, out of this opposition, a synthesis emerges that negates, preserves and elevates the opposing elements. This synthesis then becomes the thesis evoking another antithesis, giving rise to yet another synthesis, and so on, as both thought and history evolve. With Marx, Hegel's dialectical *idealism* is brought down to earth, as it were, taking the form of a dialectical *materialism* in which the clashing elements are not ideas, but socioeconomic classes, the thesis being the bourgeoisie, the antithesis the proletariat, and the synthesis the socialist state destined to "wither away" with the emergence, at the end of history, of the final communist utopia (Singer, 1980). Against the idea that dialectical thought must envisage a synthesis that necessarily negates the real autonomy of the elements composing it (rather than also preserving and elevating them), Adorno (1966) offers a "negative dialectics," while Gilles Deleuze and Alain Badiou describe a "disjunctive synthesis" or a "synthesis that separates" (Lecercle, 2010).

It is important to contrast the dialectical approach with both monistic and dualistic frameworks. In monism no fundamental conflict is recognized; there is a single force, principle or process of development, as for example, in Freud's libido theory during that brief period between the breakdown (Freud, 1914) of his initial instinctual dualism (sexual vs. self-preservative drives) when only the sexual drive was recognized before dualism was reaffirmed with the introduction (Freud, 1920) of the final dual-drive theory (*Eros vs. Thanatos*). In dualism, the clash of opposites is fundamental and although the form of the conflict may be modified, as from less adaptive to more adaptive compromise-formations (Brenner, 1982), conflict itself is built-in to the very nature of reality or the psyche and no fundamental transcendence is possible.

In dialectical thinking, by contrast, conflict is recognized as a necessary but intermediate stage in a three-step developmental process in which an initial monism gives way to a dualistic clash of opposites, which is then transcended, however momentarily, in a higher-order synthesis of some type. Whereas the figures *one* and *two* are central to monism and dualism respectively, the figure *three* is fundamental in dialectical thought, whether the "trinity" be mother, child, and father; or object, self, and the boundary separating them from one another; or Father, Son and Holy Spirit. In this perspective, both monism and dualism reflect flight from and resistance to triangulation or oedipalization (Lacan, 1977).

An argument can be made that whereas Freud's thought entails a mixture of dialectical and dualistic elements—the former being reflected in, for example, his epigenetic model of development and the latter in his instinctual dualisms of sexual vs. self-preservative drives and *Eros* vs. *Thanatos*—Kohut's thinking displays both monistic and dualistic trends. In his monistic theory of motivation, for example, Kohut (1977) seeks to abandon a view of human nature based on the conflict model in favor of a perspective emphasizing the centrality of ambition, aspiration and hope in human subjectivity—a view of "Tragic Man" who, unlike the conflict-driven "Guilty Man" of Freudian theory, is a goal-directed being seeking the "realization ... of the blueprint for his life that had been laid down in his nuclear self" (p. 133) through relations with his selfobject milieu. Beyond this, however, self psychology has presented a range of dualisms: development of narcissism *vs.* object love; narcissistic *vs.* object-instinctual transferences; deficit *vs.* conflict; self-disorder *vs.* structural neurosis; mirroring selfobject *vs.* idealized selfobject; pole of ambitions *vs.* pole of ideals; and so on.

The differences between monistic, dualistic and dialectical thinking may account for the fact that the proponent of the latter is likely to be misunderstood by both Freudian and Kohutian colleagues. Whereas the former will regard him as a Kohutian fellow-traveler, the latter will suspect him of unresolved Freudian or Kleinian tendencies. Although there is something in both these views, the deeper truth is that the dialectical thinker rejects both dualism and monism in whatever form or tradition they appear. He is always looking for the third term, the synthesis, not as any utopian final end to conflict, for allowing that conflict is inevitable, he nevertheless insists that conflict is not all. In dialectical thinking, *development through differentiation and integration* is also a reality; evolution is real. Whereas Hegel, justifiably or not, has frequently been seen as positing an attainable final synthesis, more recent dialecticians, such as Adorno (1966), envisage a progressive, but essentially interminable development toward an ultimately incompletely knowable whole (Carveth, 1984b, 1987).

For the dialectician the enduringly valuable aspect of Freud's thinking is not the dualism at the root of his pessimism, but rather his epigenetic model (Freud, 1905b; Erikson, 1950, 1959), in which conflicts at one level give rise to a synthesis permitting advance to a higher stage where conflicts emerge once again and so on as development proceeds. Naturally, devolution as well as evolution, regression as well as progression, occurs. The point is only that, against the monists, conflict is a reality; but against the dualists (including the dualistic elements of Freud's own thinking), conflict is neither the only nor the ultimate reality. Refusing views of reality in which conflict is either denied or totalized, the dialectician insists that just as it is possible to regress to a primitive monism below conflict, so one can progress to a state beyond it, at least until conflict emerges once again on this higher level. The dialectician's favored image of living systems is the spiral, which in health ascends, but in illness yields to fixation, stasis or premature decline.

Dialectical thinking is essentially allied to Klein's (1946) depressive position in which the either/or thinking (splitting) characterizing the paranoid-schizoid position is transcended. Since the attainment of the depressive position makes truly oedipal conflict in which the rival is both hated and loved (instead of merely hated as in preoedipal triangular conflict), the neurotic has the potential for dialectical thinking whereas schizo-paranoid (severely narcissistic, borderline and psychotic) patients do not (at least without substantial therapeutic development). Being able at times to transcend splitting the neurotic may sometimes suffer from paralyzing ambivalence, "holding a candle," as it were, for both Saint George and the Dragon. The dialectician strives to transcend such paralysis by working out a synthesis between the opposing views. When Freudians attack self psychology, the dialectician defends it. When Kohutians attack Freudianism, the dialectician upholds it. The dialectician sees virtue in both perspectives and yet, because she also sees both as one-sided, she says, "a pox on both your camps." She wants each to move toward the ultimately incompletely attainable synthesis. For the dialectician, advancing toward the synthesis (i.e., the depressive position) is our job. Freudian reductionists will say of the dialectician, here is someone determined to get mother and father together again; while Kohutian reductionists may regard her as a fence-sitter with an inordinate need to be accepted by everyone. But recognizing that mother and father rightfully belong together reflects the very oedipal resolution Freudians espouse; and only a peculiarly masochistic fence-sitter would risk alienating both camps by openly disagreeing with each. One is more likely to find the dialectician impaled on the fence rather than sitting on it.

Both monistic and dualistic perspectives give rise to either/or thinking, that is, to the splitting that characterizes Klein's paranoid-schizoid position and the Lacanian Imaginary. For, on the one hand, if there is a unitary principle of right, then everything else must be wrong and, on the other hand, if all that exists are the two poles of a binary opposition, then one must choose either Scylla or Charybdis. By at least acknowledging both horns of such binary dilemmas, dualistic thinking occasionally gives rise to a dialectical recognition of possible ways of passing between them. As I have argued elsewhere (Carveth, 1984b, 1987), a defining feature of regressive mental functioning is the privileging of one or the other pole of such binary oppositions, affirming thesis over antithesis or vice versa. Correspondingly, the psychoanalytic method may be conceptualized as, in part, a process of dialectical deconstruction (Barratt, 1984) in which the repressed complementarity and mutual dependence of the opposing terms is exposed.

If, as I believe, the foundational opposition constructing psychic reality is *Similarity/Difference (Connection/Separation)*, some people (the linkers) will tend to privilege the former term over the latter, while others (the separators) will tend to reverse this hierarchy. In contrast, the mark of mature mental functioning is the capacity to achieve and hold the synthesis in which neither pole is concretized or absolutized. Here, instead of the sense of connection or similarity regressing to the level of absolute oneness or identity, and the sense of separation or difference regressing to the level of absolute opposition or antithesis, the recognition of connection within separation and of difference within similarity is retained. Translated into clinical terminology descriptive of the "borderline dilemma" (Carveth, 1993), this refers to a person's capacity to experience separation without abandonment and connection without fusion or engulfment.

Because both analysts and analysands have to struggle with the existential dilemma of oneness vs. separateness, one fruitful way to think of the differing theoretical and technical stances that divide the psychoanalytic community is in terms of their respective biases toward one or the other pole of this fundamental opposition. If the Freudian, Kleinian, and Lacanian traditions can be said to manifest a bias toward separation or dis-integration (*Thanatos*) in their emphases upon abstinence, frustration, boundary-maintenance, and confrontation with the facts of separateness and "lack" through interpretation leading to insight, mourning and ultimate accommodation to the reality principle, then various relational and self-psychological perspectives may be said to reflect a bias toward integration (*Eros*) in their stress upon the importance of affect attunement, empathic linkage or connectedness, holding, and positive containing as the prerequisites for "transmuting internalization" of the analyst as a good object or selfobject.

Whereas analysts of the Freudian and related schools tend to define pathology as excessive symbiosis (Langs, 1978) or "forbidden mixture" (Chasseguet-Smirgel, 1984) and, consequently, regard the cure as one or another form of renunciation, resignation, or "acceptance of castration" (Lacan, 2002), those who lean toward the relational and self-psychological schools, regarding states of disconnection and fragmentation as the essence of pathology, prescribe "therapeutic symbiosis" (Searles, 1965), empathic attunement, and the self-selfobject connection entailed in "transmuting internalization" as the very basis for "the restoration of the self" (Kohut, 1978). By way of contrast, from a dialectical point of view our task is to deconstruct the privileging of either the *Thanatic* or the *Erotic* orientation and instead to work toward a synthesis in which the former is tempered by the latter and the latter fortified by the former. In terms of the analyst's concrete struggles with countertransference (broadly defined) in the heat of the analytic situation, the dialectically deconstructive method is one wherein the analyst intentionally "shifts gears" at crucial moments, decentering from the perspective she has been employing and surveying the situation as it appears from the opposing, but complementary point of view.

A by-product of Kohut's unitary theory of motivation as the search on the part of the self for attuned selfobject responsiveness is the either/or thinking in which a view of the subject as conflict-driven is opposed to a view of it as pursuing its ambitions, aspirations and hopes. But why cannot the human subject be seen as both conflict-driven and goal-oriented? In my view "Tragic Man" usually turns out to be "Guilty Man" on a deeper level. If by the conflict model we mean the drive model, the idea that the subject is fundamentally driven by somatically-based instinctual drives of sex and aggression as opposed to being fundamentally motivated by attachment or selfobject needs, then the conflict model would have to be abandoned. But why is the conflict model necessarily associated with the drive model? Historically, of course, this was the case, but this association is not a necessary one. We can reject the drive model and yet preserve the conflict model. But here, conflict is not between defenses on the one hand and somatically-based drives on the other, but between defenses and the narcissistic rage, archaic longings, and "disintegration products" emerging from frustrated selfobject needs—and also, I would insist, from the inevitable frustration arising from our existential predicament as self-conscious *being-toward-death* (Heidegger, 1927).

It is not only possible for attachment theorists and self psychologists to retain the conflict model while rejecting the classical drive model, it is necessary for them to do so. For the fact is that people who have had their fundamental attachment and selfobject needs frustrated—by "basic" frustration (the unavoidable existential minimum), "surplus" frustration (due to environmental failure), or both—suffer from varying degrees of conflict. This distinction between the "surplus" frustration arising from environmental or selfobject failure and the "basic" or existential frustration arising from the human condition as such is necessary in order to combat yet another instance of either/or thinking characteristic of psychoanalytic theory in general. For although virtually everyone pays lip service to the idea that the nature/nurture controversy rests on an essentially false dichotomy and that both hereditary and environmental factors interact in the causation of human behavior, what remains largely missing from psychoanalytic discourse (except in the work of the existential analysts, Fromm, and Lacan) is any adequate recognition of the reality of *Dasein*, human *being-in-the-world* (Heidegger, 1927), as a uniquely human, existential condition of symbolic self-awareness, freedom and time-consciousness that is emergent from, but irreducible to the interaction of biological and environmental factors.

It remains the case that most schools of psychoanalytic thought, in their general theory if not in their clinical attitude and praxis, lean heavily toward either a biologism that privileges the somatically-rooted drives or an environmentalism that privileges a range of relational factors in the understanding of personality development and psychopathology. There is no need to underestimate the role of biological and environmental factors and their interaction in the determination of human behavior in order to recognize "the uniqueness of man" (Huxley, 1943, 1947) and the distinctively human *passions* (Carveth, 1996) arising from our predicament as symbolling animals living not only in the inorganic (pre-biological, *lithosphere*) and organic (biological, *biosphere*) worlds, but also in the superorganic (post-biological, *noösphere*) world of self-consciousness, signification and culture.

Drawing on the philosophical ideas of Dilthey (1961), Weber (1953) and other members of the so-called *verstehende* school of historical and sociological thought, Kohut (1959) alludes to the distinction between the *Naturwissenschaften* (the natural sciences) and the *Geisteswissenschaften* (the human or cultural sciences) and argues that as a member of the latter group psychoanalysis necessarily approaches its subject matter—which he defines as the subjectivity of human beings—not from an external, objective or positivistic point of view, but rather from an internal, subjective or empathic-introspective perspective. The advocates of the intersubjective approach have carried these Kohutian tenets to their logical (from a dialectical standpoint I would say illogical) extreme while claiming that their work represents an advance over self psychology in that it is open to the discovery of organizing principles structuring the patient's subjective experience other than those of the self-selfobject unit. Once again the question is, why either/or and not both/and? Certainly if its claim to transcend self psychology through openness to principles organizing subjective experience other than "Tragic Man's" search for selfobject support is valid, then the intersubjective perspective should be able to include the intrapsychic conflicts of "Guilty Man" within its purview. (While the Hegelian *both/and* (thesis) is inevitably complemented by the Kierkegaardian *either/or* (antithesis), the very refusal to privilege either of these orientations over the other entails an affirmation of both/and thinking on the higher level (synthesis) on which the necessity and validity of each in different contexts is acknowledged.)

Although it is true that much of our work as analysts focuses on the patient's and our own subjective *experience* and therefore, relies on the empathic-introspective method, we are also interested in the patient's and our own *behavior* and, hence, resort to objective observation. Attachment theory was greatly influenced both by observation of primate behavior and the "strange situation" laboratory set up for the observation of children and their mothers (Ainsworth, Blehar, Waters, & Wall, 1978). Both self psychology and intersubjective studies have themselves been influenced by and draw support from observation of preverbal infant-mother interactions recorded by elaborate video technology (Beebe & Lachmann, 1988). Even in strictly therapeutic work, analysts observe their patients— and are observed by them—as a central element of the act of empathizing with them. In a real sense, observation and empathy are inseparable, for the latter entails and depends on the former. Beyond this, however, it is a mistake to seek to confine the psychoanalytic method to the empathic study of the patient's subjective world. In optimal psychoanalytic work, we need to move back and forth between viewing our patients as subjects and as objects. The intersubjectivists (Atwood & Stolorow, 1984a) acknowledge the influence of the existential phenomenology of Sartre (1943). But, for Sartre, the peculiar nature of the human being lies in its partaking of both *being-for-itself* and *being-in-itself* (i.e., of being both a subject and an object), denial of either aspect entailing "bad faith." Certainly any psychoanalysis carried on in a Sartrean spirit would in no way confine itself to the exploration of the subject's subjectivity, but would seek to expand that subjectivity through confrontation of the subject with its reality as an historically and socially situated object whose *being-for-others* (including the analyst) and rootedness in *being-in-itself* are as much a part of its reality as its *being-for-itself.*

It is true that whereas we can only view inanimate things from the outside as objects, by employing the empathic-introspective method we are able to view persons (and perhaps, to a degree, animals) as subjects.

It is the capacity of the human being existing on the superorganic level of *mind* (noösphere), which depends upon, but is irreducible to the organic level of *brain* (biosphere), to "take the role of the other" (Mead, 1934) that constitutes the socio-psychological foundation for the biblical doctrine of charity and its corollary, the Kantian categorical imperative, as well as for the *verstehen* or empathic-introspective method in the human sciences. But it remains the case that we can and need to view people as objects as well as subjects. In addition to attuning to and empathizing with the subjectivity of both experiencing patients and experiencing analysts (i.e., their pre-reflective experience), I believe it is necessary for analysts to attempt to maintain (or recover if it has been lost) the necessary triangulation of the analytic situation entailed in viewing each of these from a tertiary perspective: that of the observing, including the self-observing (self-reflective), analyst. In so endeavoring to maintain or recover their own "observing ego," analysts simultaneously encourage the development or reestablishment of their patients'. Hence, in addition to exploration of patients' subjectivity I believe it is necessary for analysts to keep in mind in very broad, tentative and shifting terms such things as their character structure, the quality of their reality-testing, the level of their object relations, the degree of their regression and capacity to internalize, the state of the therapeutic alliance, the nature of the transference and the countertransference and their interpenetration, and other such considerations.

Psychoanalysis helps people not only by assisting them to become more attuned to their subjective, especially their affective, experience, but also by enabling them to, in a sense, step outside their subjectivity and view themselves as objects from the standpoint of another (Mead, 1934). It is not at all necessary to assume that this other has privileged access to objective reality in order to recognize the truth in the adage that—phenomena such as *folie-à-deux* aside—two heads are generally better than one. I cannot see the back of my own head—without a mirror, that is. The analyst is a mirror (albeit inevitably a flawed one to a greater or lesser extent) in which patients can view themselves in otherwise unavailable ways. Just as a fish living entirely surrounded by water is in no position to know it is all wet, so with the help of our analysts we are enabled to escape subjective self-enclosure to some degree and acquire some approximate knowledge of the sort of objects we may be. Being enabled in this way to see ourselves more objectively, for better and for worse, is an essential element (but by no means the whole story) of how analysis works.

To someone whose training before becoming an analyst was in the sociology of Max Weber (1953) and the symbolic interactionist social psychology of George Herbert Mead (1934), the psychology of the self with its emphasis on empathic immersion in the perspective of the other (Weber's *verstehen* and Mead's *role-taking*) represents a welcome contribution to the development of a more fully interactional perspective in psychoanalysis. Contributors to selfobject theory and the intersubjective approach add their voices to the critique; developed over many decades by diverse writers in several disciplines, of what Stolorow and Atwood (1992) call "the myth of the isolated mind." In seeking to transcend the unacceptable individualism of traditional psychoanalysis in favor of a more thorough understanding of the inextricable interconnectedness among *Mind, Self and Society* (to employ the title of Mead's [1934] best-known work), selfobject theory and the intersubjective perspective join a tradition including a wide range of object-relational (Greenberg & Mitchell, 1983; Mitchell, 1988), interpersonal (Sullivan, 1953), bipersonal (Langs, 1976), attachment (Bowlby, 1969–1980), and developmental systems (Stern, 1985; Beebe & Lachmann, 1988) perspectives each of which advocates in one way or another (and of course their differences in approach are as important as their similarities) a more thoroughly social understanding of human nature and of the self. But while adding their voices to the continuing critique of "one-body" psychology and contributing significantly to the evolution of a more sophisticated and clinically valuable alternative perspective, the intersubjectivists neglect to situate their contribution within the tradition of the discipline, thus, remaining faithful to the time-honored practice in self psychology, beginning with Kohut himself, of failing to enter into dialogue with or even, often enough, to cite the work of predecessors (an exception being Bacal and Newman [1990]).

A central implication of both self psychology and the intersubjective approach is that analysts must seek continually to "decenter" sufficiently from their own perspective and taken-for-granted organizing principles to be able to empathize with and accurately understand the viewpoint of the other. This point is lucidly illustrated in the discussions of the cases of Peter, Robyn, Alice and Sarah in *Contexts of Being* (Stolorow & Atwood, 1992, chapter seven). Each of these cases illustrates how unconscious organizing principles governing the experience of the analyst sometimes link up with similar unconscious principles shaping the experience of the patient (*intersubjective conjunction*)—or clash with very different principles at work in the patient (*intersubjective disjunction*)—both of which may lead to empathic failures, disruptions and derailments and therapeutic impasses of varying types.

The authors argue that the way out of such difficulties is for analysts to become reflectively self-aware of how their hitherto pre-reflective organizing principles (deep assumptions, attitudes, metaphors, concretized theoretical convictions, and so on) have impaired or distorted—I will defend my use of this term later—their capacity for accurate empathic understanding of the patient's experience and, in this way, to overcome such areas of blindness and the impasses to which they lead. While I would say that in becoming more reflectively self-aware in this way analysts are becoming more objective about themselves and insist that if analysts can become more objective in these ways then so can patients, the authors themselves would never employ this manner of speaking owing to their total excommunication of any reference to objectivity and objective reality from psychoanalytic discourse.

Unfortunately, while emphasizing the therapeutic importance of accurate empathic understanding of the patient's experience, Stolorow and Atwood fail to extend this attitude toward psychoanalytic colleagues of other theoretical persuasions. Even if we exempt them from the task of situating their work within the ongoing dialogue that constitutes the collective psychoanalytic self, we cannot absolve them of their responsibility to adopt a respectful and empathic stance toward those psychoanalytic writers to whom they do refer—such as Edith Jacobson, Heinz Kohut, Roy Schafer and Otto Kemberg—whose work they quote out of context, caricature and exploit as a foil against which to claim the superiority of the intersubjective approach. Ironically, in their mode of offering "interpretations" to their fellow psychoanalysts, the intersubjectivists resemble the standard self-psychological caricature of the classical analyst—and the cause of intersubjectivity is ill-served in the process. Schafer (1976), for example, is accused of substantializing and universalizing the experience of personal agency and elevating this to "the ontological core of psychological life" (p. 15). But an examination of *A New Language for Psychoanalysis* reveals that in addition to his focus upon excessive *disclaiming* of personal agency, Schafer recognizes the existence of excessive *claiming* of responsibility as well, thus, refuting the charge that he is blind to the limits of personal freedom.

The "straw man" strategy is again evident in the course of the authors' argument that the "idolatry [*sic*] of the autonomous mind finds vivid expression in Jacobson's (1964) description of the experiential consequences of superego formation" (p. 13). They state that:

> prior to this developmental achievement, according to her view, the child's self-esteem is highly vulnerable to the impact of experiences with others. As a result of the consolidation of the superego, by contrast, self-esteem is said to become stabilized and *relatively* [their term, my emphasis] independent of relations with others, so that [and here they quote Jacobson herself] it "cannot be as easily affected as before by experiences of rejection, frustration, failure and the like" and is "apt to withstand ... psychic or even physical injuries to the self."
>
> (p. 13)

But having themselves said that she saw self-esteem becoming only *relatively* independent of relations with others after superego consolidation, and having quoted Jacobson herself saying that it "cannot be as *easily affected as before* [my emphasis]," the authors proceed to summarize her view as follows: "The autonomous ego of the healthy older child or adult ... is presumed to have achieved immunity from the 'slings and arrows' encountered in experiences of the surround" (p. 13). In other words, where Jacobson speaks of *relative* independence and of varying *degrees* of being affected by others, the authors radicalize her position and attribute to her a view of the immunity of the self from influences from the surround that it was never her intention to suggest. Against Kohut's theory of self-structure formation through "optimal frustration" and "transmuting internalization," which they regard as a variant of the myth of the isolated mind, Stolorow and Atwood (1992) describe improved psychological functioning in terms of "increased affect integration and tolerance" (p. 13); but these attainments would, no doubt, enable the healthier individual, not to be entirely self-reliant, but certainly to rely in less archaic and urgent ways on the selfobject milieu for assistance in affect regulation—which is, after all, what both Jacobson and Kohut had in mind.

The problem is not that Stolorow and Atwood fail to present detailed accounts of the alternative perspectives of these colleagues; that is not the sort of book they set out to write. Rather, the problem is that in choosing to refer to the writings of colleagues to illustrate their adherence to "the myth of the isolated mind," their work is read in a one-sided and polarizing way so that they can be fitted to the authors' stereotype. It is because I share Stolorow and Atwood's view of the importance of sustained empathic inquiry into the subjective world of the other that I believe the method ought to be applied not only in our dealings with patients, but with colleagues as well.

Turning to Stolorow and Atwood's (1992) reconsideration (Chapter 2), in terms of intersubjectivity, of the concept of unconscious mental processes: instead of viewing the repression barrier as a relatively fixed characteristic of the individual mind, they view it in "two-body" terms as fluid and variable from one intersubjective context to another. This is because, in their view, the motive for repression involves maintaining a tie to a needed object, a tie that would be threatened by self-experiences unacceptable to the object and that therefore, come to be dissociated, repressed, or defensively withheld from symbolization (as in Dorpat's [1987] theory of cognitive arrest). Given a different intersubjective situation—say, that of the relationship with the analyst in which the needed tie is ideally less threatened by such self-experiences—the repression barrier may be lifted to a greater or lesser degree. This it seems to me is a useful reconceptualization of the nature of repression, as are Stolorow and Atwood's (1992) distinctions among the "three realms of the unconscious": the pre-reflective unconscious, containing "the organizing principles that unconsciously shape and thematize a person's experiences"; the dynamic unconscious, containing "experiences that were denied articulation because they were perceived to threaten needed ties"; and the unvalidated unconscious, containing "experiences that could not be articulated because they never evoked the requisite validating responsiveness from the surround" (p. 33).

Although I believe the positing of these three realms, together with the theory of the intersubjective context of repression, goes some way toward refuting the charge that the intersubjective approach, like self psychology in general, denies the unconscious, for me there is a crucial element missing from this account. Specifically, there is as yet in both selfobject and intersubjective theory no adequate account of primary process mentation and the peculiar laws that structure it which Freud (1900) discovered—namely: condensation (which Lacan, following Roman Jakobson, recognized as metaphor); displacement (metonymy); plastic representation; symbolism and secondary revision. No listening stance can be truly intersubjective unless the analyst is able to decode the primary process encodings of the patient's raw perceptions, affects and phantasies concerning the analytic interaction. As Langs (1978), following Searles (1975), pointed out long ago, if, "listening with the third ear" (Reik, 1948), we know how to *hear* what patients are saying about us and about what they think is going on in us and between us and them on the unconscious level—messages that they frequently expect to be so threatening to their needed tie to us that they must be deeply encoded in a primary process disguise—then the patient's unconscious can serve as the supervisor of the analysis by pointing out to us, often in almost unbearably blunt terms, what may really be going on, or at least what the patient imagines is going on, in the interaction on deeper levels.

Although Freud originally linked the idea of the primary process to notions of psychic energy, drive theory, the economic point of view, and so on—concepts now regarded as problematic if not rejected altogether by many contemporary theorists—the important point is that, despite theorizing his insight in terms that many now find unacceptable, he at the same time discovered the existence of another language, another semiotic register, in the mind, to which he gave the name the primary process. Any psychology worthy of being called psychoanalytic must recognize that we are all (at the very least) double in this sense, split between a self that communicates in secondary process categories and one that communicates in primary process terms. Psychoanalysts do understand something about the laws and mechanisms of this second language permitting us, not to *know* with any authoritative certainty how to decode its messages, but at least to hazard a range of intelligent and plausible interpretive guesses that will be either supported or disqualified in light of the patient's own associations.

Although, speaking of defensively sequestered affective states, Stolorow and Atwood (1992) refer to "the necessity for disguise when such states are represented in dreams" (p. 31), they fail to explain the mechanisms of such disguise. In speaking of experience that remains unsymbolized or that is defensively withheld from symbolization because it is perceived to threaten a needed tie (p. 33), the authors fail to explore the possibility that such experience may sometimes be symbolized after all—only not in the everyday, secondary process form, but in the archaic language Freud described as the primary process. In discussing a dream as reflecting "a child's expression in metaphorical symbols of the increasing threat to her psychological survival" (pp. 37–38) in the context of sexual abuse by her father, and of psychotic delusions and hallucinations as encoding previously unconscious features of the patient's traumatic history, the authors have insufficient to say regarding the operation of such metaphorical symbols and their decoding. Perhaps the intersubjectivists simply accept and take for granted Freud's theory of the primary process, minus its outmoded energetic accoutrements; if so, it would be nice to hear them say so. If not, there is a deficit in their theory.

The discussion of phantasy formation in Chapter 5 does little to remedy this lacuna. Just as Brandchaft (1993) began to speak of "ghosts" in the psyche at the root of repetitive self-negating processes (p. 12)— thus rediscovering what in other psychoanalytic frameworks is the role of the archaic superego, internal bad objects, the antilibidinal ego or internal saboteur, and so on, in the compulsion to repeat—so in *Contexts of Being* (chapter five), Stolorow and Atwood reaffirm the concepts of internalization and an internal world and revive the concept of the "introject." Here we are witness to the continuing process whereby self psychology comes to reinvent the wheel. But although this chapter does have the virtue of edging toward a rapprochement with object relations theory by recognizing the existence of the introject, the discussion does not really address the issue of the primary process per se. Parenthetically, unlike the case vignettes in Chapter 7, which so well illustrate the usefulness of the self-psychological principle that analysts must "decenter" from their own perspective and open themselves to that of the other—a principle that the intersubjectivists seem to wish to appropriate and claim as their own— the discussion of the case of Jessica in Chapter 5 seems quite traditional. The material could equally well have been formulated in the language of object relations theory, separation-individuation theory or even the language of superego analysis. One wonders where is the distinctiveness of the intersubjective framework here? The contribution of the analyst's experience and organizing principles to the therapeutic process is left entirely in the dark.

Perhaps Stolorow and Atwood are reluctant to confront the issue of the primary process precisely because its existence and the analyst's special knowledge of its laws are seen to constitute a basis for the very type of analytic interpretive authoritarianism that the intersubjectivists most deplore. But the fact that knowledge can be abused is no reason to pretend that it does not exist. Besides, his knowledge of the primary process does no more than suggest interpretive possibilities. Except for his (fortunately only partial) embrace of the "essentializing" method utilized by dream dictionaries and Jungians and to which, following Stekel, he fell victim in the area of the so-called universal language of symbols, Freud's (1900) method was predominantly a "contextualizing" one (Burke, 1939). In this approach, despite his knowledge of primary process mechanisms, the analyst is entirely dependent on the patient's associations to provide the psychic context outside of which interpretation is merely "wild." This is not to deny, however, that many traditional analysts have in practice fallen victim to essentialism and the authoritarianism that follows from it—as, for that matter, have many revisionists; it is merely to insist that this is a departure from rather than an instance of legitimate analytic technique.

Contrary to the idea that any application of knowledge of the primary process must lead to interpretive authoritarianism on the part of the analyst, I think few practitioners have not enjoyed the experience of their patients employing *their* knowledge of the primary process in the conscious interpretation of their therapist's parapraxes, symptomatic actions, nonverbal behavior and so on. In my experience, this is not a rare event at all and it indicates that the interpretive sword *can*—and on the unconscious level always *does*—cut both ways. Although I have major reservations about other aspects of his work, I think Langs (1980), following Searles (1975), simply hit the nail on the head when he spoke of the fact that sometimes the designated analyst is the functional patient and the designated patient is the functional analyst. But whereas Langs was speaking of a situation he regarded as undesirable, I tend to agree with Searles that, to a degree (and here matters of degree are everything), this is a normal and necessary aspect of every analysis. In a sense, to "listen with the third ear" to what the patient as unconscious supervisor of the analysis is saying is to place oneself in the position of patient to the analysand's unconscious as analyst.

This tendency on the part of intersubjectivists to throw out a valid concept because it may lend itself to authoritarian misuse while remaining blind to its possible employment in a democratic way that undermines authoritarianism is most evident in regard to their rejection of the idea of objective reality. Although Stolorow and Atwood have stated that they are only denying the relevance of this concept insofar as psychoanalytic therapy is concerned and have ridiculed as a misunderstanding reflecting *The Fear of Loss of Reality* the idea that they are doing more than this, I think their work is more ambiguous on this score than they wish to acknowledge. On reading chapter one of *Contexts of Being* I was momentarily reassured that its authors had pulled back from what I viewed as their earlier epistemological subjectivism (Stolorow, Brandchaft, & Atwood, 1987) in view of their critique (pp. 18–20) of Basch's "radical constructivism verging on solipsism" (p. 19) in which, according to the authors, "even one's mother and father are seen as not possessing any literal existence in a world apart from the self but are regarded instead as examples of 'imaginary entities that exist only in the brain'" (p. 19). Stolorow and Atwood (1992) cogently argue that Basch's position involves a self-contradiction:

> [I]t contains on one level a claim that at another level it denies. On one hand, Basch denies the literal truth of the individual's experience of the independent existence of objects outside the boundaries of the self; he argues that such objects are only "constructions" localized inside the human brain. On the other hand, Basch does accord independent existence to one class of such external objects; the brains themselves.
>
> (p. 19)

Unfortunately, two pages later, in the context of their critique of Sullivan's concepts of "parataxic distortion" and "consensual validation," Stolorow and Atwood (1992) return to their earlier critique of the idea of "a mind separated from an 'objective' reality that it either accurately apprehends or distorts" (p. 21). In offering this critique the authors give little indication as to whether they mean to restrict it to knowing within the psychoanalytic situation or apply it to knowing in general. Hope arises that they do not mean to deny objective knowledge when they go on to state that in the intersubjective framework "it is assumed that one's personal reality is *always* codetermined by features of the surround and the unique meanings into which these are assimilated" (p. 21). Here, as in their gestures toward a Nietzschean "perspectivalism" as opposed to "radical relativism" (pp. 123–124), Stolorow and Atwood appear to reject radical constructivism—which they rightly critique in Basch—by acknowledging that there does exist a "surround" and that its features are sufficiently potent to "codetermine" one's personal reality. Although the correspondence theory of truth has frequently been associated with a Naive Objectivism or positivism that ignores the role of the subject in construing reality, I believe the very "perspectivalism" to which Stolorow and Atwood pay lip service itself entails a sophisticated version of the correspondence theory. Rejecting either pole of the binary opposition Naive Subjectivism/Naive Objectivism, we embrace a *Perspectivalism* that acknowledges the reality of the object but also that it can only be known from the standpoint of multiple perspectives. Despite the association of this epistemology with continental phenomenology and existential philosophy, I believe it shares a substantial measure of agreement with Popper's (1972) conception of objective knowledge as an evolutionary process in which our conjectures or approximations are progressively accommodated to an ultimately incompletely knowable reality.

In this light, it seems legitimate to ask to what degree one's personal reality corresponds or fails to correspond to "features of the surround." In the final section of chapter one, entitled: *The Genesis of the Sense of the Real*, Stolorow and Atwood (1992) express the view that the child's sense of the Real develops "through the validating attunement of the caregiving surround" (p. 27). However, this begs the question of the degree to which the child's *sense* of the Real is realistic. One can agree with the view that the sense of the Real develops from validation (which I regard as inseparable from invalidation because to validate one thing is necessarily to invalidate something else), but at the same time be moved to ask what happens if hallucinations are validated as real? If classical Freudian theory is validated as true by members of the New York Psychoanalytic Institute, does that make it true? I have no doubt that the nonexistence of the Holocaust is psychologically real to those whose experience is validated by the revisionist historians. Does that mean that the Holocaust did not occur?

That such questions are not frivolous and unnecessary is evident from the fact that in a subsequent edition of *Faces in a Cloud*, Atwood and Stolorow (1984b) state as one of three interrelated principles of intersubjectivity the assumption that "no personal reality is more true or valid than any other" (p. 189). To me, this is simply a bizarre and indefensible thing to say, not least because it expresses the very radical relativism the authors claim to eschew in their brief and rather belated gesture toward perpectivalism in the "Epilogue" to *Contexts of Being*. If one truly believed this dictum, therapeutic work would be pointless because a patient's post-therapeutic "reality" would by definition be no more true or valid than his or her pre-therapeutic perspective. If the authors actually believed what they claim, it would be hard to understand why they bother to write, because the intersubjective perspective they so energetically advocate—which they acknowledge "symbolically crystallizes ... the interplay between our respective worlds of experience through which our theoretical perspective came into being" (*Faces*, 1984b, p. 190)—would, by their own principle, be no more valid or true than the psychoanalytic approaches they reject, which similarly embody the personal realities of their authors.

In chapter six of *Contexts* (written in conjunction with Brandchaft) Stolorow and Atwood (1992) state that "the only reality relevant and accessible to psychoanalytic inquiry (that is, to empathy and introspection) is *subjective reality* [original emphasis]" (p. 92). When, therefore, in chapter two they acknowledge the "codetermining impact of the analyst on the organization of the patient's experience" (p. 34) and emphasize the importance of "always taking into account what the patient has perceived of the analyst that has leant itself to the patient's anticipations of retraumatization" (p. 34), one would naturally assume the authors mean to beg the question of the relative accuracy or inaccuracy of such perceptions. For to imply that such perceptions may sometimes be accurate (as I, for one, would acknowledge) would be to move beyond the patient's subjective reality to what they regard (but I do not) as unacceptable assertions of correspondence with objective reality. However, in contradiction to their own restriction of psychoanalytic work to the field of subjective reality, the authors nevertheless speak of "the kernel of truth" (p. 101) contained in the patient's perceptions and phantasies. There is simply no way that such a kernel of truth can be recognized in a psychology that has ruled reference to objective reality out of court and restricted itself to the exploration of the patient's subjective experience.

In the clinical illustration offered in chapter two, Stolorow and Atwood (1992) state that "commencing at the age of two, her father had used his daughter for primarily oral sexual gratification several times each week"

(p. 36). This does not sound to me like a statement regarding the patient's experience; it sounds like a statement of objective fact. If pressed by the patient to say whether or not they believed her about this, would the authors hedge and say only that they believed this was her experience? And, if so, what would they reply if she pressed and said: "I know you believe it was my experience, but do you believe my experience corresponds to objective fact or not? Do you believe my father sexually abused me?" Faced with this question, an intersubjectivist might reply: "Yes, I believe your father abused you," while inwardly maintaining the reservation that in so answering he was doing no more than offering a report on the content of his own subjective reality. However, if in so "validating" his patient's experience he were to make this inner reservation explicit, the patient might well ask: "I believe you believe that I was abused, but is your belief valid or not?" To this the intersubjectivist might well reply: "I believe so," thus, leading the discussion into an infinite regress.

Alternatively, an intersubjectivist might feel forced in this situation to reply: "I don't know." Although not exactly "validating," this would nevertheless be an honest answer. The analyst is frequently not in a position to independently verify or falsify various beliefs of the patient. However, against the authors' denial of the very possibility of objective knowledge in psychoanalysis, I would argue that sometimes in clinical as in applied psychoanalysis corroboration of claims about events both within and outside the therapy can be achieved (Hanly, 1991). For example, if the patient's conviction of having been abused were to be supported by, say, her father's admission of having done so and, perhaps, by her mother or sister coming forward and confirming her memories of key events, then the analyst would be justified in going beyond acknowledging his subjective belief in her account to acknowledging that, in want of evidence to the contrary, the account may plausibly be regarded as objectively true. In speaking of attainable objective knowledge I refer, like Popper (1972), not to anything resembling absolute truth, but rather to conjectures or approximations that, for the moment at least, resist falsification or, *contra* Popper, enjoy some degree of verification. I find it interesting that here I am the defender of the possibility of validation of the patient's experience through objective verification, whereas Stolorow and Atwood are required by their restriction of psychoanalytic inquiry to the field of subjective reality to join the (caricatured) classical analyst in begging the question. But just as the *patient's* experience can sometimes be validated in this way, so can the *analyst's*, even when the validation of the latter's experience entails the invalidation of the former's. Naturally, the validation of the patient's experience may at times invalidate the analyst's.

In chapter six, Stolorow and Atwood (1992) state that:

> the belief that one's personal reality is objective is an instance of the psychological process of concretization, the symbolic transformation of *configurations of subjective experience* [original emphasis] into events and entities that are believed to be *objectively* [original emphasis] perceived and known.
>
> (p. 92)

To me this indicates that, although claiming adherence to a perspectivalism transcending both subjectivism and objectivism, in combating the latter the authors have succumbed to the former, thus, regressing from a tertiary or dialectical position into dualism. Regarding the patient discussed previously, they state (chapter two) that two decades of analytic work validating the experience of having been abused resulted in the patient's acquisition of a "felt reality" (p. 39) of having been sexually abused. We now learn, however, that such convictions regarding objective reality amount to concretizations of subjective experience. Is this the sort of progress the therapist intended? Is the aim of therapy to promote the concretizations that allegedly underlie the sense of the Real, or is it to undermine such concretizations and, hence, the sense of the Real? Or could such theoretical difficulties stem from a defective epistemology, which holds that the sense of the Real necessarily rests on concretization, rather than on *correspondence* between the subject's experience and the real nature of the object, because the latter position has in practice, if not in rhetorical gestures toward perspectivalism, been rejected in both the intersubjective and self-psychological frameworks?

When Stolorow and Atwood (1992) go on to rail against the concept of distortion that accompanies the appeal to the idea of an objective reality, I am moved to ask with regard to the patient's father—who "pressured her to enjoy the sexual episodes, which he said were akin to the practices of royal families during other historical eras" and who "told her that what was taking place between them heralded the future of parent-child relations" (pp. 36–37)—was he engaged in distortion or was he not?

I'm sure what he described reflected his subjective experience, his "felt reality," but was that experience a distortion of the reality of abuse that was taking place or was it not?

Stolorow and Atwood assume that if the notion of an objective reality is allowed into the therapeutic discourse, the analyst will necessarily claim to enjoy a privileged access to it and will dismiss the patient's differing views as distortion. For some reason, the authors appear to believe that the only way to combat this is to rule out of court in psychoanalysis the idea of an objective reality by the standard of which anything might be judged to be a distortion. But this entirely ignores the democratic possibility that analyst and patient share a belief in the existence of an objective reality, but one that is extremely difficult to perceive and about which the best we ever have are approximations (Popper, 1972) and that even to arrive at our best approximations we have to perpetually seek to purge our conceptions of reality of purely subjective distortions—which are as likely to be present in the analyst's views as in the patient's. In this alternative viewpoint (which differs little from the perspectivalist epistemology that the authors claim but actually fail to sustain), analyst and patient engage in a mutually corrective dialogue in an attempt to approximate the reality of their ongoing encounters; of the patient's psychological, interpersonal and existential situation; and of his or her past. In this perspective the concept of distortion carries no authoritarian connotation, for it is recognized that in certain cases of disjunction the analyst may be distorting more than the patient. In this view, every analysis constitutes for the analyst a continuation of the training analysis, for in being open to the patient's messages regarding the analyst's distortions of reality—especially when such messages come from the patient's unconscious—the analyst receives ongoing assistance in reality-testing and ongoing help in recognizing the subjective sources of tendencies to distort in his or her insufficiently analyzed unconscious organizing principles. I think the foregoing account is in the spirit of true intersubjectivity, and I recommend it as a way out of the authors' self-contradictory epistemological *cul-de-sac*.

From this alternative epistemological perspective, Stolorow and Atwood's (1992) claim that "when analysts invoke the concept of objective reality along with its corollary concept of distortion, this forecloses and diverts the investigation of the subjective reality encoded in the patient's communications" (p. 93), is seen to have no necessary validity. For I can deny the objective reality of aspects of my patients' perceptions and suggest that they are distorting reality and, at the same time, explore with them the meaning of their experience, of the subjective reality encoded within it, and so on. Similarly, I can seriously consider their claim that I am distorting reality and, if I come to feel this is the case, I can explore, either privately or openly with the patients, the subjective reality encoded in such distortions. In other words, there is no need to assume that disbelief in the objective reality of the patients' or the analysts' perceptions must result in an authoritarianism that closes off inquiry. If patients and I can agree about reality, and even if we cannot, we can nevertheless, explore the possible symbolic meanings encoded in the patients' experience. It is not necessary for me to subscribe to their experience or even to beg the question as to its validity in order for us to analyze it, any more than I have to mistake a dream for a reality, or at least remain open to the possibility that it is more than just a dream, in order to proceed to its analysis.

According to Stolorow and Atwood (1992), "the analyst's acceptance of the validity of the patient's perceptual reality ... is of inestimable importance in establishing the therapeutic alliance" (p. 94). They write:

> Any threat to the validity of perceptual reality constitutes a deadly threat to the self and to the organization of experience itself. When the analyst insists that the patient's perception is a secondary phenomenon distorted by primary forces, this, more than any other single factor, ushers in the conflictual transference-countertransference spirals that are so commonly described as resistances to analysis or negative transferences.
>
> (p. 94)

Although I would agree that total invalidation of the patient's experience would constitute such a threat, as would authoritarian statements about what it *really* means, my point is that one can disconfirm the patient's experience on the literal level as distortion without invalidating it altogether, provided one accompanies the disconfirmation with an expression of one's conviction that it must mean something on another level and of one's genuine interest in working together to learn what that might be. In my own experience, and that of many other analysts, certain patients feel "held" and positively "contained" by early interpretations that disconfirm their (sometimes but not always) paranoid fears of the therapist and of therapy and that clarify reality—interpretations that, often enough, permit a therapeutic alliance and a positive selfobject transference to emerge. Again, in my experience, patients sometimes feel reassured and protected when therapists communicate their recognition of the patients' disordered reality-testing and offer to assist them to become more objective—provided this is done with humility, kindness, and in a truly democratic spirit in which therapists remain open to being helped by patients with their own problems in reality-testing.

As part of their critique of the practice of pointing out distortions of reality to patients, Stolorow and Atwood speak of the threat this constitutes for people who are already uncertain about the reality of their experience because it was never validated or had to be disavowed out of a sense that it threatened a needed tie. But, for some reason, the authors seem not to realize that pointing out distortions is a necessary element in the process of helping patients to become more certain of the reality of their experience by validating what is true in that experience and invalidating what is illusory or false. Ironically, in connection with their criticism of the practice of pointing out distortions, Stolorow and Atwood refer to the "gaslight" genre (p. 95). *But to "gaslight" someone is to distort reality for them, not to help them clarify what is real.* In fact, in the "gaslight" genre in addition to the villain who distorts and mystifies reality for the victim there is usually a hero who works with the victim to dispel the distortions and to clarify the reality, that is, to validate what is real and invalidate what is false or illusory. *This surely is the role of the analyst, just as in regard to humanity's collective self it is the role of science.*

But Stolorow and Atwood fail to see that validation (which they regard as good) and invalidation (which they view as bad) necessarily go together. For to arrive at the truth it is necessary, on the one hand, to validate what is real and, on the other, to invalidate what is false. Aside from this failure to recognize that validation and invalidation imply one another, the devaluation (not to say demonization) of the latter reflects a failure to appreciate the relief experienced by both children and adults when a trusted other invalidates one's distorted persecutory perceptions or nightmare fears. Surely it is of little help to patients suffering from uncertainty regarding the validity of their experience to withhold from them our assistance in reality-testing. The authors seem to assume that analysts (of other schools) are themselves deluded, perhaps by rigid adherence to ideological Freudianism or Kleinianism, and that their attempts to dispel distortions and to clarify reality will necessarily amount to attempts to invalidate patients' valid experience and indoctrinate them with the analyst's ideology. I do not doubt that this occurs, but I hardly think we need to subscribe to the authors' one-sided and self-contradictory denial of the legitimacy of appeals to objective reality in psychoanalytic work in order to critique such ideological abuses of the therapeutic relationship.

It seems to me that if parents sometimes have distorted views of what their children are experiencing, and if analysts sometimes have distorted views of what their patients are experiencing, then it is fair to assume that patients sometimes have distorted views of what their parents and analysts, among others, were or are experiencing. The attempt to clear up some of these distortions is an aspect of the therapeutic process. The authors write that "a milieu in which the patient's perceptual reality is not threatened encourages the patient to develop and expand his own capacity for self-reflection" (p. 96). But I submit that what threatens patients is not the questioning of the validity of their perceptions and beliefs per se, but rather the *spirit* in which such an investigation is carried out—whether it is conducted respectfully, democratically, with an openness to the possibility of one's own views being faulty and a willingness to have one's own distortions corrected with the patient's help, or whether it is conducted in an authoritarian manner.

Writing of Freud's conclusion that phantasies of sexual abuse amounted to mental representations of instincts rather than real events, Stolorow and Atwood (1992) point out that "Freud's dilemma was a false one," for "such fantasies often encode experiences of traumatic developmental derailment," and that "it is common for experiences of abuse and seduction of a non-sexual or covertly sexual nature to be concretized and preserved in sexual symbolism" (p. 101). They go on to state that "this insight into the kernel of truth encoded in a patient's fantasies opens up a whole new pathway for exploration, one that remains foreclosed when a patient's perceptions are dismissed as distortion" (p. 101). As indicated previously, it is, to say the least, inconsistent to speak of "the kernel of truth" contained in a patient's perceptions while at the same time arguing that the idea of objective reality has no place in psychoanalytic discourse. But for Stolorow and Atwood the notion of objective reality appears acceptable if what is being talked about is the element of truth in a patient's perceptions, but unacceptable when the element of distortion in those perceptions is being discussed. Naturally, the possible kernel of truth in analysts' views—especially in their conviction that patients are distorting—is entirely ignored. Not only is this impossibly one-sided, but it fails to appreciate that in order to even recognize the kernel of truth embedded in distortions, it is necessary to separate this kernel from the distortions in which it is embedded.

Atwood and Stolorow (1984b) support and themselves engage in the practice of tracing psychoanalytic theories to their subjective origins in the personal psychology of their authors. (Although, in a certain sense, *ad hominem*, this strategy is unavoidable in the psychoanalysis of knowledge, including psychoanalytic knowledge. It is perfectly legitimate provided it is clearly understood that psychoanalytic explanation of the subjective foundations of theoretical claims tells us nothing about their scientific validity or invalidity.) They contribute to the psychoanalysis of their own perspective by noting in the new edition of *Faces in a Cloud* that their postulate that "no personal reality is more true or valid than any other" serves as a "solution to a relentless early experience of invalidation and psychological usurpation" (p. 189). In this light, it seems legitimate to wonder whether the theoretical problems outlined previously, especially the unquestioning association of objectivist epistemology with authoritarianism, may reflect both the compulsion and the dread of repeating (Ornstein, 1974) the struggle with an authoritarian parent. If so, such a failure to work through, mourn, and in this way move beyond such transference of the early experience of invalidation would have the effect of partially removing the authors' work from the "conflict-free" ego sphere and keeping it embroiled in conflicts of personal origin. I am not claiming that intersubjective theory is flawed because it may be subjectively motivated by unresolved conflicts with an authoritarian parent. Rather, I have sought to demonstrate its flaws on rational theoretical and clinical grounds alone. Only then have I offered a conjecture regarding the possible basis of these flaws in its authors' taken-for-granted subjective organizing principles.

There is an ironic sense in which refusal to work with the idea of objectivity because of its association with authoritarianism (while remaining blind to its democratic uses) itself leads to authoritarianism. For whenever rational and collaborative inquiry into the objective truth is closed off, unquestioned assumptions and arbitrary actions tend to replace it. Having ruled the concept of objective reality out of court in psychoanalysis, instead of engaging with the patient in a joint search for the objective facts of the case, intersubjectivists may succumb to the assumption that they know what these are and proceed to act accordingly. In this situation, it is as if it is legitimate to *act* as if objective reality exists and one knows what it is, but not to *speak* of this reality, even if to do so opens up the possibility of a genuinely collaborative search for the truth.

As usual, at the root of the theoretical difficulties that bedevil both selfobject and intersubjective theory lies the either/or thinking that entails privileging one or the other term of a false dichotomy. In the present case such binary oppositions as Subjective/Objective, Empathy/Observation, and Validation/Invalidation, among others, are in operation. In each case, the former term seems to be privileged over the latter, when in reality they require and complement one another. However much the intersubjectivists may believe they have transcended self psychology, insofar as both orientations fall victim to these types of either/or thinking they suffer from a common affliction.

Summary

Three patterns of psychoanalytic reasoning are outlined: monism, dualism and dialectics. Whereas Freud's thought is a mixture of dualistic and dialectical trends, Kohut's thinking manifests both monistic and dualistic elements and displays a marked tendency toward either/or thinking. Various examples of the latter in self psychology are discussed, such as the view that one must be either conflict-driven (Guilty Man) or motivated by the goal of self-fulfillment (Tragic Man). Why not both? Similarly, against the view that psychoanalysis must study human beings purely as subjects via the empathic-introspective method, it is argued that they must be approached—even in psychoanalysis—as what they in fact are: both objects and subjects; in any case, empathy is inseparable from observation. Again, in relation to the intersubjectivist celebration of validation over the invalidation of experience, the two imply one another, for to validate one thing is by implication to invalidate something else and vice versa.

It is argued that Stolorow and Atwood's belief (1992) that "analysts embracing an objectivist epistemology presume to have privileged access to the essence of the patient's psychic reality and to the objective truths that the patient's psychic reality obscures" (p. 123) is false. One can embrace a sophisticated objectivist epistemology or perspectivalism without assuming the analyst has privileged access to reality, assuming instead that patient and analyst engage in a mutually corrective and democratic dialogue in search of closer and closer approximations to an ultimately incompletely knowable reality. Just as it is a basic principle of Freudian theory that in any conflict it is easier to swing from one pole to the other—as, for example, from saint to sinner and back again—than to genuinely master the conflict, so Naive Subjectivism and Naive Objectivism, although manifestly opposed, frequently enjoy a secret symbiosis, a kind of unholy alliance. Epistemological subjectivism on the level of theory may frequently coexist with an unquestioning and authoritarian objectivism on the level of practice.

Despite these and other serious theoretical deficiencies, both self psychology and the intersubjective approach contribute, together with a range of other psychoanalytic perspectives, to the evolution of a more thoroughly social conception of the self and the therapeutic encounter and to the enhancement of our understanding of the nature of therapeutic impasses and the ways in which they may be overcome.

Chapter 5

Lacanian theory
Appreciation and critique

In *The Triumph of Religion*, Lacan (1974) writes:

> What I have noticed ... is that, even if people don't understand my *Écrits*, the latter do something to people. I have often observed this. People don't understand anything, that is perfectly true, for a while, but the writings do something to them.
>
> (pp. 69–70)

In confessing my failure to comprehend Lacanian theory *in toto*, I accept my castration. But, unlike Heidegger, who reportedly (Pound, 2007, p. 49) said: "I haven't so far been able to get anything at all out of this obviously outlandish text" (*Écrits*), the struggle to understand Lacan did something to me. If it liberated my desire to return to Freud *via* Melanie Klein (in order to balance "paternal" with "maternal" function) it at the same time exercised a permanent influence upon my understanding of all things human.

Prior to encountering Lacan, with G.H. Mead (1934) I already recognized humans as language-animals, as well as the difference between the "I"-subject and the "me"-object poles of the self; and with Jean-Paul Sartre (1943) appreciated the gap between *being-for-itself* and *being-in-itself*; understood that "man is the being by whom nothingness comes to the world" (p. 60); recognized desire as grounded in "lack"; and grasped the tension between my "being-for-others" and my "being-for-myself." If Lacan read Freud through Ferdinand de Saussure, he also read him through the work of the previously dominant poet of Paris. As a Christian atheist I felt quite at home with Lacan's secularized and psychologized Catholicism, if not with his abstruse, deliberately vague and grandiose mode of communication. Although Lacan's so-called "return to Freud" failed to transcend the latter's patriarchalism, his defects are, like Freud's, offset—to some degree at least—by the important ideas he generated.

The question of obscurantism

Chasseguet-Smirgel (1984, chapter seven) opens her essay: *A Psychoanalytic Study of Falsehood*, by summarizing Hans Christian Andersen's story, *The Nightingale*. An ordinary-appearing bird whose exquisite singing initially brought tears to the Chinese Emperor's eyes has its place at court usurped by a jewel-encrusted mechanical substitute "which could sing thirty times over the same tune at a tempo the real nightingale could not sustain" (p. 67) until, that is, the day the usurper's mechanism jammed. As the story goes, the dying Emperor's life was only saved by the sweet song of the real nightingale who reappears in its master's time of need. Chasseguet-Smirgel informs us that:

> This fable is said to have been written in honor of Jenny Lind, called "The Swedish Nightingale," whose success had been overshadowed for a while by the more precise technique of some Italian singers; their technique, in fact, hid a lack of real talent.
>
> (p. 68)

In light of various comments in her own writings and in those of Grunberger (1979), which might be interpreted as oblique critical allusions to Lacanism, when Chasseguet-Smirgel states that: "I happen to live in a country, in a town and at a time when false values—aesthetic and intellectual as well as ethical—seem to be gratified with admiration and success at the expense of 'true' values" (p. 66), one wonders whether in addition to commenting critically upon the fads and foibles of the Parisian scene in general she might also be expressing a feeling that the unpretentious, ordinary-appearing nightingale of mainstream psychoanalysis had been temporarily displaced, especially in certain avant-garde intellectual circles in France, by an initially impressive, but ultimately disappointing and inauthentic Lacanian usurper.

Despite the notorious obscurity of Lacan's (1977, 2002) language, which is riddled with puns, multiple meanings, obscure allusions to abstruse philosophical ideas and wide-ranging cultural references, such that it constitutes a kind of museum of European culture and demands for its decoding a breadth of scholarship and cultural sophistication that exceeds both the capacity and the patience of many contemporary readers, his writings, not to mention his mystique (Clement, 1983; Schneiderman, 1983; Turkle, 1978), continue to be an object of fascination for intellectuals in a variety of fields in the humanities and social sciences, especially literary and cinematic theory, as well as in psychoanalysis itself (Smith & Kerrigan, 1983). As Gallop (1985) suggested, one of the most significant things about Lacan was his capacity, something not to be sneezed at in a psychoanalyst, to evoke a range of transferences, not all by any means exclusively positive or idealizing, from those who come into contact with him, either personally (now no longer possible since his death in 1981), or through his arcane writings, or even through his reputation alone. I suspect there are few psychoanalysts today who, even if they have not read a single word of Lacan, have not formed some opinion or affective disposition toward him.

But someone's mere ability to evoke transferences is in itself no indication of his value, authenticity or good faith: after all, most con men rely upon this capacity. Freud himself for a time thought Fliess was a genius. And who, after a love affair has terminated, has not scratched his (or her) head in puzzlement over what he (she) could ever have seen in her (him)? As we all know, one of the functions of our analytic abstinence and relative silence is to cloak ourselves in a certain obscurity the better to evoke the analysand's transference phantasies, a process that might well be aborted if the patient were prematurely and traumatically presented with the dismal evidence of our human-all-too-human selves.

While Lacan did not refrain from speaking and writing, some might think he might just as well have done, for he seems to have evolved a mode of expression that at times seems even more impenetrable than the most determined of analytic silences. Reminding us of: "The snare laid by the Sphinx with its riddles, obscuring ... understanding with sybylline language and oracular ritual," Grunberger (1979) points out that:

> Enigma per se is a sadistic genre, for posing a riddle is always laying an anal trap. One confronts the other with a problem or obstacle, while enjoying absolute mastery oneself.... Obscurity is in itself an anal trap: one "hoodwinks" one's victim or "keeps him in the dark."
> (pp. 300–301)

The Lacanian text not only frustrates by its obscurity, frequently having led me at least to the point of giving up in exasperation and angrily dismissing the man, but to make matters simultaneously better and worse, every so often it seemed to offer a comprehensible insight of sufficient importance to make it impossible to overcome the transference attachment to this frustrating yet fascinating object. Perhaps, one felt, if only one read on, tried harder, consulted yet another secondary source promising to elucidate the Lacanian mysteries, sources, which themselves, I found, were increasingly more obscure than the object they promised to illumine—perhaps then all would become clear and one would find oneself in possession of a rare and valuable type of psychoanalytic wisdom of which Lacan and the Lacanians appeared to hold a monopoly. Once again, Grunberger's (1979) remarks are of relevance, whether or not the Sphinx this French psychoanalyst had in mind was his officially defrocked, and thereby all the more eminent, colleague Lacan:

> For one thing, the obscurity of the oracle's language permits all sorts of interpretations in terms of the narcissism of the person inquiring, even if he must pay with fear and trembling, which at a deeper level, moreover, are really linked to pleasure. (The technique of doling out obscurities is familiar to those who abuse the public's credulity, and an unbroken line leads from sorcerers and seers to astrologers, diviners, conjurers and fortunetellers.) Fortunetellers both conceal and promise, lead on and then put off until tomorrow, which assures them a faithful and permanent clientele. They are constantly making out drafts against the future, a system that allows them to remain in the abstract, the vague and hazy, in allusions, paradoxical statements, and slogans, in order always to leave a window open onto a future where everything will be possible, where there will be a free lunch, and where, finally, the donkey will get to eat the carrot.

> Contact with the astrologer or fortuneteller immediately plunges the subject into the primary process where reason and logic lose their power. A few seductive gestures suffice, but also merely ambiguity or obscurity (the language itself must be marked by the ineffable). With regression thus established, one is carried away in rapture and the doors open onto a narcissistic universe of infinite possibilities—one only need believe. But, if the diviner installs the subject in that universe, at the same time he deprives him of the necessary means to

get out of it. The subject will not move, but he will escape the anguish that accompanies maturation.

(p. 300)

But these are indeed equivocal words of criticism coming from a psychoanalyst, for as Grunberger surely recognizes, that unbroken line leading from sorcerers to fortunetellers leads on to hypnotists and then to psychoanalysts, who must also be masters of the art of leading on and then putting off until tomorrow, of remaining at crucial moments in the vague and hazy, of dealing in allusions and paradoxical statements, but hopefully not in slogans, and never—Heaven forbid!—promising a free lunch (Freud's offerings of herring to the impoverished Wolf Man notwithstanding). The point is that if there was something of the mystagogue about Lacan, perhaps, as psychoanalysts, we recognize something of ourselves in this.

But surely, a voice emanating from a sense of the real seriousness and dignity of our calling insists, there is more to the art of analysis than those elements that a scientific psychotherapy has inherited from its, best forgotten, distant ancestors, the practitioners of the black arts? And at this point we find ourselves faced once again with the question: Is there nothing more to Lacan than obscurantism and a mystifying appeal to our narcissism?

Since I, for one, find the best way to dispel the transference effects, to return from regression, the primary process and the narcissistic universe, is to think and eventually write about the infatuation—or is it that I am only able to think and write once the infatuation has already been dispelled?—the earliest version of the following reflections embodied something of my attempt to settle accounts with Lacan and move on. But, of course, I had already moved on: that is why I was then able—only temporarily as it turns out—to settle accounts. One of the exasperating and fascinating things about Lacan is that he himself has taught us about this very process and given us the means to conceptualize it. He would say that after a period of Imaginary identification, one sometimes manages to return to the Symbolic. And Lacan leaves us with the impression that, as with every psychoanalyst worth his salt, the very transference effect he works upon us, the very regression he induces, is ultimately in the service of a wider degree of self-knowledge: ideally, one returns from an infatuation with Lacan, as from any good analysis, with, among other things, a deeper understanding of the processes of regression, transference, narcissism, identification and fascination. Just as, even while excommunicating them, Freud seemed to respect the more independent-minded of his students over his slavish followers and imitators, so the best students of Lacan can hardly remain ideological Lacanians, though so many of them do (Roustang, 1976).

Reading Freud through Christian culture

At the very moment when psychoanalysis was being relegated to the margins of an ever more biologically reductionist psychiatry, the Freud industry was booming in the universities. Regrettably, however, the academic assimilation of psychoanalysis frequently took the form of impossibly intellectualized, abstracted and affectively isolated versions of analytic theory bearing little resemblance to psychoanalysis as it is understood and experienced by those of us who are daily engaged in analytic dialogue with people who are in pain. The term "patient" shares with "passion" the common Latin root *patiens*, from the verb *pati*, meaning "to suffer." For the most part our patients are sufferers—except for those who prefer to induce others to do their suffering for them. My struggle to make some sense of Lacan's highly intellectualized, abstruse and intentionally frustrating texts has certainly been painful. Lacan himself, in both his writings and filmed interviews and lectures, seems more clever than compassionate, as interested in keeping the reader at a distance as in communicating.

If, as Colette Soler (2016) argues, it is unfair to say Lacan ignored affect (after all he devoted an entire seminar to anxiety), it is certainly true that he privileged the Symbolic over what Julia Kristeva (1988) called the semiotic. Kristeva writes:

> Insofar as that form of analytic discourse known as "free association" involves transferential, that is, amorous, language, it ceases to be merely intellectual and becomes, implicitly, emotional. Hence it cannot be understood in terms of a linguistic model that divides verbal signs into "signifier" and "signified."
>
> (p. 2)

In so saying, Kristeva is recapitulating a point central to the Kleinian development—namely that psychoanalysis can in no way be reduced to a "talking cure" in that, in addition to their verbalizations, analysands communicate non-verbally through processes of emotional induction or projective identification. As contributors to the Klein-Lacan dialogues (Borossa et al., 2015) have noted, there are some congruences in the thought of Klein and Lacan, between the paranoid-schizoid position and the Imaginary and the depressive position and the Symbolic, as well as in the conception of the cure as acceptance of lack and loss. But both Melanie Klein herself and Wilfred Bion bring a distinct emphasis upon what we may call the "maternal" or containing function that is sorely absent in the Lacanian stress on *le-nom-du-père* and "paternal" function.

Since I feel we cannot afford to dismiss or ignore Lacan, I will attempt to give some indication of what I find of value in his work. In doing so, I am in no way claiming any particular expertise, nor even any adequate understanding of his work as a totality, not least because so much of it remains obscure to me. But the early work on "the mirror stage" and the child's misidentification with the Imaginary (specular) ego as idol, his vision of psychoanalysis as a semiotic rather than a biological science, his distinctions between organic *need* and human *desire* and between the penis and the phallus, the three registers of the Imaginary, the Symbolic and the Real, and his later idea of psychosis as a coming undone of the three rings of the Borromean knot and the *sinthome* as knitting them together again (Thurston, 2002) are intriguing concepts even aside from their theological resonance.

As Burston (2017) points out, Lacan was "a Catholic intellectual who was not widely known for being a Catholic intellectual" (p. 1). The Borromean rings, symbolizing the Trinity, appear on the coat of arms of the family of Saint Charles Borromeo (1538–1584), Cardinal and Archbishop of Milan. Early in my study of Lacan it became clear to me, as to my colleague Paul Roazen (1996), and many others (Burston, 2017; De Certeau, 2006; Pound, 2007; Davis, Pound & Crockett, 2014; Dunlap, 2014; Gale, n.d.), that Lacan's teaching is laden with Christian signifiers. Lacan's brother was a Benedictine monk to whom he dedicated his doctoral dissertation: "To the Reverend Father Marc-Francois Lacan, Benedictine of the Congregation of France, my brother in religion" (Roazen, 1996, p. 324). His brother described Lacan as having had "a very deep personal Christian culture"; Lacan took steps to ensure that his children were baptized (p. 324). He later asked his brother "to intercede with papal authorities in the hopes of gaining Catholic approval and thereby doing 'homage to our common Father'" (Lacan as quoted by Pound, 2007, p. 10; citing Roudinesco, 1999, p. 205).

In Pound's view the dedication of the dissertation reveals "Lacan's unconscious desire, hidden in full view"; it serves as "the hermeneutical key to his work, that it is a theology" (p. 24). Burston (2017, p. 2) points out that, despite his avowed atheism, Lacan's final wish was for a Catholic burial. Rejecting the idea that he was conflicted about Catholicism, Burston suggests he simply "wanted to have it both ways—to be, and to be perceived as a loyal Catholic, and to be an atheist, simultaneously." He asks: "What else are we to make of this bizarre history?" At the risk of identifying Lacan with aspects of my own secular Christianity, I think it most likely he did not want to be a Catholic in the religious, but only in the cultural sense. Most people have little difficulty grasping that Freud was both a proud Jew and an atheist. Why is it hard to imagine Lacan as a proud Christian and, like Freud, an atheist?

For Pound it is "only by becoming theology proper" that Lacan's work can "become psychoanalysis proper, that is, speak the truth of its desire" (p. 24)—a clear statement of Pound's desire to employ Lacanian ideas to reduce (he, of course, means elevate) psychoanalysis to Catholic practice. But it is a mistake to conclude that Lacan offers anything like a justification of the faith. On the contrary, speaking of the relations between psychoanalysis and religion, he says:

> They are not very amicable. In sum, it is either one or the other. If religion triumphs as is most probable—I speak of the true religion and there is only one which is true [i.e., Roman Catholicism]—if religion triumphs, this will be the sign that psychoanalysis has failed.
> (Pound, 2007, pp. 8–9; citing Richardson, 1986, p. 75)

Writing that although: "It would appear ... that Lacan offers little advance on Freud, defining religion as a form of neurosis," Pound suggests he "arguably maintains a more nuanced approach." Yet, in Roudinesco's (1999) view:

> Lacan was not really renouncing atheism, but he knew that his way of reading Freud in the light of philosophy and from a non-biological point of view might attract a lot of Catholics, who didn't accept the

"materialistic" aspect of the master's own teaching. When they read Lacan they felt on familiar ground, that of a Christian evaluation of human personality.

(p. 205)

What Pound, like many others, doesn't understand—doesn't *want* to understand—is secular Christianity. Many Christian atheists, myself included, are, like Lacan, steeped in and deeply value Christian culture, just as Freud was steeped in and deeply valued Jewish culture. A secular Christian may well embrace the Judeo-Christian evaluation of human personality while having long abandoned Christian religion. Pound asks: Why would Lacan want to attract Catholics in the first place if he was not at root advocating the religion? It does not seem to occur to him that secular Christians share a great deal with their fellow Christians—*just not their religion*. Here, I am following Beit-Hallahmi's (2014) definition of religion as "a belief system which includes the notion of a supernatural, invisible world, inhabited by gods, human souls, angels, demons, and other conscious spirit entities" (p. 3). In repudiating supernaturalism the secular Christian rejects religion, but not necessarily Christian ethics, the Judeo-Christian understanding of human personality, or the profound existential insights contained in the central Christian metaphors of crucifixion, resurrection and new life. Secular Christianity insists on the separation of Christian philosophy from Christian religion that orthodoxy seeks to prevent. This insistence upon an either/or—either one is a religious Christian or an atheistic non-Christian—is an undialectical form of reductionism seldom applied to Jews (either one is a religious Jew or not a Jew at all) used to invalidate secular Christianity, a move that can be useful evangelically in convincing potential converts that the only way to be a part of Christian culture and community is to (attempt to) embrace the religion. Naturally, in referring to Lacan's secularized Christianity I am in no way defending what I see as distinctly "un-Christian," arrogant and uncharitable aspects of his approach.

Whether his theory of the mirror phase can be empirically validated or not, and despite whatever academic misdemeanors he may have committed in advancing it (Billig, 2006), Lacan's critique of the idolatry of the Imaginary ego and his conception of the analytic cure as its displacement in favor of the living, albeit fragmented, subject through "acceptance of castration" (read "crucifixion") holds great appeal for those of us who appreciate the critique of narcissism implicit in the Judeo-Christian evaluation of human personality, as in varieties of existentialism, Buddhism and Vedanta. Unlike Freud, the Bible does not naturalize or biologize human destructiveness, instead recognizing it as a misuse of our uniquely human freedom and self-awareness—that is, it maintains an existentialist, rather than a biologically and/or environmentally determinist view (Fromm, 1941, 1973; Herberg, 1957; Niebuhr, 1957). Though claiming to represent a "return to Freud," Lacan presents a vision of the central human problem that is radically distinct from Freud's and closer to that of Melanie Klein. Instead of conceiving it, as did Freud, as a fundamental conflict between body and mind (somatically-rooted drive *vs.* defense, soma *vs.* psyche, nature *vs.* culture, the animal *vs.* the human, id *vs.* ego-superego), like Klein, Lacan substitutes a vision in which the central issue is human narcissism (read the sin of pride), our egoistic refusal to sacrifice our (schizo-paranoid) omnipotence and accept our (depressive position) brokenness. Without, like Pound, seeking to use Lacanian concepts to justify the magical doctrine of the transubstantiation or equally fantastic elements of the religion, both secular Christians and their psychoanalytic colleagues may find much of value in the Lacanian vision (Žižek 2000, 2003, 2009; 2015; Carveth, 2013, chapters nine to eleven).

The deliteralization of Freudian discourse

If I were to single out what to me is one of the most important contributions of Lacanian theory it would have to be: the deliteralization of Freudian concepts. The great German sociologist, Max Weber (1953), wrote of the social process he called "the routinization of charisma." This is the process whereby the living concepts and ideas of a great charismatic leader come, especially after his death, to be reduced or frozen into a range of simple, but lifeless formulae to be routinely administered by unimaginative bureaucrats in the institutions set up in the leader's name. Weber, of course, had in mind the fate of the spirit of Jesus at the hands of institutional Christianity. Lacan was concerned that something rather similar had happened to the spirit of Freud at the hands of the IPA. But the Lacanian critique goes further than that, for Lacan believed that the degeneration of Freudian thinking was evident even in the later work of Freud himself whose increasingly abstract metapsychological speculations, particularly the increasing emphasis upon the psychology of the ego, amounted to a betrayal of the fundamental psychoanalytic discovery of the workings of the unconscious as set forth at the turn of the century in *The Interpretation of Dreams* (1900), *The Psychopathology of Everyday Life* (1901), and *Jokes and Their Relation to the Unconscious* (1905a).

But even aside from the problem of the rise of metapsychology and ego psychology, Freud's clinical concepts, even at times in his own hands, occasionally succumbed to a literalism incompatible with psychoanalysis as a science of *psychic* as opposed to *material* reality. Take, for example, the theory of the Oedipus and castration complexes. Students have often told me that only once this theory was presented to them in a deliteralized (i.e., Lacanian) form, could they begin to appreciate its real human meaning and importance. No wonder the theory seems incredible and is frequently rejected in favor of other psychologies when it is presented as, the child's literal desire for sexual intercourse with one parent with an accompanying wish for the death of the other, wishes that are only repressed due to fear of literal castration or equivalent bodily mutilation at the hands of the rival parent. This literalism is particularly evident in Freud's (1924, 1925) mistaken belief that castration anxiety is restricted to males and penis envy to females on the grounds that women cannot fear a castration that has already taken place and men cannot envy what they already possess. Simply distinguishing between the literal penis and the symbolic penis or *phallus*, Lacan (1977, chapter eight) helps us see the very evident facts of female castration anxiety, as the fear of the loss of the phallus (i.e., anything that has phallic significance for a woman: her intelligence, breasts, doctorate, legs, career, looks, husband, analyst, etc.), as well as the rampant penis (phallus) envy of men (who are frequently consumed with envy of the success, women, money, automobiles, houses, publications, etc. of their rivals).

It is symptomatic of the intellectually retarding hold that such literalism has over the minds of even the most distinguished psychoanalysts, that not even Anna Freud or Charles Brenner are able to bring themselves to speak of male penis envy, even when the clinical data they are summarizing cry out for such a formulation. Writing of a ten-year-old boy who imagined he owned a circus and was a lion tamer, Anna Freud (1936) tells of his phantasy regarding a thief who shot at him. The animals banded together and punished the thief:

> They kept him a prisoner, buried him, and triumphantly made an enormous tower over him out of their own bodies.... Before they finally released him, a long row of elephants beat him with their trunks, last of all threatening him with uplifted finger (!) and warning him never to do it again.
>
> (p. 76)

Anna Freud points out that the elephant trunks and the uplifted finger were attributes of his father held to be of great importance (one thinks of the giant's three magical possessions in *Jack, the Giant Killer* in this connection), but although she states that "in his fantasy he took them from the father whom he envied and, having assumed them himself, got the better of him" (p. 77), she avoids any explicit recognition of this as a case of male penis envy.

Yet again, stating that: "We do not as a rule see anything abnormal in the small boy who wants to be a big man and plays at being 'Daddy', having borrowed his father's hat and stick for the purpose" (p. 88), Anna Freud goes on to describe a little boy who "would fall into a state of extreme ill humour whenever he saw an unusually tall or powerful man" (p. 88). He developed the habit, first of wearing his father's hat, and later of compulsively clutching a peaked cap in his hand wherever he went: on one occasion, needing his hands for something else, he placed the cap in the opening in the front of his leather breeches. Although Anna Freud writes that:

> The envy of the little boy ... was continually excited by the men whom he saw around him, so he confronted them persistently with the hat, cap or rucksack which he regarded as a tangible proof of his own masculinity.
>
> (p. 90)

She nevertheless does not formulate this clinical vignette as an instance of male penis envy. Of course, the psychodynamic situation is somewhat different depending upon whether one feels one has no phallus at all; or had one that was stolen or removed; or has one that is grossly inadequate in comparison to that of others. But while such differences must not be ignored, it is nevertheless the case that they all frequently result in greater or lesser degrees of penis (phallus) envy in both sexes.

Among the several useful and long overdue revisions to classical theory undertaken by Brenner (1982), was his recognition of the fact of female castration anxiety. Against Freud's belief in its nonexistence, Brenner writes:

> The logic of this position seems incontrovertible. One cannot lose what one does not have. Yet it is contradicted by abundant clinical experience. There are women who show every sign of intense castration anxiety.... Indeed, all women show evidence of a considerable degree of castration anxiety....
>
> (p. 97)

Brenner goes on to explain that what is involved is a phantasied penis (the Lacanian phallus), as opposed to a literal one.

> Girls in the oedipal phase regularly fantasy that they are boys. They regularly imagine that they have a penis.... Her fantasied penis ... is real to her. It is real enough that anything symbolizing the idea that it may be injured or lost arouses anxiety which is comparable to the castration anxiety of a boy....
>
> (p. 97)

But while speaking of penis envy as an outcome of the female's depressive sense of having been castrated, and while pointing out that some males (e.g., those suffering from physical defects which symbolize castration in their minds, or those who have adopted a defensive feminine identification) also suffer from castration depressive affect, from the feeling of having been castrated, Brenner still does not balance his recognition of female castration anxiety by a recognition of male penis (phallus) envy.

By distinguishing the phallus from the penis, Lacan not only liberates psychoanalysis to operate on its own appropriate level, that of *psychic* as opposed to *material* reality, but in so emancipating it from a reductive literalism, he frees it from the sexism founded upon such literalism expressed in the notion that "anatomy is destiny." Psychoanalysis is not about anatomy at all, but about the meanings and phantasies about anatomy, among other things, that shape the psychic and emotional lives of human subjects. The mere absence of a penis is no bar to feeling phallic. The mere presence of a penis is no guarantee against feeling castrated. Practically speaking, many will say, we have always known this. But why has such practical clinical knowledge not found its way more explicitly into our literature? In any case, it is precisely Lacan's concern with these issues that caused his work to be one of the major inspirations of the psychoanalytic feminism of the 1970s and 1980s (Lacan, 1982; Mitchell, 1974), however much this feminism sought to criticize Lacan's own phallocentrism (Irigaray, 1974, 1977).

The humanization of the unconscious

Not only does Lacan deliteralize Freudian concepts, but he liberates them from the biologism of Freudian instinct theory and relocates them within what is essentially a theory of narcissism or the self. For example, Lacan makes a fundamental distinction between organic *need*, on the one hand, which exists on the biological level and is shared by both human beings and animals, and human *desire*, on the other, which arising from an inner sense of absence established in the human psyche as a semiotic system of differences and distinctions (between subject and object, signifier and signified), is uniquely human. Animals and preverbal infants *need*, but they do not *desire*, for desire can only exist on the basis of the fundamental alienation, the sense of *lack*, from which it originates. This sense of lack can itself exist only on the basis of the symbolic subject/object or self/other distinction, which places a bar or gap between self and other generating a sense of the self as a lack of the other, a sense of lack or absence (*Fort!*) which gives rise to desire for that comforting presence (*Da!*) that is felt to be missing (Freud, 1920).

In redefining the castration complex to include the primal cut between subject and object that establishes the inner absence, nothingness or "lack of being"—*le néant* described in Sartre's (1943) existential phenomenology—that generates desire, Lacan re-situates psychoanalysis as a theory of desire and aggression in a semiotic rather than a biologistic context. For despite criticism of Strachey's misleading translations of key Freudian concepts (see Bettelheim, 1982, among many others), the fact remains that while Freud (1915a) did not employ the German word *instinkt* connoting a biologically fixed and relatively unchangeable animal instinct (such as that of the salmon to swim upstream or the bear to hibernate), he nevertheless insisted that the *triebe* (the "drives") arise from somatic sources, however modifiable they may be in aim and object. For Lacan, psychoanalysis is certainly a psychology of desire and aggression, but *human* desire and aggression, while obviously dependent upon a neurological substrate, have their source not in the body, but in the human mind as a semiotic system. Interestingly, Brenner (1982, chapter two) himself eventually arrived at this conclusion: since the entire human psyche rests on a neurological substrate, id is no more biological, no closer to "nature" or "human nature," than ego and superego, a view, which while certainly correct, has the consequence of undermining the ego-psychological image of the human being as a *centaur*, a creature half-human, half-animal and of psychic conflict as a battle between mind and body, culture and nature.

Both Erikson (1950) and Guntrip (1971) were justifiably critical of Freud's centaur model of man. But it has not always been noted that until the *Three Essays on the Theory of Sexuality* (Freud, 1905b) psychoanalytic theory operated virtually entirely without an instinct theory. In his revolutionary work on dreams (1900), slips (1901) and jokes (1905a), in which he traced the laws and mechanisms structuring the primary processes of the system unconscious, Freud offered a semiotic and hermeneutic theory, a theory of de-coding and interpretation of significations, symbols and meanings, rather than a biologistic or mechanistic theory of the sort that increasingly came to dominate his metapsychology. But unlike certain hermeneutic theorists, Lacan (for a time, at least) insisted upon the scientific status of psychoanalysis: while not a biological science, psychoanalysis was for Lacan a semiotic science of the structure of the unconscious mind. Against the tendency of psychoanalytic ego psychology to reduce the unconscious id to "a chaos, a cauldron full of seething excitations" (Freud, 1933, p. 73), a view that attributes all psychological form and structure to the synthetic functions of the ego, Lacan insisted, against Freud himself, upon the distinctive Freudian discovery of the structure of unconscious mental life, which for Lacan, is structured like a language. As Hanly (1986) pointed out: "Lacan ... reminds us that the roots of two of the basic form-generating devices of art are to be found in primary process thought" (p. 11).

As Lacan understood, the unconscious and its primary processes, far from representing a subhuman, asocial and pre-cultural chaos of drive energies, is already symbolically, that is, culturally structured in accordance with the very laws of condensation and displacement that Freud discovered, and that Lacan, following Jakobson (Jakobson & Halle, 1956, pp. 69–96), recognized as the laws of substitution (metaphor) and combination (metonymy), which compose the synchronic and diachronic axes of linguistic structure respectively. For Lacan (1977, chapter five), the widespread resistance to psychoanalysis does not arise from its depiction of a primitive and instinctual substrate of the mind, but rather from its revelation of the uniquely human and symbolically structured nature of the unconscious, a discovery that thwarts any attempt to find in the unconscious any purely "natural" self, any pre-social "human nature," as a basis for either a critique or a defense of the social order.

> Yet that is what we must resign ourselves to. The unconscious is neither primordial nor instinctual; what it knows about the elementary is no more than the elements of the signifier.... It is the abyss opened up at the thought that a thought should make itself heard in the abyss that provoked resistance to psychoanalysis from the outset. And not, as is commonly said, the emphasis on man's sexuality. This latter has after all been the dominant object in literature throughout the ages.
> (Lacan, 1977, p. 171)

The dehumanization of the unconscious effected by psychoanalytic ego psychology represents a regression in Freud's own thinking as well as that of later ego psychologists to an essentially pre-Freudian rationalistic philosophy of mind-body dualism and a centaur model of man that echoes Plato's vision of reason (Freud's ego) as the rider striving to control the two steeds—appetite (Freud's id) and spirit (resembling Freud's superego)—upon which it is precariously perched (Freud, 1933, lecture 31). This conception has created enormous difficulties both in clinical and applied psychoanalysis. In the former field it encourages a culturally conformist view of psychoanalytic therapy as promoting the domination, domestication or socialization of the id by a socially adapted ego and superego. In the latter, particularly in the theory of creativity, its emphasis upon the ego as the source of artistic form leads to neglect of the form-generating structures of the primary process.

The dehumanization of the primary process has led to a fear of the id based on a one-sided view of it as demonic, a conception that ignores the fact that the unconscious is also a source of wisdom, vitality, creativity and healing. Ironically, the ego-psychological dictum that the analyst ought to retain a position of psychic neutrality "equidistant from the id, the ego, and the superego" (Anna Freud, 1936, p. 28) is nullified by the bias of psychoanalytic ego psychology against the id arising from its falsely primitivized conceptualization. In Freud's (1930) pessimistic and culturally conservative sociopolitical ideology, in which the claims of culture (as represented by the ego and superego) are forever in conflict with those of nature (as represented by the id), and in which repression and resulting neurosis are the price of civilized order, we see the reactionary ideological consequences of the failure to recognize that, in a significant sense, the unconscious is always already cultural and the id is profoundly and uniquely human. For, as Freud himself taught us, unconscious mental life, far from being a meaningless chaos is meaningfully structured through condensation (metaphor) and displacement (metonymy), rhetorical tropes that represent key elements of our distinctively human symbolic behavior.

The mirror stage: a self psychology with a difference

Whereas Freud, especially in his metapsychology, tended to "biologize" his psychology, Lacan might be said to "narcissize" psychoanalysis, viewing both desire and aggression as manifestations of the struggles of the human "ego," which for Lacan is not a structure of the mental apparatus, but the self-image or self-representation, as in Freud's own pre-structural theory of the *Ich* ("I" or "me") as an object of experience or representation (whatever additional meanings were sometimes attached to it). Since the concepts of Lacanian theory have an overlapping significance, it is necessary to situate such concepts as the phallus and the process of oedipalization in the broader context of Lacan's fundamental theory of the nature and origin of the ego.

According to Lacan (1977, chapter one), at about six months of age the preverbal infant enters into what he called "the mirror stage." Experiencing itself as fragmented and uncoordinated (*le corps morcelé*: the body in bits and pieces) due to its biological prematurity or neoteny, the infant is enthralled by the cohesion and impressive unity (that is, the phallic quality) of its image in the mirror. Feeling fragmented, incomplete and castrated, a self "cut off" from the primal (m)other, the infant forms a defensive or compensatory identification with its phallic mirror-image. For Lacan, the child seeks less to *have* the phallus than to *be* the phallus for the mother. In Lacanian theory, to achieve the normal-neurotic condition a double castration is necessary. Whereas the psychotic "forecloses" or fails to register the primal alienation or "castration" entailed in assuming language, the "cut" between subject and object, the pervert accomplishes this, but fails to accept the second "castration" or separation entailed in recognizing that he cannot be the phallus for the mother—that is, that he cannot be the exclusive object of her desire. Failing to "accept castration" in not recognizing mother's desire for another, a third, he remains omnipotent (omni-potent, narcissistic) and condemned to the task of unconscious self-castration, repetitively seeking the emancipating limits unsuccessfully inscribed by the no/*nom*/*non* of the father (failed paternal function).

As the two discourses are often incommensurable, it is generally unwise to seek support for psychoanalytic ideas in empirical psychology and Lacan was foolish to do so (Billig, 2006). Instead of citing studies of pigeons and chimpanzees before mirrors, he would have done better to follow Freud's precedent and ground his theory in myth and literature—in the myth of Narcissus and Echo; in his countryman Rousseau's (1762) observations on *amour-propre* and *amour-de-soi*; and the critique of egocentricity in Western and Eastern religious traditions. Here the early Lacan's unfortunate romance with "science" led him astray. In any case, those of us who are awake require no support from empirical psychology to know that human desire is fundamentally narcissistic. Despite disagreeing with other aspects of Lacanian theory, Grunberger (1979) appears to share Lacan's reversal of Freud's (1914) view of narcissism as one of the vicissitudes of libido, instead viewing libido as one of the vicissitudes of narcissism (a viewpoint implicit in Sartre's [1943] existential theory of sexuality). As Grunberger (1979) explains:

> Instinctual life, in its many and varied manifestations, is rooted in and directed by the narcissistic factor, that is, it is both the expression of and the means of action of narcissism—hence primacy belongs to the latter. The need "to satisfy oneself" stands out in psychic relief only because the subject also wants to feel autonomous, capable of satisfying himself and deserving of satisfaction.
>
> (p. 88)

In this way, Grunberger re-presents a Lacanian idea without acknowledging a debt to his excommunicated colleague, a strategy widely employed by IPA analysts.

Lacanian theory is certainly a theory of narcissism or the self, but in contrast to theories such as that of Fairbairn (1952) that posit a "pristine whole ego" at the beginning that is only subject to splitting due to bad object relations experience, or theories that view fragmentation as resulting from "not-good-enough" mothering (Winnicott, 1960a, 1960b) or from empathic failure on the part of the early selfobjects (Kohut, 1978), for Lacan inner fragmentation, emptiness and lack are intrinsic aspects of the human condition. In promoting "acceptance of castration," psychoanalysis seeks to help us accommodate to this fact: "What does Freud tell us if not when all is said and done that what the one who follows this path will find at the end is nothing other essentially than a lack?" (Lacan, 1960–1961, Book III, p. 39).

On the other hand, Lacan's universalization or existentialization of the experience of emptiness and non-identity promotes a "metaphysics of absence" that, from a dialectical perspective, is no more convincing than the "metaphysics of presence" underlying one-sidedly optimistic schools of psychoanalytic thought that privilege inner fullness, identity and cohesion as somehow more fundamental or real than the experience of fragmentation. While the latter perspectives evade recognition of the frustration and conflict that are an inevitable feature of the human condition, the former, in remaining faithful to the Freudian tendency to privilege a "tragic sense of life" over visions of possible fulfillment, runs the risk of failing to sufficiently explore the ways in which inner disharmony and emptiness, "the basic fault" (Balint, 1968), emerge, above and beyond "the human condition," from early deprivation or traumatization of various types. In a truly dialectical perspective, neither absence nor presence, lack or fulfillment, crucifixion or resurrection, Good Friday or Easter Sunday, is epistemologically or ontologically privileged.

Rather than being either pleasure-seeking (Freud, 1905b), or object-seeking (Fairbairn, 1952), libido, for Lacan, might be said to be essentially self-seeking. Rather than wanting to possess, consume or use the other, as a means to instinctual satisfaction or to establish a relationship with the other as other, in the Lacanian view *my desire is the desire of the other:* that is, I desire to be the object of the other's desire, the apple of the other's eye. That is to say, I desire to be what the other lacks and, hence, desires. But, by definition, what the other lacks and desires is the phallus for, according to Lacan, whatever is felt to be lacking and therefore, desirable assumes a phallic significance (an equation that will be questioned below). But rather than taking the phallic image of wholeness and perfection as an ideal to be pursued—i.e., as an ego-ideal—the child, according to Lacan, mistakes the image for himself, that is, he identifies with the mirror-image, with the phallus and this mis-recognition constitutes the basis of his ego as self-image. For Lacan, then, the "ego" (the "I" or self-image—G.H. Mead's [1934] objective "me" or self-concept as distinct from his "I"-subject) emerges through a misidentification of the infant subject with its mirror-image, with the phallus of the (m)other, and, subsequently, with the images of others and the images reflected by others and by the sociocultural environment in general.

A crucial difference between Lacanian theory and both ego and self psychologies concerns Lacan's view of the essentially pathological nature of the ego or the self, which rather than needing strengthening through analysis or "transmuting internalization" (Kohut, 1978), constitutes the major obstacle to the therapeutic liberation of the "subject" from the idolatry of the ego-image by which it is captivated. Some of the seeming irreconcilability between approaches that seek to enhance ego strength or the cohesion of the self, on the one hand and, on the other, the Lacanian aim of undermining the ego or self in favor of the liberation of the subject, may be overcome when we remember that, for Lacan, "ego" or "self" refer to images or representations: what is to be undermined or therapeutically relaxed is, for Lacan, an essentially defensive and constrictive "false self" constructed out of an anal-sadistic need for mastery and control associated with the opposition of *Thanatos* to *Eros*. Clearly, the "true self," the development of which Winnicott (1960a) sought to encourage, and the "cohesive self" that Kohut (1978) sought to "restore" (implying it was there to begin with?), bear a far greater resemblance to Lacan's "subject" (Mead's "I") than to his "ego" (Mead's "me" or self-concept); while the latter would seem to more closely resemble Winnicott's (1960a) compliant or conformist "false self."

The Lacanian emphasis upon the deconstruction of the "ego" in favor of the "subject" seems to me to diverge from the Kleinian recognition that both healthy development and analytic treatment entail the internalization, the building up or re-building, of a whole, good internal object. While analysis certainly entails the deconstruction of the unconscious phantasies that "live us," enhancing reality-testing through distinguishing the inner from the outer world, it is at the same time necessary for both the child and the analysand to gain or re-gain faith in the good object and in their love for it. In this sense, psychoanalytic therapy is, at times, legitimately constructive. While the Kleinian and Kohutian perspectives are often seen as radically incompatible, the former's stress upon the need to build or re-build an internal good object is echoed in the latter's emphasis upon the role of "transmuting internalization" in the therapeutic process.

For Lacan, the "ego" forever remains an alienating image, a socially constructed persona, necessarily split-off from the "subject," which as long as the ego is dominant, is subject to repression and, being unconscious, speaks only in the form of a return of the repressed. As the product of a misidentification between the subject and the mirror-image arising from a failure to differentiate or distinguish between the two, the "ego" serves as the foundation for any number of similar fusional identifications of the self with the images of others and of objects, identifications, which taken together, constitute what Lacan termed the *Imaginary* order of experience. Since, at root, Imaginary experience is a continuation of the child's illusory sense of being the phallus for the mother and of being the image in the mirror, it reflects a failure of the oedipalization process to effect a differentiation between the subject and the ego-image, on the one hand, and between the subject and the phallus, on the other. The latter distinction requires an oedipalized awareness on the part of the child that another, ordinarily the father, rather than the self, occupies the position of the phallus for the mother. Since, in the Imaginary, any fundamental difference or otherness is denied, experience is constituted either in terms of identity or opposition, for opposition is not essential difference: it is merely the negative or inverse of identity.

Imaginary experience is characterized, therefore, both by undifferentiation and fusion on the one hand and, on the other, by a kind of black and white thinking, a splitting of objects and the self (as in Klein's paranoid-schizoid position) into such binary opposites as identical/antithetical, good/bad, strong/weak, or phallic/castrated. It is to this primitive level of experience that we have regressed when, for example, we feel that the other is either for us or against us, thereby evading the ambiguity and ambivalence, which unless we advance to more differentiated and integrated levels of mentation (Klein's depressive position), we are unable to tolerate. In the Imaginary world, since there exists no middle ground between, for example, incorporation and expulsion, total identity or total opposition, intersubjective experience takes on the sado-masochistic quality of the Hegelian "master-slave dialectic" (Casey & Woody, 1983; Ver Eecke, 1983) or the Sartrean (1943) "battle to the death of consciousnesses" in which "hell is other people": since it is the narcissistic aim of each ego to be the phallus for the other, and since it seems as if only one can occupy the phallic position at any one time, experience takes on the desperation and potential violence of a game of musical chairs in which all those who have failed to occupy the phallic position are by that very fact subjected to castration. Hence, in the Lacanian view, not only is desire fundamentally narcissistic in that it is a desire to be the object of the other's desire, but aggression, far from arising from a primordial, biologically-based, death instinct or even from a simple instinct of aggression, is also essentially narcissistic in that it is a reaction to frustration of the narcissistic wish to occupy the phallic position, to be the exclusive object of the other's desire. In other words, in the Lacanian view, as in that of Kohut (1972), aggression amounts, to all intents and purposes, to narcissistic rage.

For Lacan, the preverbal mirror phase and the Imaginary order of experience that is its psychic continuation are, on the one hand, narcissistic and fusional and, on the other, divided or split into primitive binary oppositions because the gap or bar that both separates self and other, and that itself constitutes a third term between or above the polar opposites, is insufficiently established in the psyche. But somewhere around eighteen months the mirror phase normally gives way before the process of oedipalization or socialization through which the social and linguistic distinctions between mother and infant, male and female, adult and child, which make up the Symbolic or cultural order of experience begin to be internalized. For Lacan, our patriarchal cultural order is constituted by the Law of the Father, the incest taboo, which in Lacanian theory is less a matter of the prohibition of literal incest than the interdiction of that type of mental incest represented by the subject-object confusions and oppositions, identities and antitheses, characteristic of the Imaginary as opposed to the Symbolic.

The oedipalization process disrupts both the fusional identifications and the splitting or binary organization of the Imaginary through a process of triangulation: the Symbolic father enters the scene as a third term and performs the phallic function of disrupting the symbiosis, opening up a space between mother and child and, at the same time, as a third term, displacing the purely binary divisions of the Imaginary in favor of the triadic structure of the Symbolic. It is important to realize that, for Lacan, what is at stake here is not the appearance of a literal father, but rather the operation of the Symbolic father, the paternal function or metaphor, that Lacan refers to as *le-nom-du-père*, the Name-of-the-Father, which is homophonic in French with *le-non-du-père*, the "No" of the father (a phrase that, for many, inevitably also brings to mind the other two "persons" of the Trinity, the Son and the Holy Spirit). The paternal or phallic function, whether literally performed by father, mother, sibling or anyone or anything else (it can, for example, be performed by "Father Time" who disrupts the Imaginary fusion of analysand and analyst by reminding both that "that's all the time we have for today"), is to prohibit both the fusional identifications and the binary oppositions that constitute the Imaginary order. The parallels between Lacan's Imaginary and Symbolic orders and Klein's paranoid-schizoid and depressive positions indicate a degree of convergence between these perspectives (Borossa et al., 2015) despite their differences.

Phallocentrism

While Lacan appears to have viewed the equation of anything valued with the phallus in the context of an apparently universal patriarchal culture, some have felt that he failed to make sufficiently clear the phallocentric basis of this association. In addition, it can be argued that he failed to sufficiently emphasize the fact that the primary object of desire during the preoedipal or matriarchal epoch preceding the superimposition of a patriarchal revaluation of all values during the oedipalization process is the breast-mother. Her value is later suppressed in favor of the phallus—the preoedipal mother even being retrospectively accorded a penis so that the patriarchal law (where there is power there must be a penis; where there is no power there can be no penis) may in this way be maintained. Here lies the basis for a feminist critique of Lacan's phallocentrism, his failure to be sufficiently aware of the longing for origin, for the mother, behind the desire for the phallus (Irigaray, 1974, 1977).

On the other hand, since, for Lacan, one's desire is not to *have* the penis, but to *be* the *phallus* for another, originally for the mother, the claim that he neglects the infant's preoedipal involvement with the mother is equivocal, to say the least. If, for the sake of argument, we accept Lacan's view of desire as primordially narcissistic, that is, that the infant's desire is to be the object of the mother's desire, then it is perhaps legitimate to say that he insufficiently emphasized the fact that the association between the object of the mother's desire and the phallus, that is to say, the phallic signification of the object of the mother's desire, the idea that the mother desires the phallus and that one must therefore, be the phallus in order to be the object of her desire, is a phallocentric and patriarchal equation superimposed upon the valuations of the preoedipal, matriarchal universe. Perhaps, primordially, the child simply wants to be the object of the mother's desire, the apple of her eye. The notion that to be valued is to be phallic would certainly appear to be a function of the dominant codes of a phallocentric cultural order.

On the other hand, it can be argued that one of the strengths of the Lacanian perspective, like Melanie Klein's, is its rejection of the either/or thinking that falsely separates oedipal from preoedipal issues, neurotic pathology from narcissistic or self pathology, and its insistence on the interrelatedness of oedipal and identity (or separation-individuation) issues as two aspects of a single psychic complex. By deliteralizing or metaphorizing the Oedipus complex as the division of an Imaginary unity into a duality (through the boundary established by the entry of a third), Lacan, like Klein, extends it into what in other perspectives is considered the preoedipal period, regarding selfobject differentiation as an oedipal issue.

There can be little doubt, however, that the work of Lacan, like that of Freud himself, is pervaded by a patriarchal bias that, broadly speaking, takes the form of what I have called (Carveth, 1984b) a *metaphysics of absence*. In contrast to the *metaphysics of presence* that Derrida (1976; Culler, 1982) views as central to our Western "phallogocentric" tradition that privileges presence (*Da!*) over absence (*Fort!*), and the matriarchal values of union and similarity over the patriarchal virtues of separateness and difference, the metaphysics of absence, rather than transcending these binary oppositions, simply reverses the hierarchies. In the metaphysics of absence there is denial, not of absence, separation and lack (as a defense against castration anxiety), but of the presence, connection and plenitude that constitute a threat to a patriarchal order of differences, distinctions and separations. As Gilligan (1982), among others, has pointed out, whereas women in our culture tend to define themselves in terms of their connections with others and, hence, are preoccupied with their responsibilities to others and threatened by the dangers of separation and individuation, men are more likely to define themselves as separate and autonomous and are anxious to defend their rights and freedoms against the danger of incursions by others, a threat that evokes fears of engulfment, undifferentiation and loss of self in the face of relationship.

On a deeper level, the patriarchal insistence upon the facts of separateness and difference, its emphasis upon boundaries and limits, and upon the gap, space, nothingness or "lack of being" between self and other, subject and object, can be seen as a desperate distancing defense against both the threat and the temptation of merger, whether the defense is mainly against an oedipal desire for an incestuous union, a preoedipal symbiotic desire for merger with the primary object, or an unconscious need and longing to be the object of the empathic look and adoring smile of the archaic mirroring selfobject—and presumably all of these meanings can operate simultaneously—the fact remains that the very intensity of these fusional wishes can give rise to a reactive or compensatory insistence upon boundaries, separateness and difference. The unconscious longing to eliminate the space between the "I" and the "not-I," to close the gap between subject and object, and to transcend the self as a lack of the other, can certainly return from repression in such disguised forms as: fears of incestuous entanglements, infantile regressions, and incursion or engulfment by others; an anxious and moralistic insistence upon the importance of boundaries and limits, a "health and maturity morality" (Kohut, 1979, p. 12); in short, in the metaphysics of absence that privileges separateness, difference and lack as somehow ultimately more real than presence, connection, similarity and plenitude. In other words, adherence to the patriarchal virtues not infrequently defends against a profound unconscious longing for the mother, a desire that, I believe, following both Lacan and Kohut, is essentially a narcissistic wish to be the object of the (m)other's desire, that is, a wish for the exclusive, devoted and loving attention of the archaic mirroring selfobject.

In privileging lack as ultimately more real than plenitude; in viewing the therapeutic task as that of encouraging "the acceptance of castration"; and in subordinating the Imaginary denial of difference to the Symbolic order of distance and division; Lacan remains faithful to the patriarchal Freudian insistence upon the castration complex as a kind of psychic "bedrock" (Freud, 1937), the coming to terms with which entails a virtuous disillusionment and renunciation of unrealistic and impossible desires, a facing of reality, enabling one to achieve that degree of mental health in which, "sadder but wiser," one has succeeded in transforming "hysterical misery into common unhappiness" (Freud, 1895, p. 305).

Perhaps without realizing the degree of agreement between Lacan and Freud on this score, Grunberger (1979) offers acute criticism of the Lacanian (Freudian) version of the psychoanalytic cure:

> If we acknowledge ... that a person enters analysis with the unconscious hope of recovering his narcissism ..., what are we to think of a psychoanalytic theory that, like Catholicism, is postulated on the renunciation of that restitution? As a matter of fact, the mystical investment of "acceptance of castration" takes on in the unconscious the connotation of phallic acquisition. The subject is lured into renunciation. Actually, it is a matter of satisfying a fundamental human desire by masking the theory with the defence against that very desire, which is bound to contribute markedly in its success, a mechanism that religions employ to the full, and which also constitutes the basis of masochism....
>
> (p. 279)

Whether in the guise of achieving an acceptance of castration, or accomplishing an "instinctual renunciation" (Freud, 1930) in the face of the reality principle, one may unconsciously be displaying a phallus as a defense against a deeper sense of castration, that is, a deeper narcissistic depression that is warded off through the narcissistic gratification to be had from a view of oneself as possessing sufficient courage and realism to embrace, stoically, the "tragic sense of life." But, for Grunberger, "... the neurotic is not at all a person who has not accepted castration as inherent in the 'human condition'; rather, he is a person who has failed to recover his lost narcissistic integrity ..." (p. 203).

Psychopathology

Although Lacan, like Freud, clearly privileges the Symbolic over the Imaginary, the patriarchal virtues of separation over the matriarchal values of connection, he at the same time argues that no one is so successfully oedipalized as to be completely reconciled to the Symbolic order of differences, distinctions and higher-order integrations. A part of each of us forever exists in the Imaginary. While such tendencies are clearly regressive in his eyes, Lacan recognizes that, to some extent, we all continue to yearn for the perfect merger between subject and object that Freud (1930) believed was illusorily entailed in romantic love, in mystical union or "oceanic experience," and that, to some degree, we are all prone to regressively divide or split our objects and ourselves. But rather than simply manifesting universal, normal-neurotic longings in a pathologically intensified form, so-called borderline and psychotic personalities are seen by Lacan as suffering from a more fundamental failure of oedipalization, resulting in a condition in which such symbiotic longings and splitting are relatively unmodulated and extreme. As a range of theorists working in other psychoanalytic traditions have pointed out (Laing, 1960; Guntrip, 1971), in such conditions a human relationship becomes an all or nothing affair characterized by both an intense longing for merger that can tolerate no difference, distance or separateness on the one hand and, on the other, an equally intense fear of engulfment and self-annihilation and a resulting need to retreat altogether from relationship into a schizoid aloofness.

According to Lacan (1977, chapter six):

> We will take *Verwerfung*, then, to be foreclosure of the signifier. To the point at which the Name-of-the-Father is called ... may correspond in the Other [the unconscious], then, a mere hole, which, by the inadequacy of the metaphoric effect will provoke a corresponding hole at the place of the phallic signification.
>
> (p. 201)

> It is in an accident in this register and in what takes place in it, namely, the foreclosure of the Name-of-the-Father in the place of the Other, and in the failure of the paternal metaphor, that I designate the defect that gives psychosis its essential condition, and the structure that separates it from neurosis.
>
> (p. 215)

Muller (1983) elucidates the Lacanian theory of psychosis (including so-called borderline phenomena) as follows:

> What experience is cut short here? For Lacan (as for Freud) it appears to be the experience of castration, of the mother's apparent castration as well as one's own. In psychotic development castration is foreclosed: the child remains in a dual, symbiotic union with the mother in which the child identifies with being the all-fulfilling object of the mother's desire. For Lacan, the signifier of the mother's desire is the phallus. Thus, in attempting to be the imaginary phallus or completion of the mother the child rejects the limits implied by castration. These limits are the constraints invoked by the Law of the Father, the symbolic father who intervenes in this dual relation.... When the mother fails to affirm the Law of the Father, makes no room for the intervening role of the symbolic father, or when the real father himself has a hypocritical relation to the Law, the Name-of-the-Father as signifier is foreclosed, and therefore the symbolic castration involved in giving up the position of the phallus and becoming subject to the Law is also foreclosed....
>
> (p. 23)

To my mind, Muller here conflates two "castrations," the first of which establishes self/object differentiation, the foreclosure of which results in psychosis, and the second of which establishes awareness that one cannot be the phallus for the mother as another occupies this position, the failure of which results in perversion. Lacan finds the roots of psychosis in a fundamental failure of oedipalization to establish in the unconscious the signifier of the phallus, the Name-of-the-Father, as the primal cut or castration dividing infant and mother and opening up a space for symbolization. But this theory is rendered equivocal by his positing of a literal hole in the unconscious, thereby failing to recognize this "hole" as itself a signifier, the signifier of absence or lack. As we have seen, Lacan succumbs to a metaphysical view of absence as somehow constituting an ultimate reality beneath or beyond signification. As we will see in the next chapter, this is the same problem that bedevils the work of Ernest Becker and Peter Berger who reify death anxiety and anomy as realities beyond signification. It is this metaphysical bias, which prevents Lacan from seeing that the "hole" in the unconscious results not from a failure of the primordial cut, but from its successful, but overwhelmingly traumatic, registration. Similarly, when Muller asks what is cut short here, I am inclined to respond that to cut short is nevertheless to cut. The child can only reject castration if its signification has already been encountered. The hole, gap or lack is already the registration of castration. In this respect, Lacan himself falls prey to the literalism that bedevils other psychoanalytic theories that posit a literal "defect" in the ego as the basis of the more severe forms of psychopathology.

On the psychotic and borderline levels of regression, far from there being any "foreclosure" of the psychic gap or lack of being, it is the very traumatic, overwhelming and annihilating intensity of the inner sense of emptiness and absence that gives rise, on the one hand, to the urgent symbiotic longings and, on the other, to equally intense fears of annihilation through engulfment by the other. Such symbiotic longings and fears arise not from a failure to register the fact of differentiation, not from any lack of an inner sense of lack, but rather from an overwhelming sense of inner absence that precludes any coming to terms with either separation or relationship through evolving a sense of separateness that does not preclude connection and of relationship that does not entail engulfment. In this situation, the sense of castration is so overwhelming that there may well be a desperate effort to defensively deny or disavow it. However, to mask or desperately attempt to fill the gap (as in the so-called restitution phase of psychosis) is nevertheless to recognize it. The psychotic or borderline personality is not fundamentally different from the neurotic or so-called normal, but simply engaged in a more extreme struggle with the universally human dilemmas of connection (*Eros*) on the one hand, and separation (*Thanatos*) on the other.

In this view, the borderline dilemma does not concern either term of the binary opposition Absence/Presence (*Fort!/Da!*) exclusively. Rather, it arises from a tendency to literalize or reify both terms, such that any absence becomes a devastating isolation and any presence threatens annihilation or engulfment. The problem concerns not the non-registration of either separation or connection, but rather the literal or Imaginary rather than metaphorical or Symbolic nature of their registration. In other words, when the issue of presence and absence becomes deadly serious, the *Fort!/Da!* game is no longer a game: for outside the symbolic or "transitional area" (Winnicott, 1953, 1971a), it becomes a matter of life and death. In his later work, Lacan contributes what is to me a more interesting conception of psychosis as a de-linking of the Borromean rings and of the *sinthome* as a means of reconnecting them (Fink, 1995b; Thurston, 2002).

Conclusion

It would seem to be the case that psychoanalysts, no less than their analysands, suffer from a tendency to regress from the Symbolic to the Imaginary and to literalize or privilege one or the other pole of such binary oppositions as Imaginary/Symbolic, cohesion/conflict, or integration/contradiction that constitute the inevitable basis of psychic life. However, just as some individuals are more successful than others in the never-ending task of differentiation (overcoming the fusions) and integration (transcending the splits) that constitutes the dialectical process of personal development, in my view it is necessary in psychoanalytic theory to transcend both the metaphysical pessimism of those who cry *Fort!* on the one hand, as well as the metaphysical optimism of those who cry *Da!* on the other, in order to get on with the *Fort!/Da!* game of differentiation and integration, the playing of which constitutes the dialectical process of psychic development. Provided it does not become frozen into a repetitive circularity by fixation upon thesis or antithesis, such development can take the form of a spiraling process resulting in that ever-expanding and mobile synthesis that constitutes a healthy self.

Chapter 6

The melancholic existentialism of Ernest Becker

A 2003 documentary film, *Flight From Death: The Quest for Immortality* (www.flightfromdeath.com), introduces viewers to the burgeoning subfield of social psychology called "terror management theory" grounded in the work of the psychoanalytic anthropologist Ernest Becker (1973). The following critique is in no way intended to apply to Becker's total *oeuvre,* but restricted to what I see as the excessive pessimism of *The Denial of Death.* Becker's *The Birth and Death of Meaning* (1962), for example, represents an important contribution to philosophical anthropology that offers insights that mainstream psychoanalysis has yet to fully appreciate.

Based primarily on the work of Otto Rank (1932, 1936, 1958) and Norman O. Brown (1959), Becker's work elaborates an existential psychology in which human beings suffer from a primary death anxiety that is, *contra* Freud, irreducible to infantile fears. Like Pascal, Kierkegaard and others in the existentialist tradition who write of our constant need for diversion from the dismal reality of our condition, Becker argues that our primary death anxiety necessarily and quite literally drives us to distraction. Repression, if not imposed by civilization, would be self-imposed due to our need to deny the body that, in a variety of ways, especially in its anal functions, is a constant reminder of the mortality we cannot face. Society offers a range of possibilities for heroism in which death is denied and an illusion of immortality constructed. The traditional psychoanalytic animus against Marxism here reaches a new pitch of intensity as Becker asks what new distractions a revolutionary society would offer its liberated proletarians to keep them from going mad. Following Rank, Becker offers an existential psychoanalytic apology for religion as the least destructive form of the universal and necessary denial of death. The despairing schizophrenic is in some ways more honest than we self-deceived and adjusted ones. In this view, the fundamental contradiction undermining the therapeutic project of psychoanalysis lies in the fact that the analysis of defenses and illusions that is supposed to liberate us in reality exposes us to unbearable truths in the face of which defenses and illusions are indispensable.

A decade before Becker worked out his psychoanalytic version of melancholic existentialism, Peter Berger (1963, 1967) had developed a sociological version. Although Berger defined sociological consciousness as relativizing and inherently debunking, an application of the "art of mistrust" characteristic of the Western "tradition of suspicion," his theoretical perspective failed in its own terms in that it did not consistently practice the relativizing it preached. While criticizing the "epistemologically privileged position" adopted by others—e.g., the Freudian who fails to produce a psychoanalysis of psychoanalysis, or the Marxist who fails to do a Marxian analysis of Marxism—it at the same time epistemologically privileged and exempted from relativization the *anomy* that it saw as the unbearable underlying truth, the terrifying meaninglessness and chaos characterizing human existence in this world, against which society defends us by means of the "shield against terror" that is the socially constructed "nomos" or social order that constitutes a "precarious vision" of meaning and order in a meaningless and chaotic universe.

Like Becker, Berger grounded his perspective upon the theory of neoteny or postnatal fetalization, the image of the human being as the instinctless and world-open animal. In this perspective, our very freedom from instinctual preadaptation conditions the helplessness anxiety of the uprooted human creature that enters the world in a painful state of anomy or chaos—Lacan's (1977) *le corps morcelé*, "the body in bits and pieces"—an originary fragmentation from which it ever after seeks to escape through the use of various personal and social mechanisms that function as defensive "shields against terror." The social construction of reality is viewed as the creation of a *nomos* or social order, a "named world," in the face of chaos and anomy and this *nomos* is supported and legitimated by being seen as grounded in and in harmony with a sacred *cosmos* whose structure, pattern and laws it reflects (the process of *mimesis*). In this way, religion, the positing of a sacred cosmos, is seen as the fundamental support for the precariously constructed social world that, in the face of secularization, is increasingly threatened with the anomy underlying and perpetually threatening it.

In reading both these authors, one soon becomes aware of the one-sided nature of their argumentation. For Becker, not only death, but man's anality, the human body and life itself are for the most part represented negatively as frightening, disgusting or absurd phenomena and seldom is there recognition that sometimes people delight in their bodies, secretly enjoy their anal functions and, if not exactly "half in love with easeful death" (Keats, *Ode to a Nightingale*), at least having managed to achieve what Erikson (1968) describes as "integrity versus despair and disgust" and having fully lived, are able to face the prospect of personal extinction with acceptance. In its rejection of all such attitudes as "healthy-minded" forms of denial or outright Pollyanna-ism, and in its depressed and angry bitterness toward human existence, Becker's work might better have been titled "the denial of life."

This epistemological privileging of existential anxiety and refusal to recognize the other side of the ledger of human experience in which we find despair countered by delight, pain with pleasure, hate with love and bitterness with thanksgiving, calls to mind Nietzsche's (1886) view of philosophy as a "disguised subjective confession." Becker and Berger appear to work with depression as their major unquestioned premise. Dismissing all positive attitudes toward human existence as founded upon denial and illusion, they inevitably fail to question their own negative postulates. Why was Becker unable to recognize the one-sidedness of his attitude of despair and disgust? Why was Berger unable to see that *anomy* is itself another *nomos*—an interpretation of experience as vulnerable to relativization as any other? If the psychoanalytic relativization of false claims to universal validity by tracing them to their origin in particular attitudes of specific personalities was ever necessary, it is called for here. For while capturing many valid insights into the dark side of the human condition, these perspectives become increasingly unreal in their exclusive adherence to a one-sided construction of reality.

In seeking to deconstruct Becker's ontology of anxiety or basic mistrust and his melancholic outlook—as well as his gnostic type of religiosity that from a biblical point of view is heretical in its devaluation of the Creation—I in no way intend to reject his existentialist understanding of our unique predicament as symbolling and self-conscious beings, but only his one-sided interpretation of the human situation. In viewing, as I do, the "rapprochement crisis" as the "fulcrum" in psychological development (Mahler et al., 1975) in which the human subject emerges from the pre-biological (World I, inorganic, *lithosphere*) and biological (World II, organic, *biosphere*) levels of being into the post-biological (World III, superorganic) realm of the *noösphere* as a symbolling being self-consciously aware of its separateness and, soon enough, of its impending demise, I in no way regard such awareness as intrinsically unbearable, let alone as justification for a "leap" into a consolatory and gnostic religion of illusion. For the same symbolic consciousness that awakens us to a knowledge of our separateness and ultimate death at the same time awakens us to a knowledge of our connectedness and of the gift of life.

Just as for the Lacanians—William Richardson (1986) proving the exception in this regard—the *Real* is usually associated with horror and seldom with the sublime and awe-inspiring, so for Becker, the reality outside socially and personally fabricated illusion is usually associated with terror and seldom with awe or joy. But while certainly opening up the potential for despair, symbolic consciousness at the same time opens up the possibility of *jouissance*. Although in earlier sections of *The Denial of Death*, Becker does write of the awe-inspiring aspect of reality encountered outside repression and denial, he at the same time regards this as overwhelming and paralyzing and needing to be defended against by the individual simply in order to function. As his argument proceeds, this positively overwhelming aspect of the *Real* is increasingly displaced by its negatively overwhelming aspects—its association with disintegration, anality and death.

In my view, Becker's ontology of anxiety is a contemporary manifestation of the gnostic heresy that Judaism and Christianity have both sought to reject, even while being infected by it, to a greater or lesser degree, in the process. According to the Bible, the Creation is good, but for Becker it is a meaningless, chaotic realm of disorder, disintegration and death against which human beings need to be protected by illusions of meaning, by a gnostic religion positing another, more orderly and meaningful world, "beyond" this vale of tears. This gnostic devaluation of the Creation, together with its splitting of the realms of darkness and of light, has always been resisted by monotheism. Not only orthodox versions of Christianity, but also its demythologized, existentialist and "religionless" variations are capable of affirming *both* Good Friday *and* Easter Sunday, both *Thanatos* and *Eros*, without privileging either over the other—that is, of transcending paranoid-schizoid splitting and part-object functioning for the whole-object orientation of Melanie Klein's (1946, 1948, 1959) so-called depressive or reparative position.

It is often overlooked that Freud himself contributed to an existentialist perspective while developing an argument for his sociological views that is quite distinct from his instinctualism. In his later works, especially in *The Future of an Illusion* (1927) and *Civilization and Its Discontents* (1930, chapter two), even while advancing what Erik Erikson (1950, p. 192) described as his "centaur" model of man as a creature torn between the forces of nature (id) and the claims of culture (ego and superego) and his psycho-biological view of the mind as a control apparatus for the management of "the beast within," Freud at the same time draws attention to the problem of anxiety, not in the face of man's instincts or their punishment by the superego, but to his creaturely anxiety in the face of disease, accident, aging, the cruelty of others and finally of death itself. Here is the all-too-seldom recognized existentialist Freud who, aside from all instinctualist and biologistic considerations, is calling our attention to man's ontological predicament. Earlier, in *Inhibitions, Symptoms and Anxiety* (1926), Freud had taken a giant step away from his instinctualist psycho-biology when he replaced his earlier view of anxiety as transformed libidinal energy with a humanistic theory of anxiety as an intelligible human response to a danger situation and went on to enumerate the archaic fears of loss of the loved object, loss of the object's love, castration and superego condemnation.

Freud (1923, pp. 64–66; 1926) argued that since the nature of death must of necessity remain a mystery to the living thinker, whatever attitudes we have toward it are likely to be influenced by unconscious phantasy and, hence, will tend to vary with the nature of the phantasy underlying them. When death is phantasied as the ultimate abandonment and helplessness, it assumes a terrifying aspect in light of our displaced separation anxiety. Similarly, when phantasied as the ultimate castration or superego punishment (or, to add a Kleinian perspective, as a persecutory attack by an all-bad part-object), death becomes an uncanny and horrifying prospect. But sometimes death is phantasied in much more positive terms as we saw above: as reunion and refusion with the primal mother or other lost objects; as the eternal bliss of oneness with God in Heaven; etc. One need not minimize the significance of man's unique situation as an animal burdened with the knowledge of its impending demise in order to accept the psychoanalytic idea that our attitudes toward our mysterious fate are significantly influenced by unconscious phantasy.

The fact that Ernest Becker and Peter Berger produced such one-sidedly dark and pessimistic visions of human existence suggests the nature of the persecutory phantasies that may have gripped them. This might explain their essentially nihilistic and cynical view of religion as necessary illusion. Like T.S. Eliot (1944), these authors believe "human kind cannot bear very much reality" (*Burnt Norton*, No. 1 of "Four Quartets") and, like Miguel de Unamuno's (1956) *Saint Emmanuel the Good, Martyr* and Dostoevsky's (1880) Grand Inquisitor, they would gratify mankind's alleged need for consoling illusion, "magic, miracle and authority." According to Paul Tillich (n.d., as quoted by D. Mackenzie Brown): "History has shown that the Grand Inquisitor is always ready to appear in different disguises, political as well as theological." Today, he appears in the guise of "therapists" who, in the name of empathy and compassion for human weakness, seek to support or even join, rather than resolve, defenses (self-deception) and the resistance to facing inner and outer reality. In defiance of Christ's assertion that: "Ye shall know the truth, and the truth shall make you free" (*John* 8:32), the Grand Inquisitors, old and new, patronize humanity, offering us consoling illusion rather than liberating truth, while seeking, as always, to crucify those who would undermine their compassionate work.

Conceiving religious faith in Hellenistic terms as *belief* rather than in Hebraic terms as *trust* (in the sense of Erik Erikson's (1950) attitude of "basic trust"), and focusing almost exclusively on its literalistic and supernatural rather than demythologized forms, many post-Enlightenment Western thinkers find themselves unable to embrace what they view as sheer wish-fulfilling illusion, however much they, like Rank and Becker, may regard such illusion as indispensable to mental health. If, in addition, they suffer from some degree of personal depression and experience of life as persecutory, they will be unable to summon an attitude of trust and gratitude.

But while the bad part-object certainly exists, so also does the good part-object. When splitting is overcome and ambivalence (Klein's misnamed "depressive position") achieved, when the forces of love (*Eros*) are dominant over the forces of envy and hate (*Thanatos*), these part-objects are integrated into a whole, creatively repaired, good object. Confidence in one's capacity to love and make reparation for one's hatred and destructiveness establishes this whole good object, identification with which makes possible an equally holistic and integrated sense of self. Though "fallen" and "broken" and perpetually falling back into paranoid-schizoid dynamics, the self comes to be experienced as capable of repairing and of being reparable and, hence, as fundamentally good. Here is the basis for an attitude of basic trust in the goodness of existence and of the self. This is the essence of a mature faith and is no illusion.

The ideology that makes everything a defense against death anxiety defends against recognition of neurotic anxiety stemming from other sources, such as unconscious guilt. It "existentializes" or universalizes what may often be a very personal anxiety state that might be relieved by personal analysis. Often people prefer to justify their anxiety by grounding it in the human condition, the universal anxiety of death, etc., rather than facing their need for psychoanalysis to get at the real roots of their chronic anxiety instead of rationalizing it. People who have come to terms with their conscience and made substantial progress in resolving other neurotic conflicts and have acquired the capacity to give and receive love are sometimes able to accept the natural ending of life; they have been able to lead relatively fulfilled lives and are tired and willing and able to say goodbye—just as, if we are not too greedy, after a satisfying meal we are happy to push away from the table.

Research conducted in connection with "terror management theory" (Greenberg et al., 2004) has provided useful support for the idea of the defensive function of belief systems. But belief systems defend against a wide range of anxieties. It is the privileging of death anxiety as the Ur anxiety in "terror management theory" that is the problem. This type of reductionism, this sort of "master theory," is very appealing: it captures the imagination and saves people the time and trouble involved in seeking deeper self-knowledge.

Chapter 7

Concordant and complementary countertransference
A clarification

The mind of the psychoanalyst, like that of the analysand, experiences tensions and conflicts between id (impulses, affects and wishful phantasies of love, hate and their varying combinations), ego (relatively rational and reality-oriented mental processes), and superego (moral demands, ideals and prohibitions, including guilt and needs for either punishment or reparation). Anna Freud (1936) argued the analyst should maintain a position "equidistant" from the analysand's id, ego and superego, a position of neutrality from which the operations of each agency and their varying combinations may be objectively observed and analyzed.

As an ideal this implies that the analyst will engage in a range of primarily conscious or preconscious "trial identifications" (Fliess, 1942, p. 213; Olinick et al., 1973, p. 243) with the conflicting elements of the analysand's mind without overly and unconsciously identifying with any particular component of the conflict. In my view, this is what empathy consists in: the analyst's relatively conscious and preconscious, not unconscious, trial identification with both conscious and unconscious elements of the analysand's mind—that is, with the analysand's wishes, fears, phantasies and self- and object-representations. Empathy, as the act of imagining oneself "in the other's shoes," as it were, is to be distinguished from sympathy as caring or compassion, though it is possible to engage in both simultaneously. For Kohut (1959), empathic introspection is the psychoanalyst's primary data-gathering method. In regarding empathy as a means to the end of understanding there is no need to deny that it may be felt as or even be therapeutic in and of itself.

Today it is widely recognized that our personal conflicts bias us in various respects and generate countertransference identifications that, in contrast to the conscious and preconscious trial identifications that constitute empathy, may take the form of more global, concrete and unconscious identifications with specific elements of the analysand's mind. While conscious and preconscious trial identifications are available for the analyst's self-reflection, unconscious identifications with the analysand's, conscious or unconscious self- or object-representations or specific mental structures constitute the basis of potentially problematic countertransference leading to enactments, empathic failures, blind spots and analytic impasse. This is not to suggest that such countertransference or even its enactment is *always* destructive to the analytic process or to deny that it may occasionally even be seen, after the fact, to have been useful in some respects. But such exceptions do not "prove the rule." Although, as Smith (2000) points out, all our listening is conflictual in that the analyst's own conflicts are continually being stirred up, in normative analytic work it is desirable for as much of our countertransference as possible to be available for relatively conscious self-reflection, even if as Renik (1993) suggests we sometimes only become aware of it after it has been put into action. Smith (2000) writes: "if our conflicts always influence our perceptions, it remains crucial to what extent as analysts we can observe and use our conflictual responses as data" (p. 107).

In what Racker (1957) called *concordant* countertransference identification, the analyst identifies with the analysand's id on the basis of his or her own id, and with the analysand's superego on the basis of his or her own superego. But such concordant identifications may be conscious, preconscious or unconscious. Only if they are conscious or preconscious can they be said to constitute empathy (a point that Racker fails to make clear). By contrast, in *complementary* countertransference, the analyst identifies (again, consciously, preconsciously or unconsciously) with the agency the analysand is disidentifying with and emotionally inducing, evoking or projectively identifying into the analyst. For example, the patient is identifying with her superego and disidentifying with her id with which the analyst is in complementary countertransference identification; or *vice versa*, the patient is identifying with her id and the analyst is in complementary countertransference identification with the projected superego. If such complementary identifications are relatively conscious or preconscious they constitute empathy, but not if they are relatively unconscious.

In saying that in her countertransference the analyst is in complementary identification with the patient's projected id or superego there is no intent to suggest the patient is entirely responsible for such (conscious or unconscious) reactions, having "put them into" the analyst through projective identification. The patient stirs up or evokes the analyst's id, ego or superego responses. Projective identification or emotional induction is understood to involve the analyst's "role-responsiveness" (Sandler, 1976). Countertransference is always a joint production with relative and varying contributions from the analyst and the analysand.

Clinical vignette #1

An analysand is experiencing conscious sexual impulses toward someone other than his wife. In a mild conscious concordant counter-transference the analyst empathizes, id with id. But since the analyst suffers conflicts of his own in this area, he overly identifies with the analysand's impulses and then defensively represses this concordant countertransference, which as a result is no longer available to his empathic introspection. The analyst proceeds to succumb unconsciously to a complementary countertransference based on identification with the patient's projected superego. Since this identification is unconscious, he begins both to feel and intervene moralistically.

One of the things that render Racker's work difficult to comprehend at times is that he employs both the language of ego psychology—the structural model of id-ego-superego—as well as the language of internalized object relations. Sometimes he speaks of concordant countertransference identifications as those in which analyst and analysand identify with the same psychic structures (id with id, ego with ego, superego with superego), and complementary countertransference identifications as those in which they identify with different structures (id and superego, ego and id, superego and ego). At other times, however, he speaks of countertransference in the language of self and object: the analyst identifies either with the analysand (the subject) or with the analysand's projected object. In both cases, like Helene Deutsch (1926), Racker describes the *concordant* countertransference as empathy since it involves the analyst identifying with the analysand's self-state, as distinct from identification with what he is disowning through projection (*complementary* countertransference), whether the latter is conceived as one of the three mental structures or as an internal object.

According to Racker:

> The complementary identifications are closely connected with the destiny of the concordant identifications: it seems that to the degree to which the analyst fails in the concordant identifications and rejects them, certain complementary identifications become intensified. It is clear that rejection of a part or tendency in the analyst himself,—his aggressiveness, for instance,—may lead to a rejection of the patient's aggressiveness (whereby this concordant identification fails) and that such a situation leads to a greater complementary identification with the patient's rejecting object, toward which this aggressive impulse is directed.
>
> (p. 311)

This is precisely what we saw in the first vignette. The analyst rejected concordant identification with his patient's adulterous inclinations and as a result his complementary identification with the patient's projected superego intensified. Again, reference to the analyst's countertransference identification with the patient's projected superego is intended to mean no more than that the patient's disidentification with his superego and identification with his id in some way stimulates, stirs up or evokes a superego reaction in the analyst. The patient is not being seen as the sole manufacturer of the analyst's response, and no magical, transpersonal process is envisaged.

Because he views the analyst's concordant identification as empathy, without specifying whether such identification is relatively conscious, preconscious or unconscious, Racker feels compelled to argue that it should nonetheless be included in the category of countertransference: "Usually excluded from the concept countertransference are the concordant identifications—those psychological contents that arise in the analyst by reason of the empathy achieved with the patient and that really reflect and reproduce the latter's psychological contents" (p. 311). Racker sees failures of empathy—i.e., failures of concordant identification—as generating the problematic complementary countertransference identifications. But I submit that empathy consists only in those concordant countertransference identifications that are relatively conscious or preconscious, together with those complementary countertransference identifications that are also relatively conscious or preconscious. My argument is (1) that

Racker erred in confining empathy to concordant identification, when conscious or preconscious complementary identifications are also empathic; and (2) in regarding only complementary countertransference as problematic when both concordant and complementary countertransferences are equally problematic when they are relatively unconscious and serve empathy when they are relatively conscious or preconscious.

Might the equation of concordant countertransference with empathy have been avoided if Racker had employed the concept of internal object relations as involving not internal "objects," but internal self- and object-*representations* (Sandler & Rosenblatt, 1962; Kernberg, 1979)? Might this have highlighted the fact that analysands can overidentify with and disidentify from specific self-representations as well as object-representations? In Kernberg's (1987) view, "patients may project a self-representation while they enact the object representation ... or, vice versa, they may project an object representation while enacting the corresponding self-representation" (p. 215). In this case, concordant countertransference might well involve the analyst identifying with a split-off self-representation of the patient's and, just as the patient may have repressed this self-representation, so the analyst may be relatively unconscious of the fact that he has become identified with it. This certainly involves a connection between analyst and patient, but it is a relatively *unconscious* connection. For those who view the goal of analysis as enhanced conscious self-understanding—and, admittedly, not everyone views it this way—such relatively unconscious connection will most likely only prove truly useful if, in the long run, it becomes relatively conscious.

With the exception of a paper by Tarnopolsky (1995) that briefly touches upon the problem (see Carveth, 2012b), the literature on countertransference seems largely to have accepted rather than questioned Racker's equation of concordant identification with empathy. Epstein and Feiner (1979), for example, simply report that: "Racker further differentiated direct countertransference into two processes: *concordant identifications* and *complementary identifications*. Concordant identifications are empathic responses to the patient's thoughts and feelings" (p. 496). In her recent review of Racker's work, LaFarge (2007) writes:

> In ... *concordant identification* [original emphasis], the analyst identifies himself with the patient by aligning his own mind with the

patient's.... In this mode, the patient's conflicts come alive through their resonance with analogous conflicts in the analyst. This kind of identification corresponds to what people ordinarily call empathy....

(p. 7)

According to LaFarge: "When the analyst fails in his concordant identification, he is, in a sense, captured by the patient's projection instead; that is, he identifies with the internal object that the patient has projected into him" (p. 8). Here LaFarge confirms Racker's idea that the problematic countertransference identifications are those with the patient's projected internal objects—the *complementary identifications* in which "the analyst identifies himself with one of the patient's internal objects...." (p. 7) —and not concordant identification with the patient's self. When the latter fails we have the empathic failure that leads to capture by the problematic complementary countertransference.

The suggestion raised above, that the equation of concordant countertransference with empathy might have been avoided had Racker employed the concept of internal object relations as involving not internal "objects," but internal self- and object-*representations*, is not borne out in the work of Smith (2000). Although he writes: "I would prefer to put it that in concordant and complementary identification the analyst identifies with aspects of the patient's self- and object-representations, respectively," Smith nevertheless, goes on to state that: "I am in essential agreement with Racker" that "concordant identification corresponds roughly to what Arlow calls empathy, and complementary identification to what Arlow considers countertransference—namely taking the patient as an object" (p. 102). Hence, conceiving of internal object relations in representational terms does not guarantee that one will overcome the tendency to think of countertransference as identification with the patient's split-off object-representations while overlooking that it may equally entail identification with the patient's self representations. Nor does it guarantee that one will overcome the proclivity to automatically associate the latter with empathy.

Whereas relatively conscious concordant trial identification with the patient's self-representation constitutes empathy, as does relatively conscious complementary trial identification with the patient's object-representation, relatively unconscious concordant identification with the patient's self-representation does not. The crucial factor here concerns the analyst's degree of consciousness, not the patient's. I believe we can and do extend empathy (conscious concordant and complementary trial identification) to both conscious and unconscious self- and object-representations of the patient. It is when our identifications, concordant or complementary, are relatively unconscious that our countertransference is problematic, for it is then that we are captured by it rather than utilizing it in the service of conscious understanding.

Later in his paper, Smith (2000) provides several vignettes in which he is "identifying simultaneously in both concordant and complementary ways—that is, with both the patient and the patient's internal objects" (p. 109). But in correctly suggesting that "the analyst is continuously identifying with both parties in the object relationship," Smith is not addressing the relative consciousness of such identifications, nor distancing himself from the tendency to see the complementary identifications as problematic and the concordant ones as empathy. I can agree that we are continuously identifying with both the patient and the patient's internal objects, but the point at issue here is to what degree am I *captured* by one or the other of such identifications—that is, to what degree does my identification qualify as a conscious or preconscious trial identification (i.e., empathy) or as domination by an identification (complementary or concordant) of which I am largely unconscious?

Toward the end of his paper, Smith (2000) suggests that the question as to whether a particular countertransference constitutes interference or facilitation of the analytic process is irrelevant in that "all our clinical moments are mixtures of both in endless variation" (p. 15). But some unconscious countertransference identifications are not at all momentary; they can sometimes last for weeks, months, even for many years. Although it is true that sometimes they can appear, after the fact, to have been necessary and in the long run productive, at other times they can constitute the basis of analytic impasse or stalemate. In this connection, Stolorow (2002), writing of intersubjective conjunction and disjunction (the latter occurring "when empathy is replaced by misunderstanding") notes that interferences in the course of treatment, sometimes to the point of impasse, may arise from either situation, "most notably when they [intersubjective conjunctions and disjunctions] remain outside the domain of the therapist's reflective awareness" (p. 331).

Kernberg (1987) occupies a unique position in relation to Racker's work. Whereas in most of the literature the complementary countertransference identifications are seen as those with the patient's projected object or object-representation and are seen as problematic, Kernberg views the complementary countertransference as identification with what the patient is projecting, whether that be a self- or an object-representation. This allows Kernberg to understand the possibility of the analyst's capture by unconscious identification with the patient's projected self-representation. But, unlike Racker, he calls this a complementary countertransference instead of a concordant one. Again, unlike Racker, Kernberg views both concordant and complementary countertransferences as capable (presumably when relatively conscious to the analyst) of "increasing empathy with a patient's central subjective experience (in concordant identification) and in maintaining empathy with what the patient is dissociating or projecting (in complementary identification)" (p. 215). This is a legitimate theoretical resolution of the problem addressed in this paper (the failure to see the danger of capture by the patient's split-off self-representations and the confusion of empathy as such with concordant and not also complementary identification). But from a strictly scholarly point of view Kernberg's solution is problematic in that it fails to make explicit its deviation from Racker's own views. Why, we may ask, did Kernberg substantially revise Racker's concepts without explicitly acknowledging the fact or stating the reasons he felt Racker's views needed such revision? Personally, I prefer to follow Racker and most of the literature in thinking of the complementary countertransference as identification with the patient's object-representation and concordant countertransference as identification with the patient's self-representation, while openly differing with Racker in recognizing that both of these may constitute empathy when conscious to the analyst and problematic when unconscious.

If we go a little further into the first vignette we can bring into focus the reasons I find Racker's equation of concordant countertransference with empathy to be problematic.

Clinical vignette #1 cont'd

Catching himself feeling or acting in an uncharacteristically moralistic way, the analyst strove to overcome his moralism, only to lose once again his capacity for flexible, conscious trial identification with all the components of the patient's conflict, instead succumbing to an excessive, unconscious concordant countertransference identification with the patient's id. He swung from warning and reproaching to offering in the name of non-judgmental empathic attunement a level of acceptance tantamount almost to a type of encouragement of the patient's acting-out.

Here we see that if retreat from concordant identification can lead to being captured by a complementary identification, so also can retreat from the complementary lead to capture by the concordant.

While Racker and others associate concordant identification with empathy, suggesting that it is therefore, therapeutically useful and relatively unproblematic in comparison to complementary countertransference identification, the factor that determines whether a countertransference identification is helpful or problematic in furthering the analytic goal of increased self-awareness on the part of both analyst and analysand is its degree of consciousness. If the analyst is relatively unconscious of her concordant countertransference identification with the analysand, this will be as much a blind spot in the analysis as unconscious complementary identification. Conversely, a complementary countertransference identification can be useful therapeutically *provided* it is relatively conscious. Racker increased our awareness of the danger of capture by the complementary countertransference. We now need to stop equating the concordant countertransference with empathy and become aware of how empathy is impaired when we are unconsciously captured by either form of countertransference identification and how both may enhance empathy when they are conscious and available to the analyst's self-reflection.

LaFarge (2007) provides a clinical illustration of how, through her awareness of her complementary countertransference identification with her patient's excluded objects and her use of this awareness in her interventions, the transference shifted and in her countertransference the analyst ceased to feel excluded. Over time, she came not only to feel included, but to feel that she and the patient were very similar in many ways. This concordant countertransference intensified to the point of a feeling of "twinship" with the patient, as if the two were now allied against the world. LaFarge refers to this as a "heightened concordant countertransference" and explains that it had the effect of warding off important dynamics. Because she subsequently became aware of its defensive role, LaFarge does not identify this concordant countertransference with empathy, but neither does she challenge Racker's equation of the two; nor does she describe her "heightened concordant countertransference" as capture by a concordant countertransference; nor does she challenge Racker's view that only the complementary countertransferences are problematic.

Clinical vignette #2

> The younger sister of a highly successful older sister was full of envy, competitiveness and hatred toward her. The analyst was so conscious of the danger of being induced into a complementary countertransference identification with this older sister that she was blind to the fact that she had fallen into an unconscious concordant countertransference identification with the patient as the younger sister. The analyst was intimidated by the patient who was unconsciously identified with the aggressive older sister. When, with the help of a consultant, the analyst became conscious of this and overcame the feeling of intimidation sufficiently to ask the patient for a long-needed increase in the frequency of sessions, the patient responded by demanding a long overdue raise from her employer—that is, she overcame her own intimidation by an object with whom she had been enacting the younger/older sibling dynamic.

In this example, the analyst is initially captured by concordant countertransference identification with the patient as the intimidated younger sister and consequently fails to grasp the fact that she is being bullied by the patient as identified with the aggressive older sister. But, again, let us continue the story a little further.

Clinical vignette #2 cont'd

> Later in this analysis, the patient reported disappointment at what she took to be the depressing ending of a film both she and the analyst had seen. The analysand complained that while the hero had managed to escape, his friends had been left behind. On inquiry it became clear that the patient had disgustedly turned off the video just prior to the *dénouement*. Because it was part of the patient's pattern in life to "clutch defeat from the jaws of victory" the analyst seized on this as a golden opportunity to interpret the repetition compulsion. In

pointing out the patient's mistake, she fell (from the patient's point of view) into an enactment of the role of the "superior" older sister that she had been avoiding. In the next session, the patient reported that she had re-rented the video and discovered the analyst was right. She then abruptly and permanently terminated the analysis.

From having at first unconsciously identified with the patient as the intimidated younger sister, a problematic concordant countertransference, the analyst was later captured by an identification with and enactment of the "superior" older sister, a problematic complementary countertransference.

What in this case is the "part or tendency in the analyst himself" that is rejected leading to a rejection of a corresponding part of the patient? At first, it was the analyst's rejection of the idea of herself as an intimidated child. She was intent on avoiding being aggressive, domineering and intimidating and was blind to the fact that she was intimidated. Later, it seems that the patient's anger and scorn toward something that meant a great deal to the analyst may have caused her to lose sight of both her own aggression and the patient's vulnerability, succumbing to an identification with the "know-it-all" sibling and unleashing her anger at the patient in the guise of a confrontation followed by an interpretation, albeit one that had a considerable degree of validity.

One might be inclined to think that a concordant countertransference identification of ego with ego would be entirely unproblematic. Although resonance between the analyst's and the analysand's rationality is certainly a *sine qua non* of successful psychoanalytic work, the analysand's rationality is frequently defensive rather than conflict-free. At times it represents a rigid defensive flight into rationality away from anxiety or guilt-producing feelings and phantasies. Unconscious countertransference identification on the part of the analyst's rational ego with the analysand's defensive employment of rational ego functioning in this sort of circumstance is a formula for an intellectualized pseudo-analysis and for stalemate. Needless to say, unconscious countertransference identifications of superego with superego or id with id are equally unproductive precisely because they are unconscious.

In providing us with the distinction between *concordant* and *complementary* countertransference, Racker added to our understanding in this field. But as important as is the differentiation between concordant and complementary countertransference, an even more fundamental distinction is that between relatively conscious and relatively unconscious countertransference. Racker associated the concordant countertransference with empathy and viewed it as unproblematic. In my view, both concordant and complementary identifications aid empathy to the extent that they take the form of conscious or preconscious trial identifications available to the analyst's self-reflection, and both will impede empathy when they are unconscious.

LaFarge provides an example of a "heightened concordant countertransference" that disturbs rather than serves empathy, but refrains from describing this as a situation in which she had been captured for a time by a concordant countertransference. Both Smith and LaFarge illustrate how we often shift between complementary and concordant countertransference identifications. LaFarge illustrates how, at times, the latter can become so "heightened" that they disturb rather than serve empathic understanding. Yet, like Smith, LaFarge avoids explicitly criticizing Racker's and the now widespread equation of the concordant countertransference with empathy and the complementary with problematic countertransference. Kernberg understands that we can be captured by countertransference identification with either the patient's split-off object- or self-representation, but he redefines the latter as capture by a complementary rather than a concordant countertransference. This allows him to appear to be in agreement with Racker's view that it is only the complementary countertransferences that are problematic. Kernberg fails to make explicit both the fact that he has revised Racker's terminology and his reasons for so doing. Tarnopolsky's (1995) *Understanding Countertransference* is the only paper I know of that identifies Racker's error as such. Tarnopolsky defines complementarity as the analyst's identification with "something that the patient disowns" (p. 185), a statement that leaves open the possibility that sometimes it may be the self that the patient disowns while at other times it will be the object. Tarnopolsky provides a clinical example of the former and writes: "The patient is therefore not always necessarily in the position of a 'child' vis-à-vis the 'parent' therapist; in the example it is the other way round" (p. 188). In saying this, Tarnopolsky, like Kernberg, recognized that countertransference identification with the patient's self, like countertransference identification with the patient's object, can constitute problematic countertransference. However, whereas Kernberg avoids overtly criticizing Racker by calling problematic countertransference identification with the patient's self "complementary" rather than "concordant" without explaining his reasons for so departing from Racker's usage, Tarnopolsky states: "This has been called complementary reaction to, or complementary identification with, the patient; but I do not follow strictly Racker's (1957) definition" (p. 187). Although he does not go on to elaborate upon the significance of this departure from Racker's usage, Tarnopolsky both saw the point and registered his deviation from Racker.

A psychoanalyst's "third ear" might well be alerted to the possibility that some unconscious conflict might underlie such apparent inhibition of clear and explicit critical rationality. Is there some unspoken and unconscious collective taboo in the psychoanalytic community that generates a scholarly inhibition when it comes to explicitly identifying and naming errors in the work of "founding fathers"? Could this have something to do with the long-standing tendency of psychoanalysts, with the exception of Loewald (1979) and a few others (Sagan, 1988, chapter five), to identify the oedipal resolution as surrendering the wish to kill the father rather than as overcoming the inhibition against doing so, thus, gaining the psychic freedom to "kill" him in sublimated ways—such as overtly identifying the errors of his ways? As Sagan points out, in Freud's (1909) case history, "Little Hans" is cured of his phobia only after he has two dreams, one in which he marries and has many babies with his mother and another in which a plumber comes and takes away his "behind" and his "widdler" replacing them with bigger ones. Yet Freud continued to speak of the oedipal resolution as renunciation rather than symbolic fulfillment of oedipal desire. This is a question that is of central importance at a time when psychoanalysis is broadly criticized for its failures to adhere to truly scientific canons of research. As Feuer (1969) and others have pointed out, a unique element of science as a social institution is its way of accommodating the oedipal "conflict of generations": ultimately, in science, the establishment surrenders to being "killed" by competitive youth when the latter prove able to back up their challenges with reason and evidence. If young scientists surrendered the oedipal desire to critique and supersede the establishment, scientific progress might well grind to a halt.

Chapter 8

Clarifying and deconstructing Winnicott

Clarifying

According to Heidegger (1927), it is by means of a "marginal experience"—such as the shocking recognition of the reality of personal death—that an individual may be shaken out of inauthentic and awakened to authentic existence. I think there is justification for associating inauthentic existence with the narcissism of relations with subjective objects (Winnicott, 1960a, 1971b, chapter six), the pathology of the "false self" (Winnicott, 1960a), and the Imaginary, "specular ego" of Lacan's (1977, chapter one) "mirror phase," and also for associating authentic *being-in-the-world* with relations with objective objects, the "true self" and the Lacanian barred subject of the Symbolic.

Contrary to the psychoanalytic fundamentalism that insists upon taking theoretical concepts exclusively on the literal level (Carveth, 1984b), I think the following equations are—no doubt at the risk of some oversimplification—nevertheless, both justifiable and useful.

One of the potential benefits to be derived from lining up disparate concepts in a chart of this type is the discovery of conceptual parallels

Table 8.1 Theoretical parallels

Freud	pleasure principle		reality principle
Freud	narcissism		object love
Klein	Ps position		D position
Lacan	Imaginary		Symbolic
Lacan	specular ego		barred subject
Winnicott	subjective object	transitional object	objective object
Winnicott	false self		true self
St. Paul	Adam (flesh; letter)		Christ (spirit)
Heidegger	Inauthentic		Authentic

that may lead us to reconsider the usual way in which a particular concept is generally understood. For example, it may at first seem strange to associate Winnicott's (1960a) "true self" with his (1971b) "objective object" and his "false self" with the "subjective object." Thinking in terms of the developmental timetable, it is tempting to associate the true self with simple somatopsychic being, which existing from the beginning, would overlap chronologically with relations with subjective rather than objective objects. Similarly, it is usual to think of the false self as a later development reflecting a certain dissociation from simple somatopsychic being; it therefore, seems strange to associate it with relations with subjective objects.

On further reflection, however—and especially in light of Winnicott's (1971c, chapter nine) knowledge of and reference to Lacan's (1977, chapter one) notion of the birth of the "ego" in a state of alienation in "the mirror phase"—it seems preferable to distinguish the true self from original somatopsychic being and from the time of relations with subjective objects and to see it, instead, as an authentic sense of self acquired precisely, like Lacan's (Symbolic) "subject" as distinct from his specular (Imaginary) "ego," through the overcoming of the narcissism inherent in relations with subjective objects. In this view, Winnicott's "false self" would correspond to Lacan's "ego" as a narcissistic structure reflecting an omnipotent denial of reality, including the reality of one's somatopsychic being as *being-toward-death.*

In *The Use of An Object and Relating Through Identifications*, Winnicott (1971b) is concerned with "the move away from self-containment and relating to subjective objects into the realm of object-usage" (p. 88). One of the confusing things about this paper is that Winnicott has an eccentric use of the terms "relating" and "usage"—he employs them in precisely an opposite sense from that in which they are normally understood. What he is really concerned with is the shift from a narcissistic attitude toward objects as extensions or projections of the self, to what most would regard as a more advanced mode of object-relating in which the object is recognized as separate and distinct from the self. Winnicott is concerned with the process whereby the subject comes to place the object "outside the area of the subject's omnipotent control; that is, the subject's perception of the object as an external phenomenon, not as a projective entity, in fact recognition of it as an entity in its own right" (p. 89).

The originality of Winnicott's contribution lies in his recognition that: "This change ... means that the subject destroys the object" (p. 89), "... that after 'subject [narcissistically–D.C.] relates to object' comes 'subject destroys object' (as it becomes external); and then may come '*object survives* [Winnicott's emphasis] destruction by the subject'" (p. 90). He continues:

> A new feature thus arrives in the theory of object-relating. The subject says to the object: "I destroyed you." "I love you." "You have value for me because of your survival of my destruction of you." "While I am loving you I am all the time destroying you in (unconscious) *fantasy* [Winnicott's emphasis]." Here fantasy begins for the individual. The subject can now *use* [Winnicott's emphasis] [i.e., relate to–D.C.] the object that has survived.
>
> (p. 90)

Winnicott continues:

> It is important to note that it is not only that the subject destroys the object because the object is placed outside the area of omnipotent control. It is equally significant to state this the other way round and to say that it is the destruction of the object that places the object outside the area of the subject's omnipotent control. In these ways the object develops its own autonomy and life, and (if it survives) contributes-in to the subject, according to its own properties.
>
> (p. 90)

In other words, because of the survival of the object, the subject may now have started to live a life in the world of objects, and so the subject stands to gain immeasurably; but the price has to be paid in acceptance of the ongoing destruction in unconscious phantasy relative to object-relating.

> Let me repeat. This is a position that can be arrived at by the individual in early stages of emotional growth only through the actual survival of cathected objects that are at the time in process of becoming destroyed because real, becoming real because destroyed (being destructible and expendable).
>
> (p. 90)

In other words, for Winnicott, the subject is only able to achieve mature relations with objective objects through a process of separation from the subjective object—a process entailing both the "destruction" of the latter and, at the same time, a giving up of the illusion of omnipotence and the need for omnipotent control that underlies both enmeshment with the subjective object and resistance to recognizing the otherness of the objective object.

Winnicott writes: "It is generally understood that the reality principle involves the individual in anger and reactive destruction, but my thesis is that the destruction plays its part in making the reality, placing the object outside the self" (p. 91). Or again:

> The assumption is always there, in orthodox theory, that aggression is reactive to the encounter with the reality principle, whereas here it is the destructive drive that creates the quality of externality. This is central in the structure of my argument.
>
> (p. 93)

Finally, according to Winnicott:

> *There is no anger* [Winnicott's emphasis] in the destruction of the object to which I am referring, though there could be said to be joy at the object's survival. From this moment, or arising out of this phase, the object is *in fantasy* [Winnicott's emphasis] always being destroyed. This quality of "always being destroyed" makes the reality of the surviving object felt as such, strengthens the feeling-tone, and contributes to object-constancy. The object can now be used [i.e., related to–D.C.].
>
> (p. 93)

This subtle complex of insights of Winnicott's seems not to have been completely assimilated by the psychoanalytic community. Some critics reject his insight into the necessary role of destruction in establishing the reality principle on the grounds of what they take to be his acceptance of the Freudian/Kleinian assumption of an innate destructiveness. Referring to this aspect of Winnicott's thought, Bacal (Bacal & Newman, 1990), for example, states that:

Winnicott's view that the object becomes usable because it survives the infant's destructiveness, and that the infant develops a capacity for concern for the object as he becomes aware of his destructive intent, would be untenable to self psychologists, as they reject the idea of a primary destructiveness.

(p. 191)

But a close reading of this essay, together with additional commentary on its central themes contained in Winnicott's (1989) posthumously published *Psychoanalytic Explorations*, reveals that Winnicott himself had a somewhat ambiguous attitude toward this assumption. In the original paper he writes that:

> It appears to me that the idea of a developmental phase essentially involving survival of object does affect the theory of the roots of aggression. It is no good saying that a baby of a few days old envies the breast. It is legitimate, however, to say that at whatever age a baby begins to allow the breast an external position (outside the area of projection), then this means that destruction of the breast has become a feature. I mean the actual impulse to destroy.
>
> (p. 92)

While it is clear that Winnicott did not see destructiveness merely as a *reaction* to the perception of the otherness of the object—for he refers repeatedly to "the actual impulse to destroy" as playing a part in the establishment of the object *qua* other—it would be a mistake to conclude that by this "actual impulse to destroy" he is simply referring to the Freudian or Kleinian idea of innate destructiveness. He writes (1971b):

> It will be seen that, although destruction is the word I am using, this actual destruction belongs to the object's failure to survive. Without this failure, destruction remains potential. The word "destruction" is needed, not because the baby's impulse is to destroy, but because of the object's liability not to survive, which also means to suffer change in quality, in attitude.
>
> (p. 93)

So not only is there "no anger in the destruction of the object to which I am referring" (p. 93), but the destruction is only potential and only becomes actualized if the object fails to survive. This idea is quite distinct from any simple notion of a primary destructiveness.

Regarding the death instinct, in his posthumously published *The Use of an Object in the Context of* Moses and Monotheism (1968b), Winnicott (1989) writes:

> To warn the reader I should say that I have never been in love with the death instinct and it would give me happiness if I could relieve Freud of the burden of carrying it forever on his Atlas shoulders. To start with, the development of the theory from a statement of the fact that organic matter tends to return to the inorganic carries very small weight in terms of logic. There is no clear relationship between the two sets of ideas. Also, biology has never been happy about this part of metapsychology while on the whole there is room for mutuality between biology and psycho-analysis all along the line, up to the point of the death instinct.
>
> (p. 242)

Even more significantly, in his *Comments on My Paper "The Use of an Object"* (1968a), Winnicott (1989) states that: "In this vitally important early stage the 'destructive' (fire-air or other) aliveness of the individual is simply a symptom of being alive ..." (p. 239). He continues:

> I realise that it is this idea of a destructive first impulse that is difficult to grasp. It is this that needs attention and discussion. To help I wish to point out that I am referring to such things as *eagerness*.
>
> (p. 240)

Hence, the infant's eagerness—perhaps its "ruthless" love (Winnicott, 1958)—is felt by the infant to be destructive if and when the object fails to survive. However, when the object does survive (and without retaliating or changing its attitude), then such eagerness and "ruthlessness" are either not felt to be destructive or, if so, such destructiveness can be integrated without disastrous consequences for self-esteem.

While some critics have dismissed Winnicott's thinking in this area on the mistaken grounds of his adherence to the concept of the death instinct, others reject what he has to say regarding the move away from the subjective through the transitional toward the objective object on the grounds that contemporary infant research (Stern, 1985) has called into question the idea of an early phase of undifferentiation between self and object that Freud's, Winnicott's and Mahler's thinking assumes. Of course, Klein had early on rejected the notion of primary narcissism in favor of the theory of object relations from the beginning. While many mainstream analysts long resisted the implications of the infant research in this respect, most felt finally forced to abandon the notion of a phase of absolute undifferentiation. Even Mahler's associate, Fred Pine (1990, chapter eleven) was prepared to do so, even while arguing that in its focus upon the most alert and differentiated moments of the infant's day, a good deal of the infant research may have neglected those other moments of somnolence in which a sort of "merger" experience may well be taking place. Certainly a moment of merger, let alone a phantasy of merger, is not at all the same thing as an alleged actual phase of oceanic oneness at the beginning, out of which two-ness and finally three-ness gradually emerge. In being forced by empirical research to surrender its foundational myth of development as separation out of primordial unity psychoanalysis demonstrates, *contra* Sir Karl Popper, that its claim to scientific status (in some areas and to some degree) can no longer be dismissed on the grounds that its central postulates are unfalsifiable.

However, in a sense, all this is beside the point. For whatever Freud may have meant by "primary narcissism" and Mahler by "symbiosis," by "secondary narcissism" and the "subjective object" Freud and Winnicott do not mean to refer to absolute undifferentiation at all; they are referring to a state in which the cognitively differentiated object is emotionally experienced primarily through projections of the subject's own phantasies and self- and object-representations and predominantly in terms of the subject's pressing needs. And they mean to contrast this sort of narcissistic object-relation to one in which the subject is more able to get beyond such projections and egocentric demands for need-satisfaction and to recognize and make empathic contact with the real otherness of the object. This entails development of what Winnicott (1963a) calls "the capacity for concern," his useful way of describing the advance into Klein's unfortunately named "depressive position"—which I prefer to call the "reparative position" since the concern (Klein's "depressive anxiety") that drives reparation has little to do with depression.

Deconstructing

In the course of writing a paper on communicating, Winnicott (1963b) found himself "staking a claim, to my surprise, to the right not to communicate." He goes on to say that: "This was a protest from the core of me to the frightening fantasy of being infinitely exploited. In another language this would be the fantasy of being eaten or swallowed up ... *the fantasy of being found*" (p. 179).

My aim here is to clarify that the fearful phantasy Winnicott is addressing is exactly that, a fearful phantasy. It is not an existentially justified and necessary fear, but a form of persecutory anxiety underlying a pathological fear of and retreat from intimacy. Yet instead of seeking to analyze and dispel the paranoid phantasy of persecution by an all-bad part-object (being prey to a predator), Winnicott seeks to rationalize or justify it.

I think it is by now widely understood by psychoanalysts that their thinking, both in the clinical situation and in their theoretical work, is like all products of the human mind inevitably influenced by their particular more or less unconscious conflicts, phantasies and biases. In *Faces in a Cloud*, for example, Atwood and Stolorow (1984b) show how the structure of a theorist's metapsychology reflects his or her subjective world. While in no way reducible to a mere subjective projection, the centrality of the Oedipus complex in Freud's thinking is nonetheless reflective of specific aspects of his personal experience and his resulting personality conflicts.

I will not speculate as to the personal basis of Winnicott's (1963b) tendency to universalize and rationalize as healthy the "frightening fantasy of being infinitely exploited" (p. 179). He refers, for example, to what he sees as "an inherent dilemma" faced by the artist involving his "urgent need to communicate and the still more urgent need not to be found." He writes, this "might account for the fact that we cannot conceive of an artist's coming to the end of the task that occupies his whole nature" (p. 185). In other words, he suggests that the reason the artist cannot come to the end is not due to her desire to communicate her true self (Winnicott, 1960a) ever more adequately and completely, to be ever more fully realized and expressed, but on the contrary reflects her fear of being found. Far from viewing the unending quest as the true self's struggle to realize and communicate itself to others, he suggests that it derives from the false self's need to keep the true self hidden.

Winnicott's rationalization of the retreat from intimacy as health rather than pathology is clear in the following passage:

> I suggest that in health there is a core to the personality that corresponds to the true self of the split personality; I suggest that this core never communicates with the world of perceived objects, and that the individual person knows that it must never be communicated with or be influenced by external reality. This is my main point, the point of thought which is the center of an intellectual world and of my paper. Although healthy persons communicate and enjoy communicating, the other fact is equally true, that *each individual is an isolate, permanently non-communicating, permanently unknown, in fact unfound* [original emphasis].
>
> (p. 187)

While acknowledging that: "In life and living this hard fact is softened by the sharing that belongs to the whole range of cultural experience," Winnicott insists that: "At the centre of each person is an incommunicado element, and this is sacred and most worthy of preservation" (p. 187). While one might agree that: "Rape, and being eaten by cannibals, these are mere bagatelles as compared with the violation of the self's core"—that is, its violation in traumatic experience of various types—*I submit that not all experiences of being found, seen and known are traumatic violations. It is Winnicott's apparent equation of being found and being violated that is in question here* (my emphasis).

Apparently, for Winnicott, as for Jean-Paul Sartre (1944), for whom "*L'enfer, c'est les autres*" ("Hell is other people"), the "look of the other" is necessarily a withering, objectifying, if not an annihilating look—and never a look of love. Why is that? Why is the other always and inevitably a persecutor? Although raised in a Methodist home:

> Winnicott's mother had been an Anglican before her marriage, as he himself was to become while he was at medical school, (Winnicott's first wife was also an Anglican and Clare Winnicott remembers that as the occasion for Winnicott being confirmed at the age of 26 or 27 ...).
>
> (Jacobs, 1995, p. 4)

For centuries Anglicans have prayed "Almighty God unto whom all hearts be open, all desires known, and from whom no Secrets are hid"

(*The Book of Common Prayer*, 1662), a prayer that surely refers to a "finding" of the self that, for Winnicott, would have had to be worse than being raped and eaten by cannibals, for it would entail "the alteration of the self's central elements by communication seeping through the defenses." "For me," he writes, "this would be the sin against the self"—against its "need to be secretly isolated" (p. 187).

Winnicott viewed the hatred of psychoanalysis as arising from the threat he felt it constitutes to this defensive need. If psychoanalysis is to be hated for this reason, then so certainly is God—or any truly intimate other. The basis of any loving intimacy, any genuine openness to the other, is what Erik Erikson (1968) called "basic trust." The fear of being found, and the equation of being found with being infinitely exploited, is a manifestation of "basic mistrust" and, in Klein's (1946) terms, of a paranoid-schizoid process of splitting in which the other is viewed as an all-bad persecutory part-object.

There is no doubt that regressed patients suffering from psychotic, borderline and narcissistic pathology—that is, operating predominantly in the paranoid-schizoid position—often find confrontation with the analyst's separateness and difference unbearable. Winnicott writes that if "we suddenly become not-me for the patient, … then we know too much, and we are dangerous because we are too nearly in communication with the central still and silent spot of the patient's ego-organization" (p. 189). This is quite true *in the case of the regressed, psychotic, borderline or pathologically narcissistic patient* (my emphasis) whose ego-organization is highly vulnerable to fragmentation. But, I submit, this does not pertain in the case of healthier patients, those operating to a greater extent in the depressive/reparative position, and whose ego-organization (or self-structure) is far more stable and sturdy. But Winnicott fails to make this distinction. Instead, he attributes the vulnerability of regressed patients to everyone. Like Ernest Becker and Peter Berger and, to an extent, Jacques Lacan (see chapters five and six), Winnicott misrepresents a pathological condition as a universal and existential aspect of human *being-in-the-world*.

In my view, it is one of the great strengths of psychoanalytic thinking to refuse such over-generalization by tracing varying beliefs and world-views to the particular psychologies of those advancing them, just as the sociology of knowledge traces beliefs and attitudes to their origins in particular social groups and socioeconomic strata. In other words, instead of justifying and normalizing the flight from intimacy experienced as traumatic, psychoanalysis views it as symptomatic. But, on the contrary, Winnicott writes: "I am putting forward and stressing the importance of the idea of the *permanent isolation of the individual* [Winnicott's emphasis] and claiming that at the core of the individual there is no communication with the not-me world either way" (p. 189).

But having thus, normalized the retreat from intimacy, Winnicott proceeds to view it as a symptom of psychosis and of the adolescent's "preservation of personal isolation" as "part of the search for identity" and goes on to say that "one reason why adolescents on the whole eschew psycho-analytic treatment" is that: "They feel that by psycho-analysis they will be raped, not sexually but spiritually" (p. 190). So, which is it? Is the retreat from intimacy a universal and existential need? Or is it a symptom of particular conditions, such as psychosis and adolescence?

At the end of his paper, Winnicott summarizes his argument in a way that, rather than clarifying this question and resolving the contradiction only deepens it. He writes:

> I have tried to state the need that we have to recognize this aspect of health: the non-communicating central self, forever immune from the reality principle, and forever silent. Here communication is not non-verbal; it is, like the music of the spheres, absolutely personal. It belongs to being alive. And in health, it is out of this that communication naturally arises.
>
> (p. 192)

So in health there is a "non-communicating central self, forever immune from the reality principle," yet it is from this non-communicating self that "communication naturally arises." Is it at all clear what this sentence means? It would seem to make sense that communication arises from non-communication. But isn't Winnicott's point that there is a normal and healthy non-communicating core that must never be found and communication with which makes being raped and eaten by cannibals seem a mere bagatelle? He continues:

> Explicit communication is pleasurable and it involves extremely interesting techniques, including that of language. The two extremes, explicit communication that is indirect, and silent or personal

communication that feels real, each of these has its place, and in the intermediate cultural area there exists for many, but not for all, a mode of communication which is a most valuable compromise.

(p. 192)

In this concluding paragraph, we no longer hear anything about the need of the healthy self not to be found. We hear only about various modes of communication that are pleasurable, interesting and valuable and that each has its place. What happened to the "fearful fantasy of being infinitely exploited" and the need NOT to communicate? Such intellectual vacillation is itself a symptom of underlying emotional conflict. As I argued in Chapter 6 with respect to melancholic existentialism: "If the psychoanalytic relativization of false claims to universal validity by tracing them to their origin in particular attitudes of specific personalities was ever necessary, it is called for here."

Chapter 9

Neo-Kleinian theory
A dialectical re-vision

Beyond Ps → D

Kleinian theory has sometimes been interpreted in a way that conveys an oversimplified conception of emotional growth as development beyond the splitting and part-object functioning characteristic of the paranoid-schizoid position, to the ambivalence and whole-object functioning of the depressive position (Ps → D). In this perspective Ps functioning is devalued, viewed as primitive or regressive, in contrast to the advance into the more complex, realistic, mature and responsible functioning characteristic of D. But in viewing Ps as all-bad and D as all-good, this perspective itself involves splitting. It not only idealizes the depressive position by, among other things, losing sight of the often quite serious psychopathology manifested by people who function to a considerable extent in D (i.e., serious neurotic pathology), but also devalues the paranoid-schizoid position by obscuring the range of personally and socially necessary capacities that require Ps functioning. "In defence of splitting: progressive politics in the twentieth century" (Gabbert, 2014) is one of the few papers I know of that recognizes the prosocial and adaptive functions of splitting. There is no need to deny its maladaptive manifestations to recognize that without at least temporary adaptive splitting we would have been unable to defeat Nazism or establish the social state now being dismantled due to widespread false consciousness and the failure of adaptive splitting that renders the masses unable to recognize and mobilize against their exploiters.

The devaluation of Ps obscures Klein's own recognition of splitting as a developmental achievement and of the paranoid-schizoid position as the first organization of mental life. By ordering experience into all-good and all-bad categories, splitting not only protects the good from being destroyed by the bad, but rescues the developing personality from the psychotic confusion prevailing when the splits cannot be held, the good going bad and the bad turning good. Psychotic patients who cannot split in any enduring way experience great confusion due to their rapidly oscillating identifications with all-good and all-bad self and object images, confusion also induced in their therapists whose countertransference is impacted via projective identification of such rapidly oscillating states.

At the beginning in order to preserve the good object it must be protected against destruction by the bad object by keeping the two clearly separated off from one another. Klein (1958) writes:

> it is essential for normal development that a division between the good and bad object, between love and hate, should take place in earliest infancy. When such a division is not too severe, and yet sufficient to differentiate between good and bad, it forms in my view one of the basic elements for stability and mental health.
>
> (pp. 87–88)

The following year Klein (1959) writes:

> persecutory anxiety reinforces the need to keep separate the loved object from the dangerous one, and therefore to split love from hate. For the young infant's self-preservation depends on his trust in a good mother. By splitting the two aspects and clinging to the good one he preserves his belief in a good object and his capacity to love it; and this is an essential condition for keeping alive. For without at least some of this feeling, he would be exposed to an entirely hostile world which he fears would destroy him.
>
> (p. 253)

As I have pointed out elsewhere (Carveth, 2013, chapter nine; Carveth, 2016a), on almost every page where Klein displays semantic loyalty to Freud by citing projection of the death instinct to account for the inevitable persecutory anxiety of even the most sensitively cared-for infant, she at the same time (e.g., Klein, 1952, p. 433) offers an alternate and far more acceptable explanation: namely, that given its cognitive limitations, the infant is bound to misinterpret every frustration as an attack and, hence, that the absent good breast is felt as a present bad attacking breast.

Contrary to the widespread misapprehension fostered by, among others, Bowlby (Bowlby, Figlio, & Young, 1986; see discussion in Carveth, 2013, chapter nine), that she ignored or minimized the role of the real parenting in health and pathology, Klein (e.g., 1946, p. 128) constantly stressed the crucial importance of good, loving care-taking, for only this can hope to offset the inevitable rage and paranoia resulting from frustration, both that which is basic and unavoidable and the surplus frustration arising from parental failure in varying degrees. While attuned, non-intrusive and non-depriving caring is, as Klein insisted, essential to mitigate such paranoia, it cannot hope to eradicate it altogether, because frustration cannot be eliminated by even the most attuned and responsive carers imaginable.

In *Envy and Gratitude*, Klein (1957) explains how intense early envy of the breast (envy that, in my view, results from a complex combination of temperamental factors and early failures of positive containment) can have a particularly destructive psychological consequence. It is one thing to be persecuted by a bad object hated for its badness; quite another to feel persecuted by a good object due to its very goodness. In the face of such envy the good is experienced as bad or persecutory and this undermines necessary splitting processes. The infant who, due to envy, "cannot divide and keep apart successfully love and hate, and therefore the good and bad object, is liable to feel confused between what is good and bad in other connections" (p. 184). Steiner (1987, p. 326) describes how when the normal splitting Klein describes, breaks down due to envious attacks on good objects, unbearable confusional states may result, giving rise to what he calls "disintegrative" splitting against which the patient may defend through retreat into a pathological organization.

In recognizing the positive and necessary role of splitting in overcoming psychotic confusion there is no need to deny or minimize the borderline pathology of those who although they escape psychotic confusion due to their capacity to split, do so excessively and cannot attain or maintain the ambivalence and whole-object functioning characteristic of the depressive position and the largely neurotic conflicts generated there. This failure to maintain ambivalence is evident in views of Ps, and of splitting itself, as all-bad and D, ambivalence, as all-good. Psychic evolution must be conceived dialectically in such a way as to be able to recognize good (in addition to bad) in Ps and bad (in addition to good) in D. In so maintaining depressive position functioning in our theorizing we no longer speak exclusively of regression into Ps, but also of regression into D from the higher-order synthesis (PsD) that it is the aim of this paper to describe. Naturally, in speaking of the Ps, D and PsD "positions" there is no intention to reify these abstractions, any more than such "structures" as id, ego, superego, ego-ideal and conscience. All such concepts are to be understood as metaphorical approaches to the understanding of mental life.

In addition to the narcissism, omnipotence, magical thinking, polarization, paranoia, persecutory guilt, literalism, concrete thinking, "beta elements" (Bion, 1963) poor reality-testing and reliance on "symbolic equation" instead of "symbolic representation" (Segal, 1957) characterizing the paranoid-schizoid position, this is also where excitement, intensity, passion, falling in love and resolute commitment in a struggle are to be found. And in addition to the "alpha function," enhanced reality-testing, awareness of separateness and dependence, decline of omnipotence, reparative guilt, capacity for concern and for mature loving ("warts and all") characterizing the depressive position, here also we encounter neurotic inhibition due to excessive fears of being harmful and an excessively dispassionate rationality that in affirming both sides of every issue (holding a candle for both Saint George and the Dragon) can at times result in overcomplexification, inducing paralysis, "fence sitting," and a relative inability to think clearly or act decisively in the face of various threats. In *Endless Deferment of Meaning: The Media's Inequitable Melee of Events and Words*, Natoli (2015) describes a pathological manifestation of D, that Britton (1998) might view as an instance of D(path):

> PBS NewsHour wonders—as if newly arrived on the planet Earth—what may be the cause and meaning of a Baltimore uprising? Here on the NewsHour, every occurrence takes us by surprise and is treated in a kind of isolation chamber. Something is happening here, a series of Black people killed by police?! Sudden violence, mayhem. What is that all about? This is our US TV in depth and wide breadth coverage of the news, steering carefully between the Scylla of the liberal rocks and the Charybdis of the neoliberal ones.
>
> Every headline event is a source of wonderment. After surprise, wonder and amazement, we go on to hear both sides of an issue after which we are told that the conversation remains open and will continue in the future, a future in which every conclusion will be

balanced by an opposing conclusion, Koch Industries and the Center for American Progress locked in an eternal struggle. We are then free to make a personal choice. We are to add our opinion in a culture where everyone knows everything and each knows it differently.

But what exactly is being balanced here? We are seeking a balance on a ship already tilted heavily to starboard. One side has the mass of the population, the other side the mass of the wealth, rather like the present state of South Africa, where minority White wealth and economic power mocks the democratic power of the masses.

(para. 1, 2 and 3)

In stating in an earlier paper (Carveth & Carveth, 2003) that: "In current post-Kleinian theory, development is no longer conceived as a unilinear progression from the paranoid-schizoid to the depressive position, but dialectically with pathology being conceptualized as breakdown of the dialectic into a fixation on either pole" (p. 464), we underestimated the prevalence of the oversimplification described above. Despite appearances, such as Bion's (1963) re-writing of Ps→D as Ps↔D, and the helpful contributions of Ogden (1986), among others, the dialectical understanding of the Kleinian model of the mind seems far from established.

In *Elements of Psychoanalysis*, Bion (1963) writes: "The process of change from one category represented in the grid to another may be described as disintegration and reintegration, Ps↔D" (p. 35). Here Ps is equated with disintegration and D with reintegration, which is odd in light of Klein's own recognition of Ps as the first step out of chaos into order in mental life, and her association of D, not merely with whole self and object images, but simultaneously with a deepened awareness of separation and dependency and with depressive anxiety. Bion subsequently refers to "the splitting and fragmentation characteristic of the paranoid-schizoid position" (p. 40), a comment that seems to belie recognition of Ps as an initial order achieved precisely through splitting. A good deal of the post-Kleinian literature appears to have been influenced by Bion's equation of the paranoid-schizoid position with fragmentation rather than order, and also by his association of the depressive position with "feelings of depression" (pp. 39, 52), an idea I consider confused in that what we find in the depressive position is never depression, but depressive anxiety or the concern arising from attained ambivalence (Winnicott,

1963a) that one may have damaged or destroyed one's good objects, leading to attempts at reparation. Any depression serious enough to merit the name is a paranoid-schizoid phenomenon in that it involves a failure of ambivalence and the splitting that results in a view of the self as all-bad. Sadness, pining and mourning belong to D; failed mourning or melancholia belongs in Ps.

Bion's revision to some extent calls into question the unilinear model by positing development as entailing oscillation between states of disintegration and reintegration. In *Before and After the Depressive Position*, Britton (1998) expands Bion's notion of mental development as Ps↔D into a theory of successive stages or levels of psychic development. He begins by quoting Bion (1970): "Any attempt to cling to what [is known] must be resisted for the sake of achieving a state of mind analogous to the paranoid-schizoid position" (p. 124). Britton goes on to say that Bion "was emphatic that this Ps state should be tolerated 'until a pattern evolves'. This 'evolved state' he called D, 'the analogue to the depressive position'…" (p. 69). "He was concerned to distinguish his Ps from the pathological paranoid-schizoid position that Melanie Klein had described. To this end he suggested calling Ps patience and D security" (p. 69).

But Melanie Klein in no way considered the paranoid-schizoid position pathological per se, though excessive defensive regression into it and an inability to advance into D would be. In any case Ps, whether normal or pathological, has little to do with "patience," a virtue far more likely for Klein to be found in D. And as for "security," a good deal of the regressive pull back from D into Ps has to do with the security offered by splitting in the face of the ambivalence, ambiguity and uncertainty encountered in D. Britton builds upon Bion's departure from Klein in this respect. He writes:

> If we describe any move from a depressive position, with its sense of psychic order, to a paranoid-schizoid position, with its quality of disorder, as regressive, then Bion's D→Ps could be seen as a form of regression necessary for development.
>
> (p. 70)

But the paranoid-schizoid position is characterized not by disorder, but by the rigid, black and white thinking we find in fundamentalist, totalizing ideologies, whereas in the depressive position a third area opens up beyond the polarities allowing for some critical self-reflection and uncertainty. In this light, D→Ps certainly represents a form of regression, but one that may well be contrary to development rather than necessary for it.

Britton links the idea of development through regression from "security" to "patience," and from order to disorder, to related contributions, such as that of Ernst Kris (1935) on regression in the service of the ego. Loewald (1971, 1981), among others, has emphasized the creative potential of primary process thought and the adaptive potential of regression, especially when secondary process functioning has become too distant from its vital roots in the unconscious. Britton (p. 71) cites Winnicott's (1954) idea of an organized regression that provides "a new opportunity for an unfreezing of the frozen situation" (p. 283). The validity of these ideas of adaptive regression melting a frozen structure and opening up new possibilities for creative change and growth is not in doubt. What is in doubt is Bion's and, following him, Britton's conception of the frozen situation as D and its unfreezing as involving a creative regression into Ps.

The frozen order providing security is composed of paranoid-schizoid, concretized, literalistic, black and white thinking. It needs to be unfrozen, deconstructed through the de-literalizing processes that open up the depressive position and evoke a subject capable of self-reflection and toleration of ambivalence and ambiguity. This is an often painful process of facing and bearing the insecurity involved in letting go and mourning lost certainties, replacing oversimplifications with complexity and allowing what is new and different to come into being. Such "patience" is found not in Ps but in D. This is not at all to deny that a mere swing of the pendulum in the opposing direction may be equally pathological; an excessive and one-sided depressive position functioning alienated from the passion and intensity of Ps might well turn "patience" into complacency, inaction, even paralysis.

Britton's description of the process of creative psychic growth as moving "from integration, to disintegration, followed by reintegration" (p. 73) is unproblematic. What is problematic is his writing of ongoing psychic development as: $Ps(n) \to D(n) \to Ps(n+1) \to \ldots D(n+1)$, in which a primary stage of disintegration $Ps(n)$ is followed by a first integration $D(n)$, which gives way via a creative regression to a new state of disintegration $Ps(n+1)$, a "wilderness," which after many such cycles of disintegration and reintegration, results in arrival at "the promised land"

D(n+1), attainment of which initiates a new struggle. The problem is not with the conception of psychic evolution as from certainty to uncertainty to a new certainty, then a new uncertainty ... etc., but with the conception of certainty as D and of uncertainty as Ps.

Somehow, following Bion, Britton came to think of "an emergent position of uncertainty and incoherence" as Ps rather than D when dogma and certainty reside in Ps and uncertainty, ambiguity and ambivalence (which can feel like incoherence) are attainments that are more or less bearable in D. Britton refers to development as "leaving the security of depressive position coherence for a new round of fragmented, persecuting uncertainties" (p. 73). I submit it is the other way round: development requires leaving the security of paranoid-schizoid, rigidly held coherence, dogma founded usually on black and white thinking and the suppression or repression of one term of a polarity over the other, for a new round of depressive position uncertainties. In the face of such persecuting uncertainty one either regresses into paranoid-schizoid certainty, or learns to tolerate ambivalence, ambiguity and complexity along with the rest of the mental pain (loss, separation, dependence, guilt, regret ...) to which life in the depressive position is heir. At the same time, we must recognize that to escape a one-sided Ps certainty into an excessive and paralyzing uncertainty in D is no advance; it is merely to exchange Ps(path) for D(path).

It was only a superficial reading of Bion (1963) that earlier led us to assume that his re-writing of Ps→D as Ps↔D represented a move toward a more truly dialectical understanding of mental development. While having the arrows point both ways might suggest something positive in Ps as well as in D, as does Britton's model of developmental advance through cycles of disintegration and reintegration (despite the confusion involved in associating order with D and disorder with Ps), neither achieve the ambivalence that recognizes both the positive and the negative qualities of both positions or the possibility of working out a higher-order synthesis that combines what is most creative and life-enhancing in each. I propose that we write this more dialectical model as:

$$PsD$$
$$\downarrow$$
$$Ps\,(+-) \leftrightarrow (-+)\,D$$

As Ogden (1986) explains:

> A dialectic is a process in which each of two opposing concepts creates, informs, preserves, and negates the other, each standing in a dynamic (ever-changing) relationship with the other. The dialectical process moves toward integration, but integration is never complete. Each integration creates a new dialectical opposition and a new dynamic tension.
>
> (p. 208)

Ogden cites Hegel (1807) and Kojève (1934–1935) in this context, but his description of the dialectic seems to me to leave out the essential element of an elevation, an upward movement, a "sublation" or "sublimation" *(Aufheben)* involving a progressive ascent through the clash of opposites.

Although the formula thesis-antithesis-synthesis can be traced to Kant, Fichte and Schelling, Hegel himself rarely employing it, I believe it nonetheless captures the essential idea: a thesis gives rise to an antithesis and out of the resulting conflict is evolved a synthesis that negates, preserves and elevates the component elements. In its present application the clash between Ps and D, which can result in simple oscillation between them (Ps↔D), results instead in a creative sublimation or transcendence of the lower-order polarities in favor of a synthesis, which negates and yet preserves and at the same time elevates the lower-order components of the conflict. Instead of one-sidedly privileging D over Ps, or Ps over D and instead of valuing one and devaluing the other, both the merits and the demerits of both positions are recognized and a creative synthesis that unites what is valuable and life-enhancing in each is worked out. Here, for example, we might find the passion and intensity of Ps creatively combined with the care and responsibility of D (a synthesis symbolized here as PsD).

Without here going into the added complexity of further development in which PsD becomes the thesis evoking another antithesis leading on to a still higher synthesis, suffice it to say this is exactly what is implied in a dialectical model of psychic development. It must be acknowledged that in the widest sense D is ultimately privileged in this model over Ps. If *either/or* belongs to Ps and *both/and* belongs to D, a dialectical perspective will want to work out a synthesis that includes *both* either/or

(Ps) *and* both/and (D), both splitting and the overcoming of splitting. In this sense, the Hegelian both/and ultimately triumphs over the Kierkegaardian (1843b) either/or, but only ultimately so.

Happily, the psychoanalytic literature already contains a discussion that although not originally developed in Kleinian terms, lends itself to the foregoing analysis. According to Freud (1915b):

> Sexual love is undoubtedly one of the chief things in life, and the union of mental and bodily satisfaction in the enjoyment of love is one of its culminating peaks. Apart from a few queer fanatics, all the world knows this and conducts its life accordingly; science alone is too delicate to admit it.
>
> (pp. 168–169)

Robert Stoller and Otto Kernberg are two psychoanalytic scientists who are not too delicate in this respect. I recall that when, in the mid-seventies, Stoller (1975) presented at a conference on his book *Perversion: The Erotic Form of Hatred*, people seemed ready to accept his stress on the role of aggression in the perverse drama. But when a year or so later he returned to say he had concluded that sex purged of hatred, risk and danger is hardly worth having many were shocked. Stoller (1979, 1985) argued that in order for sexuality to remain exciting it must be in some measure "transgressive" (i.e., naughty). In a series of papers written a few years later, Kernberg (1991a, 1991b, 1993) agreed, arguing that in order to keep their sex life passionate partners must not allow remnants of their puritanical superegos to amplify each other to the point where they are unable to discuss, let alone play with, their transgressive phantasies. All this, of course, challenges an ideal that was at one time widely held in our culture, even in psychoanalytic circles, and that may well be resurfacing today (as part of a puritanism rising both in the East and the West): a puritanical ideal of a fully libidinal sexuality purged of aggression—a "purified" sublimely loving sexuality. Challenging this ideal and providing some support for the Stoller/Kernberg hypothesis are indications (e.g., Pope, 2009) that the phenomenon of marital "dead bed" is apparently not rare among both heterosexual and homosexual partners who have cohabited for more than about four years, by which time, according to Fisher (1994), the "sexy" chemicals generated in the earlier stages of the relationship are increasingly displaced by the "cozy" ones that mediate intimacy more than passion, unless creative ways are found to keep the latter alive. In this view, when one's "kinkiness" is entirely excluded from the marital bed, that bed may go dead over time. If so, some may seek fulfillment of transgressive desire elsewhere—in extra-marital affairs, with sex workers of various types, or in pornography and masturbation. Others may live lives of quiet desperation or elect to turn away from sexuality altogether. On the other hand, Kernberg suggests that if mutual puritanical superego reinforcement can be avoided and the couple can explore together their respective transgressive phantasies and desires, mutually fulfilling forms of erotic drama may sometimes be constructed that can have the effect of maintaining a lively sexual bond over many years—although, as Fisher suggests, constant cohabitation makes this difficult.

It is not my aim to either support or reject the Stoller/Kernberg hypothesis, to pathologize low libido or make an exciting sex life a criterion of "mental health"—a concept that, with Szasz (see my Introduction), I view as obscuring what are ethical choices in any case. My aim here is only to employ Kernberg's argument to illustrate dialectical logic and the concept of PsD as the higher-order synthesis negating, preserving and elevating Ps and D. Although he himself does not develop it in these terms, Kernberg's (1991b, 1993) argument is essentially that in order to maintain passion, the partners must relate to each other simultaneously in both Ps and D. Mere rapid cycling (Ps↔D) is not adequate to describe the kind of creative synthesis (PsD) I have in mind. On the level of D my partner is a whole-object, my cherished beloved, a person whose welfare I care about and whom I seek to protect from all danger and harm—Buber's (1937) "I–Thou" relation. But if I relate to him or her only on this level (on the Stoller/Kernberg hypothesis) sexual passion will slowly evaporate. On the level of Ps she or he is my sexual part-object, a "thing" I seek to use as a means to the end of my selfish pleasure—Buber's "I-it" relation. But if I relate to her or him exclusively on this level, love degenerates into narcissism, perversity and abuse. It is admittedly a tall order to find a way to love, hate, cherish and use more or less simultaneously, but this is what appears (on the Stoller/Kernberg hypothesis) to be necessary for sexuality to be both responsible and exciting.

Can we distinguish perversion from the type of transgressive drama operative in the kind of exciting and yet responsible sexuality that Kernberg describes? In order to qualify as a perversion as distinct from a mutually acceptable and pleasurable type of transgressive play, the staging of the sexual drama must be excessively costly or risky in terms of the potential physical and/or social pain and danger to which it exposes the subjects involved. An exciting sexual drama that is mutually fulfilling and non-perverse would be one that, in contrast to the perversion, is not excessively costly or risky, while sufficiently maintaining the elements of transgression, risk and danger that Stoller argues are essential components of sexual excitement. In other words, whereas in creative, transgressive, exciting sexuality the dialectical synthesis (PsD) is maintained, in both perversion and "dead bed" it breaks down and either paranoid-schizoid functioning or depressive position functioning predominates. In this definition, there is no privileging of heterosexuality, penetration, genital intercourse or reproduction. The criterion concerns the level of danger and risk of physical and/or social harm to which the self and the other are exposed. When partners genuinely care for each other and work out an exciting drama that is socially and physically safe and at the same time thrilling because it subsumes transgressive psychosexuality, a mutually fulfilling sex life is their reward.

Just as it is necessary to overcome the splitting entailed in older notions of Ps as all-bad and D as all-good by recognizing the good in Ps and the bad in D and the dialectical transcendence offered by the PsD synthesis, so the merits of the primary process (vitality, order, creativity, emotional intensity, the inspiration phase in creativity) and the demerits of the secondary process (excessively moderate, dispassionate, or "disaffected" states; intellectual intelligence devoid of emotional intelligence) must be kept in mind. Loewald (1971, 1981), as we have seen, emphasized the creative potential of primary process thought and the adaptive potential of regression, especially when secondary process functioning has become too distant from its vital roots in the unconscious. Another way to describe the dialectical synthesis (PsD) is to view Ps and D, primary and secondary processes, as the terminal poles respectively on a continuum, the "intermediate area" of which may be viewed, following Winnicott (1953, 1971), as a transitional position or process. In this view, the "transitional area" includes types of mental functioning that cannot clearly or consistently be assigned to either Ps or D, primary or secondary process and that seem somehow to overlap, fall between or transcend these dualistic categories. Ogden (1986) has made some progress toward integrating Winnicott and Klein along these lines.

It is commonly recognized that use of transitional phenomena requires a "willing suspension of disbelief." In actuality, it requires suspension of both belief and disbelief. Both vital experience of the arts and a transitional faith in and worship of the sacred exist between the poles of dogmatic literalistic belief (Ps) and an entirely rationalist skepticism (D) that, having been achieved, is temporarily suspended on entry into the transitional area and resumed again on exit (see Carveth, 2013, chapter ten). This suspension is precarious: it can easily collapse into either belief (Ps) or disbelief (D). To take but one example: transitional symbols of something sacred, such as bread and wine as signifiers of Christ, can easily succumb to literalization or concretization, becoming magically identified with what they are meant to symbolize, "symbolic equations" (Segal, 1957) on the paranoid-schizoid level, as in the Roman Catholic doctrine of the transubstantiation. On the other hand, to treat the Eucharistic elements as mere signifiers or "symbolic representations" on the level of the depressive position is to leave the transitional area in the opposite direction of excessive objectivity, in which case the liturgical play breaks down, as when a film breaks and the house lights come up accompanied by the groans of annoyance and disappointment on the part of a frustrated and disillusioned audience.

Having suggested how this dialectical/transitional model might be applied in the fields of sexuality, religion and the arts, I will not here attempt to apply it to the field of politics. Gabbert's (2014) recent defense of splitting has made a good start on this. Hitler was defeated by people capable of distinguishing between good and evil and confronting the latter decisively without being hampered by a maladaptive depressive position inhibition grounded in, say, awareness that he was an abused child and was kind to dogs. The so-called welfare or social state (long under threat of dismantlement under neoliberalism) was achieved by men and women ready and willing to put their lives on the line in pitched battles with the agents of reaction without being crippled by depressive position scruples that would have led to their defeat. Suffice it to say that the future of our world would seem to depend upon our finding a way to overcome political paralysis and commit ourselves to the fight against domination, corruption and exploitation without turning into our erstwhile enemies and losing sight of the transcendence we are fighting for.

Attacks on splitting

In *Attacks on Linking*, Bion (1959) is concerned with "destructive attacks which the patient makes on anything which is felt to have the function of linking one object with another" (p. 308). He provides various clinical illustrations of these phenomena. In his work on "the Grid" Bion (1963) describes learning from experience as involving the linking or mating of a preconception with a realization generating a conception. A kind of mental coupling analogous to sexual intercourse leading to biological conception is viewed as central to creative thought. Out of the intercourse of two comes a third. Out of the creative mating of container and contained comes psychological growth and change—provided such coupling can be tolerated. Those who, for whatever reason, find such a "primal scene" unbearable feel obliged to put a stop to such intercourse. In so doing they obstruct the analytic process, block productive thinking and undermine their capacity to learn from experience.

There is no doubt that such attacks on linking occur and not only in what Bion (1957) describes as the "psychotic," but also in the "non-psychotic" parts of the personality. The refusal to see similarities, to appreciate metaphors and analogies, and to make connections among phenomena that belong together, striving instead to keep them separated or isolated from one another (splitting), is a common form of resistance to mental growth. But, of course, so is the refusal to make distinctions, to recognize important differences, attempting instead to keep merged or linked phenomena that should be separated out from one another. Early in our education we all encountered tests that required us to "compare and contrast" the phenomena under study. This is because valid knowledge and proper mental functioning requires us to attend to both similarities and differences, to appreciate both links and distinctions or boundaries.

If psychopathology entails attacks on links it also entails attacks on boundaries. If it strives to prevent coupling by keeping objects apart, it also prevents productive coupling by undermining the fundamental separation that generates the two objects necessary for linking to occur in the first place. If there is only one, no linking is possible. Without implying that in focusing upon attacks on linking, Bion intended to deny or was oblivious to attacks on separating, I feel it is nevertheless worth emphasizing that it is a mistake to identify psychopathology exclusively with the former, that is, with the absolutization of difference (de-linking) that results in the antitheses that constitute splitting, for psychopathology equally results from attacks on separating, the absolutization of similarity (links) that result in the totalized identifications that constitute various states of psychological merger. However creative and life-enhancing transference may be at times, it is, after all, a form of linking that can often involve distortion of neurotic and psychotic proportions. Primary process mentation is characterized as much by absolute identity as by absolute difference or antithesis. In contrast, secondary process mentation is characterized by relative similarity and relative difference.

While Bion (1959) emphasized the psychopathology resulting from "attacks on linking" (i.e., denial of similarity, absolute difference or splitting), it is worth reminding ourselves about that which emerges from "attacks on separating" (i.e., denial of difference, absolute similarity or fusion). In marked contrast to the Bionian stress on the role of linking in human mentation, on the final page of *Knots*, R.D. Laing (1970) envisions the mind as a process of de-linking or differentiating: "All distinctions are mind, by mind, in mind, of mind; no distinctions no mind to distinguish" (p. 82). Laing was a follower of Jean-Paul Sartre (1943) who wrote that "man is the being through whom nothingness comes to the world" (p. 24) and who viewed human consciousness as "nihilating"—as having "to secrete a nothingness," a gap, lack or boundary between subject and object, knower and known.

In this light, the mystic "All is One" is a formula for an uncreative stasis: growth, development and evolution occur in time rather than eternity and require not one, but a couple through whose productive intercourse a dialectical process (thesis, antithesis, synthesis) may take place. This is a process of integration (linking), and disintegration (de-linking), through which reintegration on a higher level may occur, a synthesis that, in turn, may meet an antithesis leading to a yet higher synthesis, and so on. Sigmund Freud lived in a culture permeated by Hegelian ideas. We know he studied philosophy with Brentano and was, initially at least, enthused about both the man and his work (Brook, 2015). It is therefore, no surprise that Freudian theory is substantially dialectical. Freud's idea of development through conflict and compromise-formation, his vision of conflict as entailing the privileging of one pole of a binary opposition (thesis) and the suppression or repression of the other (antithesis), and his notion of sublimation (Hegel's sublation, *Aufheben*) as a creative, higher-order solution to the conflict is manifestly dialectical. Despite his later, and as Brook (2015) points out, rather mysterious neglect of Brentano, not to mention his many disparaging remarks about philosophy as little more than a product of the schizoid minds of "thinkers who were for the most part turned away from the world" (Freud, 1933, 175), Freud clearly owed a great debt to the dialectical ideas pervading his intellectual milieu.

It would be false to suggest that Bion (1962a, 1962b) conceived learning from experience exclusively in terms of a preconception mating with a positive realization leading to a conception. He also, like Freud himself, viewed it as a process in which a preconception encounters a negative realization, a "no-breast" or "no-thing," thus generating thought. Nevertheless, I think the Symingtons (1996) are incorrect when having described Hegel's dialectical view of historical development they write that "Bion formulated development of thought on a model which is not dissimilar" (p. 56). Certainly in *Attacks on Linking* development is conceived as linking, mating, coupling, not as conflict and contradiction. The idea of the mating of a preconception with a negative realization, a "no-thing," certainly plays an important role in Bion's thought, but the encounter of a preconception with a "no-thing" is not quite the same thing as its encounter with a direct contradiction. An unfulfilled expectation is not quite the same thing as an active negation. An absence is not the same thing as a conflicting or contradictory presence. Nowhere in Bion is the theme of development through conflict and contradiction given anything like the emphasis it receives in both Marxian and Freudian thought.

Although any two objects are inevitably similar in some respects while being different in others, some people, the linkers, are inclined to repress difference, while others, the splitters, are inclined to repress similarity. And, of course, a single person may do either at different times or on different levels of consciousness. People are motivated to repress difference or similarity in order to defend against painful feelings of anxiety and depression having to do with separation or abandonment on the one hand and intrusion or engulfment on the other. Faced with a threat of abandonment one may seek to link; faced with a threat of impingement or engulfment one may seek to de-link, differentiate, separate and individuate.

Without lapsing into any biological or even psychological essentialism, Gilligan (1982) pointed to a general tendency for women to be linkers and for men to be separators, while acknowledging there are many exceptions to this rule. Hence, a view of analysis as separating or differentiating what has been fused may reflect a "masculine" bias in favor of difference, which may in turn be motivated by unconscious fears of symbiotic merger, impingement, annihilation, undifferentiation of self and object, loss of self-cohesion, castration, or the fear of "femininity." The conception of pathology as symbiosis or "attacks on boundaries" and the corollary model of therapy as boundary-making would appear to underlie the rigid insistence upon the achievement and preservation of a clear analytic "frame" that characterized the work of Langs (1978), among others. On the other hand, an equally one-sided view of the analytic process as deconstructing absolute difference, overcoming splitting or "attacks on linking" may be motivated by a "feminine" bias in favor of similarity that we see at work in therapies that privilege connection, relationality, empathic attunement and "transmuting internalization" (Kohut, 1978) over confrontation, clarification, interpretation, insight, separation-individuation and mourning in the analytic cure. This bias is likely motivated by unconscious fears of object loss, loss of love, castration and superego condemnation, each of which in turn may threaten loss of self-cohesion.

The "linkers" have a "feminine" bias toward connection: they want everything to touch, merge and be the same and have little tolerance for differences. If they succeed in sublimating this bias toward *Eros*, they become the creative unifiers or integrators. The "separators" have a "masculine" bias toward difference: they want to differentiate and keep things apart and have little tolerance for similarity and merger. If they succeed in sublimating this bias toward *Thanatos*, they become the creative discriminators or distinguishers. But, ultimately, neither bias, to the extent that it entails a defensive repression of one or the other component of what Freud (1905b) regarded as our inherent bisexuality, can alone result in the achievement of optimal psychic functioning because this requires attention to reality in its entirety, both similarities and differences. Hence, a more adequate conception of analysis is as both metaphor-analysis and contrast-analysis: it promotes both the transformation of absolute similarity into relative similarity (by pointing to implicit difference), and the transformation of absolute difference (splitting) into relative difference (by pointing to implicit similarity). For just as different things can never be absolutely the same and yet remain different, so different things can never be absolutely different, without being similar in at least some respects. Hillman's (1972) conclusion that: "Analysis cannot constitute this cure until it, too, is no longer masculine in psychology" (p. 292), needs to be supplemented by the recognition that an opposing perspective that is exclusively "feminine" is no better. We are cured when we are no longer only either "masculine" or "feminine" in psyche—that is, when we manage to stop "essentializing" or privileging one element of our "bisexual" nature at the expense of the other.

Needless to say, the reason the terms "masculine" and "feminine" are placed in inverted commas is to indicate that the equations in which they figure belong to the Imaginary and Symbolic orders (Lacan, 1977); that is, they refer to image and symbol rather than to anything biological, to what is imagined to be masculine or feminine in the order of human culture and not to what an "essentializing" perspective might regard as being literally, as opposed to metaphorically, the case (Burke, 1939). In a "contextualizing" perspective that restricts itself to the realm of psychic reality as the proper domain of psychoanalytical concern, the human subject is seen to be inevitably only figuratively masculine or feminine and never literally so. In bringing to light the repressed "bisexuality" upon which the fictions or tropes that constitute our gender identities are founded, psychoanalysis reveals the constructed, dramatic and imaginal quality of human identity (the "ego" or "self") as such. However inclined we may be to take ourselves seriously in our roles as masculine and feminine actors, we are wise to remember that, as in all of our performances, in our sexual dramas we are never a man or a woman "as this table is a table" (Sartre, 1943, p. 64). We forget or repress this awareness only at the cost of falling into what Sartre described as "bad faith" or the "spirit of solemnity," a phenomenon that I have discussed as a defensive regression involving the literalization of metaphor and contrast (Carveth, 1984b), and that Lacan (1977) explained as the narcissistic alienation of the "ego" maintained by the primal and ongoing repression of the otherness within me (the unconscious) that would decenter my cherished identity and that, fortunately, periodically leads me to forget or mistake my lines.

The tendency for one or another image of absolute similarity or difference to hold us captive arises either from genuine ignorance of other possibilities or from a defense against the affects of anxiety and depression associated with the full range of infantile danger situations. We can only speculate about the factors contributing to a person's bias toward similarity, *Eros,* and "femininity," or toward difference, *Thanatos,* and "masculinity," and the resulting personality orientations toward saying "Yes" (agreeing, linking and merging) on the one hand, and saying "No" (disagreeing, breaking links, separating and individuating) on the other. Factors such as, for example, the role of a depressed and withdrawn mother in the early development of the "linkers" and the corresponding role of an impinging, intrusive and dominating mother, or a more general need to "dis-identify from mother" (Greenson, 1968), in the early formation of the "separators" might be important. However, such pure types are nonexistent because *Eros* and *Thanatos,* integrating and disintegrating tendencies, "femininity" and "masculinity," inevitably coexist in a greater or lesser degree of fusion; because both types of danger situation may motivate both personality orientations; and because both orientations may coexist on different levels of the personality structure and even serve to defend against each other.

These biases are reflected in psychoanalytic theory itself: while a predisposition toward linking may incline one to think of analysis as mothering, a bias toward separation may lead one to think of it as fathering. But despite its patriarchalism in other respects, it seems apparent that the bias of the "linkers," those predisposed to privilege similarity over difference, finds expression in the classical theory of the infantile danger situations, a theory that in focusing upon *loss* (of the object, its love, the phallus, superego approval) implicitly downplays those dangers having more to do with the object's overwhelming or malevolent presence than with its absence. The Freudian myth of man's eternal longing to "re-find" (Freud, 1905b, p. 222) the lost object of primary identification and re-establish the oceanic bliss or Nirvana of primary narcissism (Freud, 1920, 1930; Grunberger, 1979) is only half the story: it needs to be complemented by insight into the equally primordial and eternal wish to "re-lose" or "re-destroy" the primary object, the primary identification (Greenson, 1968) and Eden itself, regarded as a dubious paradise, more as a prison or a coffin than a haven. And despite their matriarchalism in other respects, in the work of theorists such as Klein, Winnicott and Mahler, the Freudian bias toward *Eros* (a reflection of Freud's idealized image of the mother-infant relation) is balanced to some extent by insight into wishes to destroy links, resist impingement, separate, individuate and guard autonomy, wishes associated with *Thanatos* understood as the psychic desire to separate in the service of independence or self-cohesion, whether this aim leads in the direction of literal life or death. It is perhaps at least partly in this bias of the Freudian tradition toward *Eros* (only partially corrected in 1920 with the introduction of the final dual-drive theory) that the explanation lies for its relative failure to recognize the importance of (i.e., its relative repression of) the role of the destructive mother-image (May, 2001) in the genesis of various types of psychopathology and, consequently, its tendency to privilege anxieties concerning loss over those having to do with impingement, persecution or annihilation.

According to Ricoeur (1970), "'Symbols give rise to thought,' but they are also the birth of idols. That is why the critique of idols remains the condition of the conquest of symbols" (p. 543). When relative similarities are absolutized into identities—and to cite but a few examples, women literally equated with castrated men, human motives with animal instincts, human selves with ceramic artifacts, or psychological dysfunctions with medical illnesses—the consequence is a psychic regression from the differentiated experience characteristic of the secondary process and the depressive position to the undifferentiation or fusion that characterizes the primary process and the paranoid-schizoid position. It is important, however, to recognize that in addition to involving defusion or splitting, regressive mental functioning also entails varying degrees of fusion or undifferentiation. Conversely, it is not simply that in the primary process metaphors are literalized such that analogies are reduced to identities, but also that contrasts based on recognition of relative differences are absolutized into antitheses, binary oppositions, or splits: the sexes, for example, being thought of literally as opposites; or psychosis and neurosis dichotomized; or the "drive-structure" and "relational-structure" models of the mind represented as simply irreconcilable (Greenberg & Mitchell, 1983, chapters one and twelve); or human relations forced into the reductive pattern of such (phallic-oedipal, anal and oral) binary roles as castrator/castrated, superior/inferior and feeder/fed; or the paranoid-schizoid (Ps) and depressive (D) positions of mental life (Klein, 1946) dichotomized rather than dialectically interrelated (though admittedly Kleinians have always postulated ongoing oscillation between the two positions).

The one-sided conception of psychopathology as "forbidden mixture" developed by Chasseguet-Smirgel (1984) in *Perversion and the Universal*

Law needs to be complemented by recognition of the pathologies of "forbidden separation." Whereas the Bible, as Chasseguet-Smirgel points out, certainly does proscribe regressive fusion, as in incest and other violations of the boundaries separating the sexes and the generations, it also prohibits regressive defusion, as in the splitting of the Godhead, which is the object of the monotheistic critique of dualism: "Hear, O Israel, the Lord our God is one Lord" (*Deut.*: 6:4 KJV). In my view, regressive splitting and fusion function as defenses against core anxieties of absolute incorporation or engulfment on the one hand and absolute separation or abandonment on the other. But while the fundamental anxieties motivate the various concretized associations, fixed ideas and black and white thinking—the psychic rigidification or mental totalitarianism—that serve to defend against them, they do not merely give rise to defensive reification, but are themselves manifestations of it. For such anxieties embody the myths of totalized identity (complete loss of boundaries or de-differentiation) and totalized difference (complete loss of connection or links) that always already reflect regressive fusion and defusion.

Although these twin anxieties are most evident in the borderline "need/fear" dilemma that for Mahler, Pine and Bergman (1975) represented unsuccessful resolution of the "rapprochement crisis" of separation-individuation, I believe that in more primitive and global forms they also underlie psychotic, and in milder forms neurotic, pathology as well. In other words, there is a continuum of psychopathological reactions of undifferentiation and disintegration ranging from the mild (neurotic), to the moderate (borderline and narcissistic) to the severe (psychotic). Emancipation from psychic enslavement by the myths of oneness and separateness in their varying degrees and manifestations requires a therapeutic process of demythologization or deliteralization in which "dead" or "dying" metaphors and contrasts are "resurrected" or "revived." In coming to be recognized as merely relative, the myths of absolute engulfment and abandonment lose their power to dominate our subjectivity. In returning to "life" they at the same time liberate us from the "deadly" serious, primary process world of psychotic incorporation and polarization, fusion and defusion.

Chapter 10

Beyond nature and culture
Erich Fromm's existentialism

Erich Fromm has been widely viewed as a "Neo-Freudian" member of the so-called "culturistic" school of psychoanalysis who, along with Karen Horney, Harry Stack Sullivan and others, in rejecting the "biologism" of the classical Freudian theory of the instincts, succumbed to a radically constructivist and culturally relativist "sociologism" that Dennis H. Wrong (1961) called: "The over-socialized conception of man in modern sociology." While agreeing with Wrong's critique of the one-sided social determinism prevalent in the mainstream structural-functionalist sociology of the 1950s, I subsequently argued against Wrong that to simply replace the *over-socialized* model of human nature with the *under-socialized* and overly *biologized* conception offered by Freudian drive theory is no solution (Carveth, 1984a). In my dissatisfaction with both *over-* and *under*-socialized models and my search for a dialectical solution to the *nature/nurture* polarity, I was following in the footsteps of Fromm who was quite as alert to the danger of sociological as of biological reductionism.

Sociologism, Biologism Humanistic Existentialism

Like many "symbolic interactionist" sociologists who, forgetting G.H. Mead's (1934) "I"-subject reduced the self to the socially determined "me"-object, Harry Stack Sullivan at times seemed to reduce the self to a product of the "reflected appraisals of others" (Sullivan, 1940, p. 22). For Fromm the reduction of the self to the sum of one's social roles manifests the self pathology displayed by the *marketing* type of social character produced by late capitalism. He writes:

This selflessness of modern man has appeared to one of the most gifted and original contemporary psychiatrists, the late H.S. Sullivan, as being a natural phenomenon. He spoke of those psychologists who, like myself, assume that the lack of the sense of self is a pathological phenomenon, as of people who suffer from a "delusion." The self for him is nothing but the many roles we play in relation to others, roles which have the function of eliciting approval and avoiding the anxiety which is produced by disapproval. What a remarkably fast deterioration of the concept of self since the nineteenth century, when Ibsen made the loss of self the main theme of his criticism of modern man in his Peer Gynt!

(Fromm, 1956b, p. 143)

That many sociologists accepted such a deteriorated concept of the self—a *situational* as distinct from a *substantive* theory of the self in which the self is reduced to a subjective echo of the ever-changing roles one plays and personality is reduced to performance—is a fact that itself requires sociological explanation. Sociologists of knowledge know that ideas often become established for reasons other than their truth-content. Sociological ideas arise in particular historical contexts, in this case a late capitalist society in which the marketing orientation is so dominant that individuals are loathe to invest heavily in a self that might well go out of fashion, prove difficult to shed or transform, and thus, turn out to have been a poor investment. As Lasch (1979), among others, pointed out, with the shift from productive to consumer capitalism in the 1950s, psychoanalysts became increasingly preoccupied with narcissism. In *The Obsolescence of the Freudian Concept of Man*, Marcuse (1970) argued Freud had been right, but was now wrong because the social reality had changed, no longer producing what Riesman (Riesman, Glazer, & Denney, 1950)—who as Burston (1991) points out was an analysand and later close friend of Fromm's—called an "inner-directed," but only an "other-directed" personality, i.e., a marketing, character.

Greenberg and Mitchell (1983) argue that the claim that in the interpersonal tradition "the individual is merely a cultural product ... constitutes a serious misreading" (p. 80) that mistakes Sullivan's (1950) protest against "the illusion of unique individuality" (by which they argue he means a kind of narcissistic defense against anxiety) for a denial of "the real unique individuality of each psychobiological organism—an individuality that must always escape the methods of science" (Sullivan, 1936, p. 16, as quoted by Greenberg & Mitchell, p. 113). Mead (1934) also wrote of the subjective "I" as eluding science in that any self we know will necessarily be an object of knowledge—i.e., a "me" rather than the "I"-subject doing the knowing. So here, like Fromm and Mead, Sullivan seems to recognize an existential element, as does Lacan (1977) in distinguishing a "subject" from the "specular ego," and as certainly does Winnicott (1960a) in distinguishing a "true self" from a "false self." Greenberg and Mitchell (1983) argue that Sullivan distinguishes the "self-system," a conglomeration of defenses erected to ward off anxiety, from the "personality" that contains elements of one's "psycho-biological organism" not subsumed by the defensive "good me," "bad me" and "not-me": "One's personality," they write "is what one *is* [original emphasis]; one's self is what one *takes oneself to be* [original emphasis]" (p. 96).

I remain unconvinced by these authors' defense of Sullivan against Fromm's charge. If for Sullivan and the interpersonalists, individuality is not a delusion, why did they choose for the epigraph of their chapter on this psychoanalytic tradition a passage from Nietzsche's *The Birth of Tragedy* that associates Apollo, a symbol of the *principium individuationis,* with both the veil of Maya and illusion? They go on to say that, in marked contrast to Fromm: "Sullivan was convinced that adaptation to and integration into contemporary society, despite its failings, is *essential* to mental health" (p. 112) and to acknowledge that whereas "Sullivan is a determinist: the person is a product of past interpersonal integrations ... Fromm is an existentialist: the person is continually choosing" (p. 113).

In countering biological reductionism, not with sociological reductionism, but with humanistic existentialism, Fromm anticipated the work of the existentialist sociologists Berger and Luckmann (1966) who, despite strong tendencies toward social determinism recognized this danger and adopted an existentialist solution. Instead of, like Wrong, Trilling (1955) and critical theorists such as Adorno (1968) and Marcuse (1955, 1956), resorting to Freud's somatically-based drives to counter social internalizations, they adopted a Sartrean (Sartre 1943, 1960) existentialist concept of an ineradicable element of subjective freedom to resist, manipulate or detach from social pressures—to achieve an "ec-static" consciousness that to a degree transcends the socially constructed self and world. Without giving Fromm his due, no doubt because of their ingrained sociological hostility to psychoanalysis, they like him transcended both biological and cultural determinism through a humanistic existentialism that while recognizing the forces of both nature and culture at the same time posits a human nature characterized by a degree of irreducible subjective freedom, agency and responsibility—an "I" in addition to a "me."

Such is the power of academic fashion that even someone, like myself, who had extensively critiqued the one-sided social constructionism and relativism characterizing earlier sociological thought was slow to recognize that the anti-humanist, structuralist, post-structuralist and post-modern paradigms that came to predominate in social theory for several decades represented an even more extreme and unrealistic version of the same thing. Foucault (1969) went so far as to announce "the death of Man"—the negation of any concept of a human nature or essence of the sort that grounded Fromm's (1956b) existential humanism and that enabled him to assess the relative success or failure of particular societies in satisfying what he saw as universal human needs—for *relatedness, creativeness, rootedness, identity* and *orientation and devotion*. Today, a range of contemporary thinkers are concerned to "challenge the excessive culturalism and anti-personalism which characterize most 'postmodern' thinking, whether it be structuralist, poststructuralist, or posthuman" and to promote "the *dialectical supersession* [original emphasis] of the anti-humanist paradigm" (Durkin, 2014, p. 211) in favor of a renaissance of humanism.

If Fromm himself at times exaggerated humanity's break with nature, he at least insisted our existential dichotomy involves our being immersed by our bodies in it, even while through our symbolling and meaning-making minds we transcend it. Against what amounts almost to the "nature phobia" (Benton, 2001) of many sociologists, the recognition that humans are primates and share with our primate cousins an unlearned, biologically grounded need for attachment (Bowlby, 1969–1980) is invaluable, as is recent research (Bloom, 2013) demonstrating that infants (*in fans*: beneath language) as young as three months of age distinguish right from wrong and prefer the former over the latter. While not constituting evidence of an "innate" morality, for by three months infants have already had time to identify with the loving nurturance provided by their carers, such evidence, together with research on the prosocial behavior of other species (De Wall, 1997, 2009) exposes the poverty of one-sided views of the human being as an exclusively culturally programmed "language animal" (Steiner, 1969). Against behaviorism and related forms of environmental determinism Chomsky (1957) had as early as the 1950s convincingly posited the biological grounding of language and, hence, by implication, of related dimensions of our human nature, a point of view he continued to assert against the exaggerated culturalism of Foucault and other radical constructivists (Chomsky & Foucault, 1971 [2006]).

Qualified essentialism

None of the above is meant to in any way deny the validity and importance of the critique of essentialism in social and psychoanalytic theory, of ahistorical and ethnocentric notions of an unchanging and unchangeable human nature or essence. As Fromm himself frequently pointed out, Marx (1867), and not, be it noted, merely the early Marx, distinguished between "human nature in general" and "human nature as modified in each historical epoch" (1867, Vol. 1, Chapter 24, Section 5, fn. 50). Fromm follows Marx in this distinction, adopting a "qualified essentialism" that recognizes the existence of a human nature grounded in very general, universal biological and existential aspects of the human condition, but always as shaped by particular personal, historical and cultural circumstances. Both reductive, ahistorical essentialism and reductive, extreme social constructionism are rejected in this dialectical model.

While Adorno, Horkheimer and Marcuse were also determined to resist radical social determinism and cultural relativism, they felt it necessary to defend Freud's reductionist theory of the drives in the process. They offered a manifestly self-contradictory critique of Fromm: castigating him, on one hand, for rejecting Freud's under-socialized and overly biologized theory in favor of social factors (Fromm, 1955, 1956a; Marcuse, 1955, 1956; Jacoby, 1975) and, on the other, for failing to recognize that the human essence he posited is a social product. In Ingleby's (1991) view, their attack on Fromm "is to some extent based on a misreading of his work: he does not, as Adorno claims, reduce psychology to sociology, and many of his criticisms of Freud remain more convincing than the defense offered by Adorno and Marcuse" (p. xxiv). Critical theory failed to recognize that Fromm had placed the critique of the over-socialized model on a far more solid footing than Freudian drive theory through his qualified essentialism and existentialism.

In some ways, Fromm's perspective bears significant affinities to Sartre's (1960) existential Neo-Marxism. But his emphasis upon loving human relations (Fromm, 1956c) is entirely discrepant with the earlier Sartre's (1943) vision of the sado-masochistic structure of human relations, albeit in the state of bad faith. Regrettably, this is the only state Sartre described, since the potential "radical escape" from bad faith through a "self-recovery of being" or "authenticity" (chapter two, fn. 9, p. 116) resulting in an "ethics of deliverance and salvation" (chapter three, fn. 13, p. 534), mentioned in two small footnotes in a book of some 800 pages, seems to have got subsumed by the idea of a revolutionary transformation of society in his later work (Sartre, 1960).

Fromm rejected both reductive biological and environmental determinisms in favor of an existentialist view of the human being's "emergence" as a self-conscious creature, rooted in nature by the body and yet significantly transcending it due to its capacity for symbolic processes, relatively free from instinctual determination and, hence, as in the Sartrean (1943) vision, suffering from a "fear of freedom" and a marked temptation to surrender it. Like both the early and the later Sartre (Laing & Cooper, 1964), Fromm in no way minimizes the limitations upon our practical freedom ("freedom to …") arising from the force of material and social circumstances, even while insisting upon an ineradicable degree of psychological freedom ("freedom from") possessed by human agents, at least as long as we remain subjects as yet unreduced to material or biological objects.

Fromm's qualified essentialism enabled him to distinguish human nature in general from its manifestations under particular historical and cultural circumstances. As a result, he is able to recognize a range of universal human needs and dilemmas as revealed by the human sciences. In the face of the anxiety and loneliness arising from our existential situation as both immersed in nature and separated from it, Fromm recognized five possible "solutions," four regressive and one progressive, comprising his revised version of Freud's characterology. In addition to the *receptive, exploitative, hoarding and marketing* orientations, there is the *productive* orientation that includes the capacities for love and reason.

The naturalistic fallacy

In *Man For Himself: An Inquiry into the Psychology of Ethics*, Fromm (1947) advances the idea of "objective" or "naturalistic ethics" in which "'good' is synonymous with good for man and 'bad' with bad for man" (p. 18). As Ingleby (1991, p. xxxix) and other critics (Schaar, 1961; Snippe, 1988) have argued, there is a "naturalistic fallacy" at work here. Fromm (1947) writes:

> But one can deduce norms from theories only on the premise that a certain activity is chosen and a certain aim is desired. The premise for medical science is that it is desirable to cure disease and to prolong life; if this were not the case, all the rules of medical science would be irrelevant. Every applied science is based on an axiom which results from an act of choice: namely, that the end of the activity is desirable.... We can imagine a hypothetical culture where people do not want paintings or bridges, but not one in which people do not want to live. The drive to live is inherent in every organism, and man cannot help wanting to live regardless of what he would like to think about it. The choice between life and death is more apparent than real; man's real choice is that between a good life and a bad life.
> (p. 18)

In arguing that "the drive to live is inherent in every organism and man cannot help wanting to live," Fromm appears to be forgetting his own vision of man as a "freak of nature," both rooted in and transcending it, with the freedom to negate both organismic and environmental pressures, even to the point of choosing death over life. In a footnote to the above quoted passage, Fromm argues that: "Suicide as a pathological phenomenon does not contradict this general principle" (p. 18). Without claiming that Fromm always regarded suicide, or all suicides, as pathological. I submit that calling suicide "pathological" is an obscured way of expressing the value judgment that it is a bad choice. I have argued (Carveth, 2013, chapter one and the Introduction to this volume) that it is a long-standing strategy in a de-moralizing psychoanalysis that refuses to preach what it practices to employ the language of health and pathology to cloak the value judgments undergirding its theory and *praxis* from beginning to end. The mere fact that many or even most people choose something in no way proves their choice is good. It is simply incorrect to say that "man cannot help wanting to live." Many want to die and choose suicide. Fromm's own (1973) account of the reality of *necrophilia*, the love of death, is evidence of this. Calling necrophilia "pathological" does no more than indicate one doesn't like it because of one's value preference for life. Regrettably, except for a few purists like Thomas Szasz (1961), most people working in the "psy" fields, myself included, fall regularly or occasionally into the mystifying language of the medical model, the language of health and pathology, when we ought to make our value judgments explicit instead of calling what we dislike "sick."

In recent postmodern philosophy, the claim has been made that the fact/value distinction posited by David Hume, G.E. Moore, Bertrand Russell and others—the claim that one cannot deduce an *ought* from an *is*, that reason and science are *descriptive* only and cannot be *prescriptive*—has collapsed (Putnam, 2002). But on examination what has been deconstructed is only an impossibly exaggerated version of the distinction, a fact/value *disjunction* that the modernists had never advanced in the first place. Of course one can reason about values in many ways, and even the preference for coherence over incoherence and logic over illogic are values. But none of this, including Horkheimer's (1947) essentially pre-modern celebration of a supposedly "objective" as distinct from merely "instrumental" reason, nullifies the impotence of reason to generate or authorize value judgments. The attempt to escape from freedom, from the value choices entailed in efforts to create an "objective" ethics, is both inconsistent with Fromm's existentialism and unnecessary, for an ethics grounded in the study of human nature can be developed without obscuring the value choices involved.

According to Martin Buber (1938), for Immanuel Kant philosophy is comprised of answers to four questions: what can I know? (epistemology); what should I do? (ethics); what may I hope? (religion); what is man? (philosophical anthropology). Any answer to the fourth question automatically implies answers to the other three. This is due to the power of "the argument from human nature," the syllogism in which the first of the two premises leading to a conclusion is a statement regarding the nature of human nature, while the second is the value judgment that human beings *ought* to be able to act in accordance with their nature and that society *should* be so organized as to allow or promote this. From these two premises, the second of which is an uncloaked value judgment, far-reaching moral and political conclusions may be drawn. If, for example, humans are naturally competitive, then unrestrained capitalism is the good society for it permits human beings to act according to their nature. But if humans are naturally cooperative then competitive capitalism is a bad system for it forces people to act against their nature, thus, alienating or estranging them from their true or authentic selves. The human sciences inform us as to the essential nature of human nature (apart from its widely differing historical and cultural manifestations). We then plug this data into the syllogism, the argument from human nature, and—*voila!*—important moral and political conclusions may be drawn without having to deceive ourselves about the leap beyond facts into values entailed in the second premise of our argument.

Authoritarian vs. humanistic "conscience"

Like Freud, who often used the terms superego and conscience interchangeably, in differentiating authoritarian and humanistic "conscience" Fromm (1950) was not distinguishing conscience from superego (as I do, see chapter two), but drawing attention to two very different types of superego. In seeking to replace the authoritarian by the humanistic "conscience" (i.e., superego), he was in essential agreement with Freud, Alexander and Ferenczi, each of whom conceived the therapeutic task as the "demolition" (Freud, 1940, p. 180) or "complete dissolution" (Ferenczi, 1928 [1927], p. 100) of the superego as an "anachronism in the mind" (Alexander, 1925, p. 25), an outmoded and infantilizing internalized parental and societal authority operating "like a garrison in an occupied city" (Freud, 1930, p. 123), sometimes even taking the form of a "pure culture of the death instinct" (Freud, 1923, p. 52). But in seeking to transfer the moral functions to the rational ego, Freud and his colleagues failed to understand that because reason is *descriptive* not *prescriptive* and we cannot deduce an *ought* from an *is*, the ego cannot serve as a conscience. Hence, I have argued (Carveth, 2013, 2016a, 2016b; Chapter 2 above) in favor of reversing Freud's (1923) decision to merge conscience with the superego and instead recognize it as a separate mental function originating in early identification with the nurturer while the superego is grounded in early identification with the aggressor.

While by a humanistic conscience Fromm meant a humanistic superego—failing to differentiate conscience from superego as such—there is no doubt that by a humanistic conscience/superego he had in mind something more than the rational ego that Freud, Alexander and Ferenczi mistakenly thought could take over the moral functions. Fromm's humanistic conscience/superego included love as much as reason and, therefore, although he did not ground it in our mammalian and primate heritage and identification with the early nurturers as I do, it bears a close affinity to the conscience I have proposed distinguishing as a separate structure and function with a different origin and nature from the superego as such.

We cannot entirely eliminate the hate that fuels the superego. Not because our hate is grounded in biological drive. Fromm's rejection of that kind of biologically reductionist drive theory is entirely warranted. Hate is a reaction to frustration, but there is no human existence, no infancy and childhood, without serious frustration that is *basic* or *existential* and unavoidable, in addition to the *surplus* frustration due to trauma, abuse, neglect, injustice, socialization into pathological social patterns, etc. An important element of Fromm's existentialism is his recognition of the tragic fact that a portion of our suffering is nobody's fault. Siblings are born. We all die. We cannot have our cake and eat it too. Since frustration is unavoidable even with the best carers imaginable, and since frustration generates aggression, and aggression gets both projected and turned on the self, varying degrees of persecutory guilt and paranoia are inevitable.

In asserting that our therapeutic task is to strengthen the forces of love (Fromm's *biophilia*, Freud's *Eros* and Klein's *depressive/reparative* dynamics) over hate and destructiveness (*necrophilia*, *Thanatos*, *paranoid-schizoid* dynamics) I am in no way contradicting my critique of the medical model because I do not claim this task is anything other than a moral choice: I do not choose life and love because they are healthier, but because, according to me, they are better. (My enemies, those preferring death and hate, disagree and so we fight.) But instead of conceptualizing the transformation of character we promote as disempowering the superego in favor of the conscience, mainstream psychoanalysis chose to follow Strachey (1934) rather than Freud, Alexander and Ferenczi, conceiving it as the modification of an "archaic" into a "mature" superego, *while failing to understand that we need a conscience precisely in order to know in what directions the superego needs to be modified.* Beyond this, the transformation we seek is radical; less a process of continuous than of emergent evolution; more akin to revolution than to reform. It involves the demolition of the superego, not in favor of the ego, but of the conscience.

The roots of our difficulty lie deeper than at least the early Fromm (1944) wanted to recognize. Certainly authoritarian socialization pressures that repress the true self, its sexuality, aggression and spontaneity, are important. But it is a mistake to think the problem of human guilt is reducible to such external social causes. Here Freud is, in a sense, more existential than Fromm, for he recognized that in addition to the guilt inflicted by the superego (internalization of social authority via the parental superegos and turning of aggression on the self) there exists a pre-superego guilt arising from simple ambivalence: from hating those we love. Although he mostly advanced a view of morality as socially constructed, in *Totem and Taboo*, Freud (1912–1913) described the remorse stemming from the killing of the ambivalently loved primal father that led to the establishment of the moral law in the first place. In Freud's historical myth (and implied in his account of the oedipal development of the individual) guilt, instead of resulting from the superego, precedes and motivates its formation. This is not the persecutory guilt inflicted by the superego, but the depressive or reparative guilt arising from conscience.

The Oedipus complex IS universal

Like Melanie Klein, Erich Fromm (1951) recognized the developmental importance of the preoedipal phase of the mother-infant dyad preceding the oedipal triad. Following Bachofen (1861), he posited a matriarchal phase of civilization preceding the patriarchal order. Unlike Freud and Lacan, patriarchal thinkers who privileged the oedipal over the preoedipal in personality formation and psychopathology and paternal over maternal function, Fromm advanced a theory and a clinical *praxis* that to a degree transcends this bias. His advocacy of the humanistic conscience grounded in love and care over the authoritarian conscience representing conventional norms and hierarchical institutional authority is an expression of this, as is his more egalitarian approach to clinical work.

Fromm advanced a revisionist, socially conditioned and relativistic rather than universal and existential theory of the Oedipus complex in which it is not primarily about sexual jealousy, but about authority and, in Western culture at least, about the father-son conflict. He writes:

> Freud gives a universal meaning to a feature that is characteristic only of patriarchal society ... [where] the son is subject to the father's will; ... As always, oppression leads to hate, to a wish to liberate oneself from the oppressor, and in the last analysis, to eliminate him.
> (Fromm, 1980, p. 29)

Other Marxists also made the Oedipus about hostility and domination rather than sex, utilizing Malinowski's (1927) data on the Trobriand culture where the boy's hostility is not toward the man who sleeps with mother (his father), but toward the man who holds authority over him (his maternal uncle).

Anthropologist Anne Parsons (1964) reviewed Malinowski's data and found Trobriand culture full of brother-sister incest myths, jokes and taboos, because the culture makes her brother the most important man in a woman's life. Her son perceives that while his father merely sleeps with her, he has little importance in his mother's and uncle's matrilineal and matrilocal milieu and is easily divorced. The mother's brother is the really significant man in her life. So while the Oedipus is not about narrow sexual jealousy, it *is* about jealousy in a wider and more fundamental sense. It stems from narcissistic desire more than sexual desire: *the desire to be the apple of the mother's eye.* This narcissistic desire is universal, existential, though directed differently under different kinship arrangements. So Fromm is right that the Oedipus is not fundamentally about sex, but neither is it fundamentally about authority, though resentment of authority certainly plays a part, and in our society the male authority figure also sleeps with the mother and is often the most important person in her life.

Fromm underestimated the universal narcissistic desire to be preeminent and the rivalry, jealousy, envy and aggression that result from competition. The narcissistic project is, in my view, an unavoidable by-product of attachment. While certainly not drawing on attachment theory, Lacan (1977) argues that "man's desire finds its meaning in the desire of the other" (p. 58)—that is, I desire to be desired. While such desire is universal the resulting competition is inflamed in a competitive capitalist culture, while a socialist culture could mitigate it in various ways. A qualified essentialism recognizes that the narcissistic project is reducible to neither nature nor culture, but is existential, inevitable. But it also understands that it can either be socially inflamed or tamed, channeled into positive, prosocial directions, creatively sublimated, etc.

Humanistic religion: an oxymoron?

Fromm's radical humanism had its early roots in prophetic messianism (Burston, 1991; Braune, 2014), in the Judaism that he, like Marx, broke away from in favor of an atheistic secularization of these ethical and messianic themes. Fromm (1950) chose to distinguish humanistic from authoritarian religion instead of distinguishing humanism from religion as such. Today many consider supernaturalism as religion's defining quality:

> Religion is a belief system which includes the notion of a supernatural, invisible world, inhabited by gods, human souls, angels, demons, and other conscious spirit entities.... A supernaturalist belief system does not have to refer to gods, but it does always refer to spirit entities (ancestors, ghosts, angels, etc.) which have some power over humans and can affect their lives.
>
> (Beit-Hallahmi, 2014, p. 3)

Freud demanded that adherents of demythologized, metaphoric, "As If" or secular readings of religious traditions admit that in abandoning literalism and supernaturalism they had in fact embraced atheism:

> One would like to mix among the ranks of the believers in order to meet these philosophers, who think they can rescue the God of religion by replacing him by an impersonal, shadowy and abstract principle, and to address them with the warning words: "Thou shalt not take the name of the Lord thy God in vain!"
>
> (Freud, 1930, p. 73)

Similarly, for Beit-Hallahmi (2014), as for me, if there are no supernatural elements central to the belief system it is not religion.

While some religious traditions are, doubtless, more authoritarian and less humane than others, if we define humanism as a man-centered or anthropocentric perspective it is clearly incompatible with religion as a God- or spirit-centered system of belief. In his later years, Fromm became interested in Buddhism, which unlike the Abrahamic religions is not a form of theism. But many Buddhist traditions nevertheless, qualify as religion in that they are permeated by supernatural beliefs. Forms of Buddhism and related meditative practices that are absent of any supernatural elements or claims would qualify as types of philosophy and related ways of life rather than religion. Whether they would qualify as humanistic is open to debate, since in seeking forms of transcendence of egocentricity they may in fact be seeking to transcend the anthropocentrism central I would argue to humanism as such.

Anthropocentrism

Beit-Hallahmi refers to the supernaturalist experience of "mystical union with a deity or with nature" (p. 68), as if there is no valid distinction between the former and the latter; as if all experiences of unity with nature must somehow entail supernaturalism when in fact they may reflect the expanded naturalism that recognizes our intrinsic connectedness or embeddedness in nature. Just as Freud (1930) reduced the "oceanic" experience to infantile primary narcissism prior to differentiation of self and other (a stage that, thanks to empirical infant research, we now know does not exist), so Beit-Hallahmi appears to relegate it to the realm of religion. But it is our failure to recognize our continuity with nature (a connectedness that, however celebrated by mystics, is now recognized by physicists as the "butterfly effect") that has resulted in the exaggerated sense of human exceptionalism, the anthropocentrism that I believe has contributed greatly to anthropogenic climate disruption.

Here lies what in my opinion is the major flaw in Fromm's work, the anthropocentrism that pervades it from beginning to end. Beyond his exaggeration of human uniqueness and minimizing of the intelligence and complexity of other species is the collective human narcissism that places humanity at the center with, as the Bible says, *dominion* over the rest of Creation. Is anthropocentrism not an inextricable element of humanism? Can one envisage a post-anthropocentric humanism capable of meaningfully addressing anthropogenic climate disruption in what is increasingly recognized as the Anthropocene, the likely site of the coming sixth mass extinction (Kolbert, 2013; Carveth, 2015b, 2015c)? Durkin (2014) writes that "by his last work, *To Have or to Be*, he [Fromm] is clear on the need for a relationship of balance and respect with nonhuman nature" (p. 210). If so, this came late and does not exempt the main body of his work from the charge that Durkin rejects: that it reflects "a vainglorious speciesism" (p. 210).

Following Marx, Fromm located human nature, our "species-being," in *productive activity*. Herein lies the existentialist element in both Marx's and Fromm's thought: the capacity of human beings for creative realization of their "projects"—their freely chosen, future-oriented goals or ends. Yet it is unrestrained, Promethean activity, industry and "growth" in both capitalist and "socialist" forms, that has and is destroying our ecosystems and, hence, ourselves. It is true, as Durkin (2014) points out, that:

> In all the influences Fromm draws upon, a central stress is laid on achieving greater awareness, becoming open and responsive and on the need to experience oneself in the act of being, not in having, preserving, coveting, using.... Common to all, then, is the goal of overcoming greed, narcissism, and egoism....
>
> (p. 186)

Yet to my mind Fromm's equation of mental health with *productive* activity exists in tension with his late groping toward the values of *being*. It is true that in his later years Fromm began to distinguish *being* from *having*—but notably not from *doing*. Given the centrality of productive activity in Fromm's very definition of human nature and his devaluation of passivity, I was not surprised to learn from Friedman (2013) of his hyperactive personal style (hence, Friedman's title, not *The Life* but *The Lives of Erich Fromm*).

Like Freud, Fromm was too sophisticated a thinker to simply equate masculine with activity and feminine with passivity. Unfortunately, Fromm chose not to substitute terms like "humanity" or "human" for the generic "man" used so frequently in his texts even after most scholars had become alert to gender issues. While as Kellner (n.d.) points out, Fromm's early essays on Bachofen's theory of matriarchy "contain some provocative perspectives on the question of women's liberation" and celebrate matricentric over patricentric values, his major postwar texts "either lack a discussion of gender or reproduce cultural commonplaces on the differences between men and women." The values of nurturance, care and responsibility toward the other (unnecessarily gendered as "matricentric") might have mitigated the destructiveness arising from an unbalanced embrace of the values of individuation, activity and achievement (unnecessarily gendered as "patricentric"). Our obsession with *doing* over *being* has contributed to our malaise, even perhaps to our demise. While it might have been possible for us to learn from indigenous cultures to see ourselves as *part of* rather than *apart from* nature, we chose instead to destroy them and it. Fromm offers an insightful critique of narcissism in favor of an ethic of love and concern for the other, but seldom extends such concern to Mother Nature, thus, manifesting the collective narcissism that is anthropocentrism. In its stress upon separation and individuation from "regressive" and "primitive" symbiosis with nature and community, Fromm's radical humanism, while insightfully identifying and criticizing many aspects of our cultural pathology, at the same time reflects and fails to transcend it. As Ingleby (1991) argued, Fromm's humanistic psychoanalysis "remains firmly rooted in the suspicious attitude to nature, the body, and woman, which characterizes modernism" (p. l).

Conclusion

Despite such limitations, Fromm nevertheless, has much to offer contemporary psychosocial studies both theoretically and clinically. His qualified essentialism and Neo-Marxist existential humanism offer an *Aufhebung,* an abolition, preservation and transcendence (Kaufmann, 1966, p. 144) of the polarities nature and nurture, of both biologistic essentialism and extreme social constructivism and relativism. While not as well-known as his work in social and psychoanalytic theory, Fromm offered important contributions to clinical theory, seeking to counterbalance the remote, pseudo-objective and at times authoritarian stance of the classical Freudians with his egalitarian, personalistic and humane clinical values (Buechler, 2016). His efforts to integrate Marx and Freud can helpfully contribute to healing what has recently been called "the unhappy divorce between sociology and psychoanalysis" (Chancer & Andrews, 2014). Although he conceives human love more as a solution to the existential anxiety and alienation arising from our separation from nature than as rooted in the innate needs for attachment we share with our primate cousins, his existential revision of psychoanalytic characterology has much to offer—provided the healthy orientation is redefined in terms of one of Fromm's own most prominent personal characteristics: a *caring* orientation to life.

Postscript
Dialectical thinking

"Goddess, please tell me this, and speak the truth—
is there some way I can get safely through,
past murderous Charybdis, and protect
me and my crew when Scylla moves to strike."

(Homer, n.d., Book Twelve)

Among the central themes characterizing these critical psychosocial studies the first concerns my distinction between conscience and the superego and my proposal that we reverse Freud's (1923) regrettable decision to fold five mental structures into three, thus, occluding our capacity to study the full range of conflicts, fifteen to be exact, within and among id, ego, superego, ego-ideal and conscience. Related to my advancing conscience as a separate structure and function from the superego is my claim that psychoanalysis is a fundamentally ethical enterprise, in no way a "value-free," but rather a "value-infused" "science," a discipline somehow transcending the division between *verstehen* and *erklären*, interpretive (hermeneutic) and causal explanation, *Geisteswissenschaft* and *Naturwissenschaft* (Dilthey, 1961).

Apart from a few exceptions, such as Erich Fromm, psychoanalysts have refused to preach what they practice, bending themselves out of shape to disguise under the camouflage of "health" the fact that Freud possessed "the mind of a moralist" (Rieff, 1959) and psychoanalysis is a moral enterprise from beginning to end. But just as he failed to distinguish persecutory from reparative guilt, so Freud failed to distinguish the superego from the conscience and the two fundamentally different types of morality governing each. The superego is merely normative, reflecting the often immoral values of particular societies, while the conscience manifests a universal value-orientation grounded in our mammalian and primate heritage and our universal experience as helpless nurslings responded to well or poorly by primary carers. Here lie the roots of both our caring and our carelessness. While it is not our job to enforce or advocate the normative (we must strive not to be "superego-ish" with patients), as therapists we are called to be carers and, hence, we must often carry the conscience in the treatment until those under our care become capable of assuming this responsibility themselves. In this light, I advocate more explicit attention to assessment of conscience (not superego) in the selection of candidates for training and of training and supervising analysts. More generally, with respect to the way we organize and manage our psychoanalytic institutions, we need to move away from the essentially paranoid-schizoid, sado-masochistic, authoritarian and secretive forms of organization established by Freud toward more conscientious, reparative and democratic forms.

Another theme pervading my work concerns the kind of comparative studies that seek to bring the different paradigms and traditions of psychosocial thought, research and therapeutic practice into mutually respectful dialogue so that we can compare and contrast related concepts, discovering parallels as well as differences within the "confusion of tongues" characteristic of the field. We need to break out of the "silos" in which Freudians only speak with Freudians, Kleinians with Kleinians, Jungians with Jungians, Lacanians with Lacanians, etc. Without blurring the real differences among these perspectives there are often substantial and interesting parallels and convergences as well. Both Lacan and Kohut are concerned with states of fragmentation and with reintegration of what has come undone, however differently they conceive this therapeutic task. Despite their differences with respect to the centrality of aggression in mental life, Klein and Kohut both conceive the therapeutic task, rightly or wrongly, as "transmuting internalization" and, for Klein, identification with a whole good internal object. Despite appearances there are important parallels between Winnicott's false self and Lacan's specular ego, and between the former's true self and the latter's barred subject that emerges through "acceptance of castration." We must overcome the taboo against speaking of the paranoid-schizoid and depressive positions unless we are Kleinian, of the selfobject transferences unless we are Kohutian, or of the Imaginary, Symbolic and Real unless we are Lacanian. In so saying, I am in no way advocating a theoretical *bricolage*, the sort of conceptual "stew" characteristic of "eclecticism" in the worst sense. On the contrary, I am advocating careful conceptual clarification, comparisons and contrasts that should make possible both genuine integration and clearer recognition of real disagreements. Admittedly, this is a daunting task. It is difficult enough to master one paradigm let alone several in order to make such comparative work feasible. But I see no alternative if we are to transcend the situation where having one important piece of the puzzle we pretend we have the whole.

Finally, running like a red thread through my work is my stress on the need to dialectically deconstruct the privileging of one pole of a binary opposition over the other and the need to strive toward the synthesis that negates and yet preserves and elevates both. Although the Kierkegaardian *either/or* legitimately complements the Hegelian *both/and*, Hegel is ultimately victorious in that on the level of the *Aufheben*, the higher-level synthesis that abolishes, preserves and elevates, we find a place for both *either/or* and *both/and* thinking. Sometimes we face an inescapable *either/or*: are human drives or motives grounded in a somatic source, as Freud believed or are they not? Aside from a few organically-based needs, such as those to eat, urinate and defecate, the vast range of human motives, like human sexuality, do not "bubble up" from the body but "trickle down" from the symbolling and meaning-making mind. While there are temperamental differences observable in newborns, if by aggression we mean anger and destructive wishes, these clearly arise from frustration and failures of positive containment, no matter how much they may become crystallized as elements of character.

But sometimes *both/and* thinking is appropriate and necessary. People suffer from both conflicts and deficits. Failure of provision of selfobject function produces rage, splitting, projection and paranoia. Both Kohut and Klein are essential in these cases. Ultimately the rage, splitting, projection, etc., need to be analyzed, but for this to be possible sometimes long periods of non-interpretive provision of selfobject function, mirroring and empathic attunement are essential. Psychoanalytic therapy entails work on both the level of the Imaginary and the Symbolic, involving both illusioning and disillusioning technique, "maternal" and "paternal" function. Tragic Man turns out to be guilty and Guilty Man's wrongdoing has tragic roots. Rejection of the supernaturalism that defines religion need not preclude adherence to the Judeo-Christian anthropology, Christian ethics and metaphors and central biblical insight regarding human existence. Both the complementary and concordant countertransferences are informative when conscious and problematic when not. Our mortal existence is a blessing as well as a curse. Pathology takes the form of excessive linking as well as excessive separating. There is good as well as bad in Ps and bad as well as good in D and, hence, we need to strive toward PsD. Splitting can be adaptive as well as maladaptive. We need to evolve a theory of human nature that is neither over- nor under-socialized, irreducible to the categories of nature and nurture or their combination. Transcending both one-sided determinism and excessive voluntarism is Erich Fromm's humanistic existentialism and qualified essentialism.

The identification of the binary oppositions characterizing any discourse and the refusal to privilege thesis over antithesis or *vice versa* is central to both dialectical and deconstructive method in both theoretical and clinical work. To a considerable extent it is a defining feature of Freudian thought. Freud's (1920) apparent duality of *Eros vs. Thanatos* transcends dualism through the concepts of *fusion* and *defusion* of the drives. Only in regressed borderline and psychotic states do we find radically defused libido and aggression, the all-good and the all-bad, unmodulated love and hate. For Freud, as for Klein, mental growth requires transcending totalized links and splits, overcoming the "purified pleasure ego" (Freud, 1915a) in which the self is all-good and the other all-bad, or its opposite (a "purified unpleasure ego") in which the other is all-good and the self all-bad. Freud's central idea of the symptom, the slip and the dream—and then all human productions—as "compromise-formations" (compounds, alloys or blends) embodies the idea of a synthesis, a "sublation," irreducible to the opposing forces that it negates, preserves and transcends. Here lies Freud's notion of "sublimation": while the symptom represents a problematic and often maladaptive synthesis, sublimation represents a far more creative version of the same phenomenon. I call it creative rather than adaptive for such creativity often transcends and represents a challenge to established ways and values.

Dialectical thinking is evolutionary thinking. Freud and Erikson describe psychic development as a process of *epigenesis*. At each phase there is a conflict, which results in fixation (stasis), regression (to an earlier stage), or progression toward a higher stage or level upon which conflict once again emerges. Evolutionary progress is made possible by substitution. As Sagan (1974) pointed out, cannibalism (oral devouring) gave way to head-hunting (anal collecting), head-hunting to slavery (phallic domination), and slavery (though still not eradicated) to class oppression (wage slavery). It is far from clear if and how we will overcome the latter. What less harmful substitutes (scapegoats) can we find onto which to displace our aggression? Many animals are already extinct and the natural world severely wounded in what is increasingly recognized as the Anthropocene, the era of what appears to be the coming sixth extinction. As Sagan (2001) understood, if there is historical progression there is certainly also regression: every step forward is followed by backlash: Lyndon Johnson's program for a "Great Society" and his "War on Poverty" stalled due to the Vietnam War. This was followed by the emergence of neoliberal market fundamentalism, globalization and outrageously high levels of economic inequality. Today we witness yet another instance in which capitalism in crisis produces one or another form of fascism. Thinking dialectically, Žižek (2017) is hopeful that destruction of the neoliberal elite consensus will stimulate the Left to reorganize and mobilize effectively for socialism. If this is to happen at all, it better happen quickly as our ecosystems are on their death bed.

The psychological foundation for what on the social level is socialism is conscience. Democratic socialism is the sociopolitical manifestation of conscience. It is opposed by reactionary forces analogous to the superego. It is important to distinguish the forces of love from the forces of hate. Whatever else we may think about Lacanian theory and the central role it gave to the Law of the Father, to "paternal" rather than "maternal" function, it accurately diagnosed the culturally conformist nature of Freudian ego psychology and its bias toward social adaptation as distinct from social change. Freud blurred the distinction between conscience and the superego and his followers in ego psychology are disinclined to focus upon the difference, reluctant to critique the superego, far more inclined to defend it as a needed authority or enforcer, while underestimating the bite of conscience. There can be no doubt that both superego and conscience perform needed functions and require aggression to do so, including aggression on the part of conscience in resistance to an immoral superego.

If in seeking to manage our aggression we encounter a shortage of scapegoats onto whom to displace it, we may be forced to abandon the scapegoating mechanism altogether (Girard, 1989)—that is, instead of displacing our aggression onto others, nature or ourselves, we may have to become fully conscious of it and its grounds and, finally, learn how to both moderate it by dispelling some of its irrational foundations and to manage it constructively—that is, to acquire self-control and even to accomplish positive personality change, becoming less hateful, more loving. Psychoanalysis can assist in this by helping us recognize that whatever real injuries, deprivations and frustrations fuel our aggression, it is inflamed by irrational phantasies of various sorts, and that our thinking is distorted by defensive processes such as splitting, projection, repression, displacement and turning against the self. Our compulsion to repeat is fed by a range of psychological forces of which we need to become aware, including our unconscious need for punishment for our real and imagined crimes and misdemeanors. We need to become conscious of our hate without having to act it out, learning instead how to channel it in prosocial rather than antisocial directions. We need to become conscious of our guilt without totalizing it and unconsciously seeking to destroy ourselves or others, learning instead to make creative reparation.

Our emergence as "the freak of nature" (Fromm, 1947), both rooted in yet transcending the biosphere due to our uniquely human symbolic consciousness, has blessed and burdened us with freedom and self-awareness, generating our anxiety, our destructiveness and our creativity. Lacking instinctual regulation we are free to imagine future states and to rationally plan their realization, but our planning has unintended consequences that, over time, threaten to destroy us. Inseparable from our rationality is the individual and collective irrationality that constitutes our psychopathology and our destructiveness toward ourselves, others and the ecosystems we depend on. Only the rational animal can go mad. Naturally dysregulated, we lurch, like drunkards, from one extreme to the other until, learning from experience, we occasionally, like Odysseus, manage to sail between the monsters into the harbor, but we never get to stay there very long. Given the dire situation facing us, do we have time for psychoanalysis? Without it can we hope to do more than repeat the very mistakes that got us into this mess in the first place? In the face of the plague (Camus, 1947) what else is a healer to do, but like the musicians on the Titanic, carry on? Even if, *sub specie aeternitatis*, our efforts appear futile, we need not succumb to the despair of Hardy's (1928) dark poem *Before Life and After* ("Ere nescience shall be reaffirmed/How long, how long?"), for we are free to conclude instead with Camus (1942, p. 91): "The struggle itself toward the heights is enough to fill a man's heart."

References

Adorno, T.W. (1966). *Negative Dialectics.* Trans. E.B. Ashton. New York: Continuum.

Adorno, T.W. (1968). Sociology and psychology—II. *New Left Review* 47: 79–97.

Aichhorn, A. (1935). *Wayward Youth.* New York: Viking Press.

Ainsworth, M., Blehar, M., Waters, E., & Wall, S. (1978). *Patterns of Attachment.* Hilldale, NJ: Lawrence Erlbaum Associates.

Akhtar, S. (Ed.). (2013). *Guilt: Origins, Manifestations, and Management.* Margaret S. Mahler Series. New York: Jason Aronson.

Alexander, F. (1925). A metapsychological description of the process of cure. *International Journal of Psycho-Analysis* 6: 13–34.

Alexander, F., & French, D. (1946). *Psychoanalytic Therapy: Principles and Applications.* New York: The Ronald Press.

Alford, C.F. (2001). *Melanie Klein and Critical Social Theory.* New Haven: Yale University Press.

Altizer, T.J.J. (1970). *The Descent Into Hell: A Study of the Radical Reversal of the Christian Consciousness.* Philadelphia & New York: J.B. Lippincott.

Arlow, J. (1982). Problems of the superego concept. *Psychoanalytic Study of the Child,* 37: 229–244.

Atwood, G.E., & Stolorow, R.D. (1984a). *Structures of Subjectivity: Explorations in Psychoanalytic Phenomenology.* Hillsdale, NJ: The Analytic Press.

Atwood, G.E., & Stolorow, R.D. (Eds.). (1984b). *Faces in a Cloud: Intersubjectivity in Personality Theory* (2nd ed.). Northvale, NJ: Aronson, 1994.

Bacal, H.A. (1985). Optimal responsiveness and the therapeutic process. In A. Goldberg (Ed.), *Progress in Self Psychology.* New York: Guilford, 1985, pp. 202–226.

Bacal, H.A., & Newman, K.M. (1990). *Theories of Object Relations: Bridges to Self Psychology.* New York: Columbia University Press.

References

Bachofen, J.J. (1861). *Das Mutterrecht: eine Untersuchung über die Gynaikokratie der alten Welt nach ihrer religiösen und rechtlichen Natur.* Stuttgart: Verlag von Krais und Hoffmann.

Balint, M. (1958). Sandor Ferenczi's Last Years. *International Journal of Psycho-Analysis* 39: 68.

Balint, M. (1968). *The Basic Fault: Therapeutic Aspects of Regression.* New York: Brunner/Mazel.

Barnett, B. (2007). *You Ought To! A Psychoanalytic Study of the Superego and Conscience.* Psychoanalytic Ideas Series, I. Wise, & P. Williams (Eds.), M. Parsons, (Foreword). London: The Institute of Psychoanalysis and Karnac Books.

Barratt, B. (1984). *Psychic Reality and Psychoanalytic Knowing. Advances in Psychoanalysis: Theory, Research, and Practice*, Vol. 3. Hillsdale, NJ: The Analytic Press.

Barrett, W. (1958). *Irrational Man: A Study in Existential Philosophy.* New York: Doubleday.

Becker, E. (1962). *The Birth and Death of Meaning.* New York: Free Press.

Becker, E. (1973). *The Denial of Death.* New York: The Free Press.

Beebe, B., & Lachmann, F. (1988). Mother-infant mutual influence and precursors of psychic structure. In A. Goldberg (Ed.). *Frontiers in Self Psychology: Progr. Self Psychol.*, Vol. 3, Hillsdale, NJ: The Analytic Press, pp. 3–25.

Beit-Hallahmi, B. (2015). *Psychological Perspectives on Religion and Religiosity.* London & New York: Routledge.

Benton, T. (2001). Why are sociologists naturephobes? In J. Lopez, & G. Porter (Eds.). *After Postmodernism.* London: Athlone Press.

Berger, P. (1963). *Invitation to Sociology.* New York: Doubleday.

Berger, P. (1967). *The Sacred Canopy: Elements of a Sociological Theory of Religion.* New York: Doubleday.

Berger, P., & Luckmann, T. (1966). *The Social Construction of Reality.* New York: Doubleday.

Bettelheim, B. (1982). Freud and the soul. *The New Yorker*, March 1, 1982.

Billig, M. (2006). Lacan's misuse of psychology: evidence, rhetoric and the mirror stage. *Theory, Culture & Society* 23, 4: 1–26. DOI: 10.1177/02632764 06066367

Bion, W. (1957). Differentiation of the psychotic from the non-psychotic personalities. *International Journal of Psychoanalysis* 38: 206–275.

Bion, W.R. (1959). Attacks on Linking. *International Journal of Psycho-Analysis* 40: 308–315.

Bion, W.R. (1962a). The psycho-analytic study of thinking. *International Journal of Psycho-Analysis* 43: 306–310.

Bion, W.R. (1962b). *Learning From Experience.* London: Heinemann.

Bion, W.R. (1963). *Elements of Psychoanalysis*. London: Maresfield Library; Karnac Books (1984).

Bion, W.R. (1970). *Attention and Interpretation*. London: Tavistock.

Bion W.R. (1992). *Cogitations*. Bion, F., Ed. London: Karnac Books.

Bloom, P. (2010). The moral life of babies. *New York Times Magazine*. May 3, 2010.

Bloom, P. (2013). *Just Babies: The Origins of Good and Evil*. New York: Crown.

Bonhoeffer, D. (1953). *Letters and Papers from Prison*. London: Collins.

The Book of Common Prayer. (1662). *The Order for the Administration of the Lord's Supper, Or Holy Communion*. Accessed June 18, 2017. www.justus.anglican.org/resources/bcp/1662/Orig_manuscript/hc.htm

Borossa, J., Bronstein, C., & Pajaczkowska, C. (Eds.). (2015). *The New Klein-Lacan Dialogues*. London: Karnac.

Bowen, E.S. [Laura Bohannan]. (1964). *Return to Laughter: An Anthropological Novel*. Foreword by David Riesman. New York: Doubleday Anchor Books.

Bowlby, J. (1969–1980). *Attachment and Loss*, 3 vols. Harmondsworth, Middlesex: Penguin.

Bowlby, J., Figlio, K., & Young, R.M. (1986). An interview with John Bowlby on the origins and reception of his work. *Free Associations* 1: 36–64.

Brandchaft, B. (1993). To free the spirit from its cell. The 1991 Kohut Memorial Lecture delivered to the 14th Annual Conference on the Psychology of the Self. In A. Goldberg (Ed.), *The Widening Scope of Self Psychology: Progr. Self Psychol.*, Vol. 9, Hillsdale, NJ: The Analytic Press, pp. 209–230.

Braune, J. (2014). *Erich Fromm's Revolutionary Hope: Prophetic Messianism as the Critical Theory of the Future*. Rotterdam: Sense Publishers.

Brenner, C. (1982). *The Mind in Conflict*. New York: International University Press.

Britton, R. (1989). The missing link: parental sexuality in the Oedipus Complex. In R. Britton, M. Feldman, & E. O'Shaughnessy (Eds.), *The Oedipus Complex Today: Clinical Implications*. London: Karnac, 1989, chapter two, pp. 83–101.

Britton, R. (1998). Before and after the depressive position: Ps(n)(D(n)(Ps(n+1)). In R. Britton, *Belief and Imagination: Explorations in Psychoanalysis*. London & New York: Routledge, chapter six, pp. 69–81.

Britton, R. (2003). *Sex, Death, and the Superego: Experiences in Psychoanalysis*. London: Karnac.

Britton, R. (2004). Narcissistic disorders in clinical practice. *J. Anal. Psychol.*, 49, 4: 477–490.

Brook, A. (2015). *Freud and Brentano*. Unpublished paper delivered at the annual scientific meetings of the Canadian Psychoanalytic Society, Québec City, June, 2015.

Brown, N.O. (1959). *Life Against Death: The Psychoanalytical Meaning of History.* Middletown, Conn.: Wesleyan University Press.

Buber, M. (1937). *I and Thou.* Trans. W. Kaufmann. New York: Scribner's, 1970.

Buber, M. (1938). What is man? In R.G. Smith (trans.), *Between Man and Man, Section V.* New York: Collins, pp. 148–240.

Buber, M. (1952). *The Eclipse of God.* New York: Harper & Row.

Buber, M. (1965). Guilt and guilt-feelings. In M. Friedman (Trans. & Ed.), *The Knowledge of Man: Selected Essays.* New York: Harper & Row, chapter 6, pp. 121–148.

Buechler, S. (2016). *Choosing Life: Fromm's Clinical Values.* Unpublished paper presented at a conference concerning "Erich Fromm's Impact on Psychoanalytic Thinking and Practice," NPAP (National Psychological Association for Psychoanalysis), New York, April 2nd, 2016. Forthcoming with other papers from this conference in the *Psychoanalytic Review* (2017).

Bultmann, R. (1958). *Jesus Christ and Mythology.* New York: Scribner's.

Burke, K. (1939). Freud and the analysis of poetry (pp. 73–94). In P. Meisel (Ed.), *Freud: A Collection Critical Essays.* Englewood Cliffs, NJ: Prentice-Hall, 1981.

Burston, D. (1991). *The Legacy of Erich Fromm.* Cambridge, MA: Harvard University Press.

Burston, D. (2007). *Erik Erikson and the American Psyche: Ego, Ethics, and Evolution.* Lanham, Maryland & Toronto: Jason Aronson.

Burston, D. (2017). Pharisees, Freudians and the fetishism of the text: Catholic triumphalism in Jacques Lacan. *Psychother. Politics Int.* 2017: e1400. https://doi.org/10.1002/ppi.1400

Calhoun, C. (Ed.). (2002). Sapir-Whorf hypothesis. *Dictionary of the Social Sciences.* New York: Oxford University Press.

Camus, A. (1942). *The Myth of Sisyphus and Other Essays.* Trans. J. O'Brien. New York: Vintage Books, 1991. Translation originally published by Alfred A. Knopf, 1955. Originally published in France *as Le Mythe de Sisyphe* by Librairie Gallimard, 1942.

Camus, A. (1947). *The Plague.* Trans. S. Gilbert. London: Penguin, 1960.

Carveth, D.L. (1984a). Psychoanalysis and social theory. *Psychoanalysis and Contemporary Thought* 7: 43–98.

Carveth, D.L. (1984b). The analyst's metaphors: a deconstructionist perspective. *Psychoanalysis & Contemporary Thought* 7, 4: 491–560.

Carveth, D.L. (1987). The epistemological foundations of psychoanalysis: a deconstructionist view of the controversy. *Philosophy of the Social Sciences* 17, 1: 97–115.

Carveth, D.L. (1993). The borderline dilemma in Paris, Texas: psychoanalytic perspectives on Sam Shepard. *Canadian Journal of Psychoanalysis/Revue canadienne de psychanalyse* 1: 19–46.

Carveth, D.L. (1994). Dark epiphany: the encounter with finitude or the discovery of the object in the body. *Psychoanalysis & Contemporary Thought* 17, 2: 215–250.

Carveth, D.L. (1996). Psychoanalytic conceptions of the passions. In J. O'Neill (Ed.), *Freud and the Passions*, University Park: Penn State Press.

Carveth, D.L. (2010). How today may we distinguish healthy sexuality from "perversion"? *Canadian Journal of Psychoanalysis/Revue canadienne de psychanalyse* 18, 2 (Fall 2010): 296–305.

Carveth, D.L. (2012b). Letter to the Editor. *Canadian Journal of Psychoanalysis* 20: 329–330.

Carveth, D.L. (2013). *The Still Small Voice: Psychoanalytic Reflections on Guilt and Conscience.* London: Karnac.

Carveth, D.L. (2015a). The immoral superego: conscience as the fourth element in the structural theory of the mind. *Canadian Journal of Psychoanalysis* 23, 1 (Spring, 2015): 206–223.

Carveth, D.L. (2015b). Review of *The Sixth Extinction: An Unnatural History* by Elizabeth Kolbert. *Journal of Psychohistory* 42, 3 (Winter 2015): 257–260.

Carveth, D.L. (2015c). Fromm resurrected. Review of *The Radical Humanism of Erich Fromm* by K. Durkin. *Journal of Psychohistory* 43, 2 (Fall, 2015): 146–155: *Canadian Journal of Psychoanalysis* 24 (2016): 145–154.

Carveth, D.L. (2016a). Why we should stop conflating the superego with the conscience. *Psychoanalysis, Culture & Society*. First online April 28, 2016: doi:10.1057/pcs.2016.13

Carveth, D.L. (2016b). *Expanding structural theory.* Address to the Iranian Congress of Psychoanalysis and Dynamic Psychotherapy, Tehran, Iran, November, 2016.

Carveth, D.L. (2016c). Review of *Guilt: Origins, Manifestations, and Management.* S. Akhtar (Ed.). *Canadian Journal of Psychoanalysis/Revue canadienne de psychanalyse* 24, 1 (Spring, 2016): 120–127.

Carveth, D.L. (2016d). Review of *Psychological Perspectives on Religion and Religiosity* by B. Beit-Hallahmi. London & New York: Routledge, 2015. *Journal of Psychohistory* (Fall, 2016).

Carveth, D.L., & Carveth, J.H. (2003). Fugitives from guilt: postmodern demoralization and the new Hysterias. *American Imago* 60, 4 (Winter 2003): 445–480.

Casey, E.S., & Woody, J.M. (1983). Hegel, Heidegger, Lacan: the dialectic of desire. In J.H. Smith, & W. Kerrigan (Eds.), *Interpreting Lacan, Psychiatry and the Humanities*, Vol. 6. New Haven & London: Yale University Press.

Chancer, L., & Andrews, J. (Eds.). (2014). *The Unhappy Divorce of Sociology and Psychoanalysis: Diverse Perspectives on the Psychosocial.* New York: Palgrave Macmillan.

Chasseguet-Smirgel, J. (1984). *Creativity and Perversion.* New York: Norton.

Chesterton, G.K. (1927). *The Secret of Father Brown.* In G.K. Chesterton, *The Complete Father Brown.* New York: Penguin, 1987, pp. 461–584.

Chomsky, N. (1957). *Syntactic Structures.* The Hague: Mouton.

Chomsky, N., & Foucault, M. (1971). *Chomsky vs. Foucault: A Debate on Human Nature.* New York: New Press, 2006.

Clement, C. (1983). *The Lives and Legends of Jacques Lacan.* Trans. A. Goldhammer. New York: Columbia University Press.

Coen, S. (2013). Guilt in the therapist and its impact on treatment. In S. Akhtar, (Ed.), *Guilt: Origins, Manifestations and Management.* Lanham, MD: Aronson, 2013, pp. 69–82.

Crews, F. (2017). *The Making of an Illusion.* New York: Holt.

Culler, J. (1982). *On Deconstruction: Theory and Criticism After Structuralism.* Ithaca: Cornell University Press.

Danto, E. (2005). *Freud's Free Clinics: Psychoanalysis and Social Justice, 1918–1938.* New York: Columbia University Press.

Davis, C., Pound, M., & Crockett, C. (Eds.). (2014). *Theology After Lacan: The Passion for the Real.* Eugene, OR: Wipf and Stock (Cascade Books).

De Certeau, M. (2006) *Heterologies. Discourse on the Other.* Trans. B. Massumi. *Theory and History of Literature,* Volume 17. (Minneapolis, London: University of Minnesota Press).

Derrida, J. (1976). *Of Grammatology.* Trans. G.C. Spivak. Baltimore: Johns Hopkins University Press.

de Unamuno. M. (1956). *Saint Emmanuel the Good, Martyr.* In translated and with an introduction by A. Kerrigan, *Abel Sanchez and Other Stories.* Chicago: Gateway.

Deutsch, H. (1926). Okkulte Vorgnge whrend der Psychoanalyse. *Imago*, XII: 418–433.

De Waal, F. (1997). *Good Natured: The Origins of Right and Wrong in Humans and Other Animals.* Cambridge, MA: Harvard University Press.

De Waal, F. (2009). *The Age of Empathy: Nature's Lessons for a Kinder Society.* New York: Harmony Books.

De Waal, F. (2011). Moral behavior in animals. TED talk, November, 2011. www.ted.com/talks/frans_de_waal_do_animals_have_morals#t-319556

Dilthey, W. (1961). *Meaning in History.* H.P. Rickman (Ed.), London: Allen & Unwin.

Dorpat, T.L. (1987). A new look at denial and defense. In *Annu. Psychoanal.*, 15: 23–47. Madison, CT: International Universities Press.

Dostoevsky, F. (1880). *The Brothers Karamazov.* Translated and with an introduction by D. McDuff. New York: Penguin, 1993.

Dunlap, A. (2014). *Lacan and Religion.* Durham, UK: Acumen.

Durkin, K. (2014). *The Radical Humanism of Erich Fromm.* New York: Palgrave Macmillan.

Eagle, M. (1984). *Recent Developments in Psychoanalysis: A Critical Evaluation.* New York: McGraw-Hill.

Eagle, M. (2011). *From Classical to Contemporary Psychoanalysis: A Critique and Integration.* New York: Routledge.

Edgcumbe, R. (2000). *Anna Freud: A View of Development, Disturbance and Therapeutic Techniques.* London: Routledge.

Eissler, K.R. (1953). The effect of the structure of the ego on psychoanalytic technique. *J. Amer. Psychoanal. Assn.*, 1: 104–143.

Eliot, T.S. (1944). *Four Quartets.* London: Faber & Faber.

Eliot, T.S. (1950). *The Cocktail Party.* London: Faber & Faber.

Epstein, L., & Feiner, A.H. (1979). Countertransference: The therapist's contribution to treatment—an overview. *Contemp. Psychoanal.*, 15: 489–513.

Epstein, M. (1995). *Thoughts Without a Thinker: Psychotherapy From a Buddhist Perspective.* New York: Basic Books.

Erikson, E. (1950). *Childhood and Society.* Revised and enlarged edition. New York: W.W. Norton, 1963.

Erikson, E. (1959). Identity and the life cycle: selected papers. *Psychological Issues Monogr.* 1. New York: International Universities Press.

Erikson, E. (1968). The life cycle: epigenesis of identity. *Identity, Youth and Crisis.* New York: Norton, chapter three, pp. 91–141.

Fairbairn, W.R.D. (1952). *Psychoanalytic Studies of the Personality.* London: Routledge & Kegan Paul.

Ferenczi, S. (1928 [1927]). The elasticity of psycho-analytic technique (pp. 87–101). In Balint, M. (Ed.), E. Mosbacher, et al. (Trans.), Thompson, C. (Intro.), *Final Contributions to the Problems and Methods of Psychoanalysis.* New York: Basic Books, 1955.

Fernando, J. (2000). The borrowed sense of guilt. *International Journal of Psychoanalysis* 81: 499–512.

Fernando, J. (2008). *The Processes of Defense: Trauma, Drives, and Reality—A New Synthesis.* New York: Aronson.

Feuer, L. (1969). *The Conflict of Generations: The Character and Significance of Student Movements.* New York: Basic Books.

Fink, B. (1995a). Science and psychoanalysis. In R. Feldstein, B. Fink, & M. Janus (Eds.). (1995), *Reading Seminar XI: Lacan's Four Fundamental Concepts of Psychoanalysis.* Albany: State University of New York Press, pp. 55–64.

Fink, B. (1995b). *The Lacanian Subject: Between Language and Juissance.* Princeton, NJ: Princeton University Press.

Fisher, H. (1994). *The Anatomy of Love.* New York: Random House.

Fliess, R. (1942). The metapsychology of the analyst. *Psychoanal Q.,* 11: 211–227.

Fonagy, P., & Target, M. (2003). *Psychoanalytic Theories: Perspectives from Developmental Psychopathology.* New York: Brunner-Routledge.

Foucault, M. (1969). *The Archaeology of Knowledge.* London: Tavistock, 1972.

Frattaroli, E. (2013). Reflections on the absence of morality in psychoanalytic theory and therapy. In S. Akhtar (Ed.), *Guilt: Origins, Manifestations and Management.* Lanham, MD: Aronson, 2013, pp. 83–110.

Freud, A. (1936). *The Ego and the Mechanisms of Defence.* New York: International Universities Press, 1966.

Freud, S. (1895). Breuer, J., & Freud, S. (1893–1895). Studies on hysteria. *S.E.,* 2.

Freud, S. (1900). The interpretation of dreams. *S.E.,* 4 & 5.

Freud, S. (1901). The psychopathology of everyday life. *S.E.,* 6.

Freud, S. (1905a). Jokes and their relation to the unconscious. *S.E.,* 8.

Freud, S. (1905b). Three essays on the theory of sexuality. *S.E.,* 7.

Freud, S. (1905c). Fragment of an analysis of a case of hysteria (1905 [1901]). *S.E.,* 7: 1–122.

Freud, S. (1908). "Civilized" Sexual Morality and Modern Nervous Illness. *S.E.,* 9 (1906–1908): 177–204.

Freud, S. (1909). Analysis of a phobia in a five-year-old boy. *S.E.*

Freud, S. (1912–1913). Totem and taboo: some points of agreement between the mental lives of savages and neurotics. *S.E.,* 13: vii–162. London: Hogarth.

Freud, S. (1914). On narcissism: an introduction. *S.E.,* 14.

Freud, S. (1915a). Instincts and their vicissitudes. *S.E.,* 14: 109–140.

Freud, S. (1915b). Observations on transference love (Further recommendations on the technique of psycho-analysis III). *S.E.,* 12: 157–171.

Freud, S. (1916). Some character-types met with in psycho-analytic work. *S.E.,* 14: 309–333.

Freud, S. (1920). Beyond the pleasure principle. *S.E.,* 18: 1–64.

Freud, S. (1923). The ego and the id. *S.E.,* 19: 1–66.

Freud, S. (1924). The dissolution of the Oedipus complex. *S.E.,* 19.

Freud, S. (1925). Some psychical consequences of the anatomical distinction between the sexes. *S.E.,* 19.

Freud, S. (1926). Inhibitions, symptoms and anxiety. *S.E.,* 20: 77–175.

Freud, S. (1927). The future of an illusion. *S.E.,* 21: 3–56.

Freud, S. (1930). Civilization and its discontents. *S.E.,* 21: 57–146.

Freud, S. (1933). New introductory lectures on psycho-analysis. *S.E.,* 22: 3–182.

Freud, S. (1935). Foreword to Aichhorn, A., *Wayward Youth.* New York: Viking Press.
Freud, S. (1937). Analysis terminable and interminable. *S.E.*, 23: 209–253.
Freud, S. (1940). An outline of psycho-analysis. *S.E.*, 23: 139–208. London: Hogarth.
Friedman, L. (2013). *The Lives of Erich Fromm: Love's Prophet.* New York: Columbia University Press.
Fromm, E. (1941). *Escape from Freedom.* New York: Holt, Rinehart and Winston.
Fromm, E. (1944). Individual and social origins of neurosis. *American Sociological Review* (Vol. IX, No. 4, August, 1944): 380–384.
Fromm, E. (1947). *Man for Himself: An Inquiry into the Psychology of Ethics.* New York: Rinehart.
Fromm, E. (1950). *Psychoanalysis and Religion.* The Terry Lectures. New Haven: Yale University Press.
Fromm, E. (1951). *The Forgotten Language: An Introduction to the Understanding of Dreams, Fairy Tales and Myths.* New York: Rinehart.
Fromm, E. (1955a). The human implications of instinctivistic "radicalism": a reply to Herbert Marcuse. *Dissent*, 2: 342–349.
Fromm, E. (1955b). *The Sane Society.* London & New York: Holt, Rinehart & Winston, Fawcett Books.
Fromm, E. (1956a). A counter-rebuttal. *Dissent* 3: 81–83.
Fromm, E. (1956b). *The Art of Loving: An Enquiry into the Nature of Love.* New York: Harper.
Fromm, E. (1962). *Beyond the Chains of Illusion: My Encounter with Marx and Freud.* New York: Grove Press.
Fromm, E. (1973). *The Anatomy of Human Destructiveness.* New York: Holt, Rinehart & Winston.
Fromm, E. (1980). *The Greatness and Limitations of Freud's Thought.* New York: New American Library.
Gabbert, M. (2014). *In defense of splitting: progressive politics in the twentieth century.* Unpublished paper presented at the annual meeting of the Association for the Psychoanalysis of Culture and Society, October, 2014.
Gale, J. (n.d.). Lacan and the Benedictines. *European Journal of Psychoanalysis.* Online: www.journal-psychoanalysis.eu/lacan-and-the-benedictines/
Gallop, J. (1985). *Reading Lacan.* Ithaca: Cornell University Press.
Gilligan, C. (1982). *In a Different Voice: Psychological Theory and Women's Development.* Cambridge, Mass.: Harvard University Press.
Girard, R. (1989). *The Scapegoat.* Baltimore, MD: Johns Hopkins University Press.
Gorman, H.E. (2002). Growing Psychoanalysis. *Canadian Journal of Psychoanalysis* 10: 45–69.

Gorman, H.E. (2008). An intention-based definition of psychoanalytic attitude. *Psychoanal. Rev.*, 95: 751–776.

Greenberg, J., & Mitchell, S. (1983). *Object Relations in Psychoanalytic Theory.* Cambridge, MA: Harvard University Press.

Greenberg, J., Koole, S.L., & Pyszczynski, T. (2004). *Handbook of Experimental Existential Psychology.* New York: Guilford Press.

Greenson, R. (1968). Disidentifying from mother: its special importance for the boy. *International Journal of Psycho-Analysis* 49: 370–374.

Grinberg, L. (1962). On a specific aspect of countertransference due to the patient's projective identification. *International Journal of Psychoanalysis* 43: 436–440.

Grinberg, L. (1964). Two kinds of guilt: their relations with normal and pathological aspects of mourning. *International Journal of Psychoanalysis* 45: 366–371.

Grinberg, L. (1979). Countertransference and projective counteridentification. *Contemporary Psychoanalysis* 15: 226–247.

Grosskurth, P. (1991). *The Secret Ring: Freud's Inner Circle and the Politics of Psycho-Analysis.* New York: Addison-Wesley.

Grotstein, J.S. (1996). Comments during discussion following presentation of *Autochthonyversus Alterity: Psychic Reality in Counterpoint* to the Toronto Institute for Contemporary Psychoanalysis, April, 1996.

Grunberger, B. (1979). *Narcissism: Psychoanalytic Essays*, trans. J.S. Diamanti. New York: International Universities Press.

Guntrip, H. (1971). *Psychoanalytic Theory, Therapy and the Self.* New York: Basic Books.

Hanly, C. (1991). *The Problem of Truth in Applied Psychoanalysis.* New York: Guilford.

Hanly, C. (1986). Psychoanalysis and aesthetic theory. *Psychoanal. Q.*, 55: 1–22.

Hardy, T. (1928). Before life and after. In: *Thomas Hardy: The Complete Poems.* New York: Palgrave, 2001.

Hartmann, H. (1939). *Ego Psychology and the Problem of Adaptation.* New York: International Universities Press, 1958.

Hartmann, H. (1960). *Psychoanalysis and Moral Values.* New York: International Universities Press.

Haynal, A. (1989). *Intermezzo:* Ferenczi—biographical notes. In Ed. A. Haynal (Ed.), E. Holder (Trans.), D.N. Stern (Preface), *Controversies in Psychoanalytic Method: From Freud and Ferenczi to Michael Balint.* Washington Square, New York: New York University Press, chapter 3, pp. 35–59.

Hegel, G.W.F. (1807). *Phenomenology of Spirit.* Trans. A.V. Miller. London: Oxford University Press, 1977.

Hegel, G.W.F. (1820–1829). *Hegel's Aesthetics: A Critical Exposition.* Abridged (Ed.). New York: The Classics US, 2013.

Heidegger, M. (1927). *Being and Time.* Trans. J. Macquarrie, & E.S. Robinson. New York: Harper, 1962.

Herberg, W. (1957). Freud, the revisionists and social reality. In B. Nelson (Ed.), *Freud and the 20th Century*, Cleveland and New York: The World Publishing Co., pp. 143–163.

Herrigel, E. (1953). *Zen in the Art of Archery.* New York: Pantheon.

Hillman, J. (1972). *The Myth of Analysis: Three Essays in Archetypal Psychology.* New York: Harper & Row.

Homer. (n.d.). *The Odyssey.* Trans. I. Johnston. Richer Resources Publications. Online: www.richerresourcespublications.com/Books/Classic_Books/Homer/Odyssey/Odyssey-Flipbook.htm

Horkheimer, M. (1947). *Eclipse of Reason.* New York: Oxford University Press.

Hughes, J.M. (2008). *Guilt and Its Vicissitudes: Psychoanalytic Reflections on Morality.* London: Routledge.

Hugo, V. (1862). *Les Misérables.* Trans. I.F. Hapgood, *The Complete Works of Victor Hugo (1802–1885).* Delphi Classics, 2012: www.delphiclassics.com

Hume, D. (1739–1740). *A Treatise of Human Nature: Being an Attempt to introduce the experimental Method of Reasoning into Moral Subjects.* www.gutenberg.org/ebooks/4705

Hume, D. (1748). *An Inquiry Concerning Human Understanding.* www.gutenberg.org/ebooks/9662

Huxley, J. (1943). The uniqueness of man. In J. Huxley, *Man in the Modern World.* New York: Mentor, 1948, chapter 1, pp. 7–28.

Huxley, J. (1947). Introduction. In P.T. de Chardin, *The Phenomenon of Man.* London: Fontana, 1965.

Ingleby, D. (1991). Preface to the second edition of Erich Fromm's (1956). *The Sane Society.* London & New York: Routledge, pp. xvi–lv.

Irigaray, L. (1974). *Speculum de l'autre femme.* Paris: Minuit.

Irigaray, L. (1977). *Ce sexe qui n'en est pas un.* Paris: Minuit.

Jacobson, E. (1964). *The Self and the Object World.* New York: International Universities Press.

Jacobs, M. (1995). *D.W. Winnicott.* London: Sage.

Jacoby, R. (1975). *Social Amnesia: A Critique of Contemporary Psychology from Adler to Laing.* Boston: Beacon.

Jakobson, R., &. Halle, M. (1956). *Fundamentals of Language.* The Hague: Mouton.

Jones, E. (1955). *Sigmund Freud: Life and Work.* Vol. 2, Years of Maturity 1901–1919. London: The Hogarth Press.

Kant, I. (1781–1787). *Critique of Pure Reason.* Trans. M. Weigelt. London: Penguin, 2007.

Kaufmann, W. (1966). *Hegel: A Reinterpretation.* New York: Doubleday Anchor.

Kaufmann, W. (1968). *Nietzsche: Philosopher, Psychologist, AntiChrist.* New York: Vintage.

Keats, J. (1819). *Ode to a Nightingale.* Poetry Foundation. Online: www.poetryfoundation.org/poems-and-poets/poems/detail/44479

Kellner, D. (n.d.). Erich Fromm, feminism and the Frankfurt School: reflections on Patricia Mills' *Woman, Nature, and Psyche.* Retrieved from https://pages.gseis.ucla.edu/faculty/kellner/Illumina%20Folder/kell27.htm

Kernberg, O. (1975). *Borderline Conditions and Pathological Narcissism.* New York: Aronson.

Kernberg, O. (1976). *Object Relations Theory and Clinical Psychoanalysis.* New York: Aronson.

Kernberg, O. (1979). Some implications of object relations theory for psychoanalytic technique. *J. Amer. Psychoanal. Assn.*, 27S: 207–239.

Kernberg, O. (1987). An ego psychology—object relations theory approach to the transference. *Psychoanal. Q.*, 57: 197–221.

Kernberg, O.F. (1991a). Sadomasochism, sexual excitement, and perversion. *J. Amer. Psychoanal. Assn.*, 39: 333–362.

Kernberg, O.F. (1991b). Aggression and love in the relationship of the couple. *J. Amer. Psychoanal. Assn.*, 39: 45–70.

Kernberg, O.F. (1993). The couple's constructive and destructive superego functions. *J. Amer. Psychoanal. Assn.*, 41: 653–677.

Kierkegaard, S. (1843a). *Fear and Trembling.* A. Hannay (Trans. & Intro.). London: Penguin, 1985.

Kierkegaard, S. (1843b). *Either/Or: A Fragment of Life.* London: Penguin, 1992.

Klein, M. (1946). Notes on some schizoid mechanisms. In: *The Writings of Melanie Klein*, Vol. 3. London: Hogarth Press, 1975, pp. 186–198.

Klein, M. (1948). A contribution to the theory of anxiety and guilt. *International Journal of Psycho-Analysis* 29: 114–123.

Klein, M. (1952). The origins of transference. *International Journal of Psychoanalysis* 33: 433–438.

Klein, M. (1957). Envy and gratitude. Chapter 10 in *Envy and Gratitude and Other Works 1946–1963. Int. Psycho-Anal. Lib.*, 104: 1–346. London: The Hogarth Press and the Institute of Psycho-Analysis, 1975.

Klein, M. (1958). On the development of mental functioning. *Int. J. Psycho-Anal.*, 39: 84–90. Chapter 11 in *Envy and Gratitude and Other Works 1946–1963. Int. Psycho-Anal. Lib.*, 104: 1–346. London: The Hogarth Press and the Institute of Psycho-Analysis, 1975.

Klein, M. (1959). Our adult world and its roots in infancy. Chapter 12 in *Envy and Gratitude and Other Works 1946–1963. Int. Psycho-Anal. Lib.*, 104: 1–346. London: The Hogarth Press and the Institute of Psycho-Analysis, 1975.

Kohut, H. (1959). Introspection, empathy and psychoanalysis: An examination of the relationship between mode of observation and theory. In P. Ornstein, (Ed.), *The Search for the Self*. New York: International Universities Press, 1978, pp. 205–232.

Kohut, H. (1971). *The Analysis of the Self*. New York: International Universities Press.

Kohut, H. (1972). Thought on narcissism and narcissistic rage. *Psychoanal. Study Child* 27: 360–400.

Kohut, H. (1978). *The Restoration of the Self*. New York: International Universities Press.

Kohut, H. (1979). The two analyses of Mr. Z. *Int. J. Psycho-Anal.*, 60: 3–27.

Kohut, H. (1984). *How Does Analysis Cure?* A. Goldberg, & P. Stepansky, (Eds.), Chicago: University of Chicago Press.

Kojève, A. (1934–1935). *Introduction to the Reading of Hegel.* Trans. J.H. Nichols, Jr. Ithaca, NY: Cornell University Press, 1969.

Kolbert, E. (2014). *The Sixth Extinction: An Unnatural History.* New York: Henry Holt & Co.

Kris, E. (1935). The psychology of caricature. Reprinted in *Psychoanalytic Explorations in Art.* New York: International Universities Press, 1952.

Kris, E. (1938). Review of Anna Freud's *The Ego and the Mechanisms of Defence. International Journal of Psycho-Analysis* 19: 115–146.

Kris, E. (1956). The personal myth—a problem in psychoanalytic technique. *J. Amer. Psychoanal. Assn.*, 4: 653–681.

Kristeva, J. (1988). In the beginning was love. Language and subject in psychoanalysis. *In the Beginning was Love: Psychoanalysis and Faith (European Perspectives).* Trans. A. Goldhammer. New York: Columbia University Press, chapter one.

Lacan, J. (1960). *Discourse to Catholics.* Published together with *The Triumph of Religion.* Trans. B. Fink. Cambridge, UK: Polity, 1974.

Lacan, J. (1960–1961). Transference. *The Seminar of Jacques Lacan.* Book VIII. J.-A. Miller (ed.). B. Fink (trans.). Cambridge: Polity, 2015.

Lacan, J. (1967–1968). *The seminar of Jacques Lacan.* Book XV. *The psychoanalytic act.* Psychoanalysis (Lacanian Psychoanalysis: Collected Translations and Papers by Cormac Gallagher). http://hdl.handle.net/10788/164

Lacan, J. (1973). *The Four Fundamental Concepts of Psycho-Analysis.* Ed. J.-A. Miller, Trans. A. Sheridan. Harmondsworth, Middlesex: Penguin, 1979.

Lacan, J. (1974). *The Triumph of Religion* and *Discourse to Catholics.* Trans. B. Fink. Cambridge, UK: Polity.

Lacan, J. (1977). *Écrits: A Selection*. Trans. A. Sheridan. London: Tavistock Publications.

Lacan, J. (2002). *Écrits: The First Complete Edition in English*. Trans. B. Fink in collaboration with H. Fink and R. Grigg. New York: Norton.

Lacan, J. (2016). *The Sinthome: The Seminar of Jacques Lacan, Book XXIII*. New York: Polity.

LaFarge, L. (2007). Commentary on "The meanings and uses of countertransference" by H. Racker. *Psychoanal Q.*, 76: 795–815.

Laing, R.D. (1960). *The Divided Self: An Existential Study in Sanity and Madness*. Harmondsworth, Middlesex: Penguin, 1965.

Laing, R.D., & Cooper, D.G. (1964). *Reason and Violence: A Decade of Sartre's Philosophy 1950–1960*. Foreword by Jean-Paul Sartre. London: Tavistock.

Laing, R.D. (1967). *The Politics of Experience* and *The Bird of Paradise*. London: Penguin.

Laing, R.D. (1970). *Knots*. Harmondsworth, UK: Penguin, 1970. Online: www.oikos.org/knots5.htm

Langer, S.K. (1951). *Philosophy In a New Key*. Cambridge, Mass.: Harvard University Press.

Langs, R. (1976). *The Bipersonal Field*. New York: Aronson.

Langs, R. (1978). *Technique in Transition*. New York: Aronson.

Langs, R. (1980). Truth therapy/lie therapy. *Int. J. Psychoanal. Psychother.*, 8: 3–34.

Lasch, C. (1979). *The Culture of Narcissism: American Life in an Age of Diminishing Expectations*. New York: Warner.

Lecercle, J.-J. (2010). *Badiou and Deleuze Read Literature*. Edinburgh: Edinburgh University Press.

Leon, P. (2015). Personal communication.

Levene, J.E. (1996). Conflict in a psychoanalytic class: the influence of discrete vs. comparative curriculum models on the level of class conflict. *Canadian Journal of Psychoanalysis/Revue canadienne de psychanalyse*, 4, 2: 331–340.

Levinas, E. (1961). *Totality and Infinity: An Essay on Exteriority*. Pittsburgh: Duquesne University Press, 1969.

Lifton, R.J. (1986). *The Nazi Doctors: Medical Killing and the Psychology of Genocide*. New York: Basic Books.

Lindner, R. (1950). *The Fifty-Minute Hour: A Collection of True Psychoanalytic Tales*. New York: Bantam.

Loewald, H.W. (1971). Some considerations on repetition and repetition compulsion. In *Papers on Psychoanalysis* (pp. 87–101). New Haven, CT: Yale University Press, 1980.

Loewald, H.W. (1979). The waning of the Oedipus complex. *Journal of the American Psychoanalytic Association* 27: 751–775.

Loewald, H.W. (1981). Regression: some general considerations. *Psychoanalytic Quarterly* 50: 22–43.

Lomas, P. (1987). *The Limits of Interpretation: What's Wrong with Psychoanalysis?* Harmondsworth, Middlesex: Penguin.

Mahler, M.S., Pine, F., & Bergman, A. (1975). *The Psychological Birth of the Human Infant.* New York: Basic Books.

Malinowski, B. (1927). *Sex and Repression in Savage Society.* London: Kegan Paul, Trench, Trubner & Co.

Marcuse, H. (1955). The social implications of Freudian "revisionism." *Dissent* 2: 221–240.

Marcuse, H. (1956). A reply to Erich Fromm. *Dissent* 3: 79–81.

Marcuse, H. (1964). *One-Dimensional Man: Studies in the Ideology of Advanced Industrial Society.* Boston: Beacon Press.

Marcuse, H. (1970). The obsolescence of the Freudian concept of man. In J.J. Shapiro, & S.M. Weber (Trans.), *Five Lectures: Psychoanalysis, Politics and Utopia.* Boston: Beacon Press, chapter three, pp. 44–61.

Margolis, B.D. (1994). Selected papers on Modern Psychoanalysis. *Modern Psychoanalysis* 19, 2: 131–254.

Marshall, R.J. (1982). *Resistant Interactions: Child, Family, and Psychotherapist.* Northvale, NJ: Aronson, 1997.

Marshall, R.J. (1998). Hyman Spotnitz and Heinz Kohut: contrasts and convergences. *Modern Psychoanalysis* 23, 2: 183–196.

Marx, K. (1867). *Capital: A Critique of Political Economy.* Vol. 1. Introduction by E. Mandel, B. Fowkes (Trans.). London: Penguin, 1976.

May, U. (2001). Abraham's discovery of the "bad mother": a contribution to the history of the theory of depression. *Int. J. Psycho-Anal.*, 82: 283–305.

McLaughlin, N. (2001). Critical theory meets America: Riesman, Fromm, and the lonely crowd. *The American Sociologist* 32, 1: 5–26.

McWilliams, N. (1994). *Psychoanalytic Diagnosis: Understanding Personality Structure in the Clinical Process*, (2nd Ed.). New York: Guilford, 2011.

McWilliams, N. (2004). *Psychoanalytic Psychotherapy: A Practitioner's Guide.* New York: Guilford.

Mead, G.H. (1934). *Mind, Self, and Society.* C. Morris, (Ed.). Chicago: University of Chicago Press.

Menand, L. (2017). Why Freud survives. He's been debunked again and again—and yet we still can't give him up. *The New Yorker.* August 28, 2017. www.newyorker.com/magazine/2017/08/28/why-freud-survives

Menninger, K.A. (1938). *Man Against Himself.* New York: Harcourt, Brace & Co.

Mills, C.W. (1959). *The Sociological Imagination.* New York: Grove.

Mitchell, J. (1974). *Psychoanalysis and Feminism: Freud, Reich, Laing and Women.* New York: Vintage.

Mitchell, S.A. (1988). *Relational Concepts in Psychoanalysis: An Integration*. Cambridge, MA: Harvard University Press.

Mitchell, S.A., & Black, M.J. (1995). *Freud and Beyond: A History of Modern Psychoanalytic Thought*. New York: Basic Books.

Muller, J.P. (1983). Language, psychosis, and the subject in Lacan. In J.H. Smith, & W. Kerrigan (Eds.), *Interpreting Lacan. Psychiatry and the Humanities*, Vol. 6, New Haven & London: Yale University Press.

Natoli, J. (2015, May 16). Endless deferment of meaning: the media's inequitable melee of events and words. *Truthout*. Retrieved from www.truth-out.org/opinion/item/30719-endless-deferment-of-meaning-the-media-s-inequitable-melee-of-events-and-words

Niebuhr, R. (1957). Human creativity and self-concern in Freud's thought. In B. Nelson, (Ed.), *Freud and the 20th Century*. Cleveland and New York: The World Publishing Co., pp. 259–276.

Nietzsche, F. (1882, Book Five added 1886). *The Joyful Wisdom*. Trans. T. Common. Introduction by K.F. Reinhardt. New York: Ungar, 1960.

Nietzsche, F. (1886). On the prejudices of philosophers. *Beyond Good and Evil: Prelude to a Philosophy of the Future*. Trans. W. Kaufmann. New York: Vintage, 1966.

Nietzsche, F. (1901). *The Will to Power*. W. Kaufmann (Ed.). New York: Vintage, 1967.

Ogden, T.H. (1986). *The Matrix of the Mind: Object Relations and the Psychoanalytic Dialogue*. Northvale, NJ: Aronson.

Olinick, S.L., Poland, W.S., Grigg, K.A., & Granatir, W.L. (1973). The psychoanalytic work ego: process and interpretation. *Int. J. Psycho-Anal.*, 54: 143–151.

Ornstein, A. (1974). The dread to repeat and the new beginning. *Annu. Psychoanal.*, 2: 231–248. New York: International Universities Press.

Orwell, G. (1949). *Nineteen Eighty-Four*. Thomas Pynchon (Foreword); Erich Fromm (Afterword). Plume, 2003.

Paglia, C. (2016). The modern campus has declared war on free speech. (http://heatst.com/culture-wars/camille-paglia-free-speech-modern-campus-protest/?mod=sm_tw_post# 7/30/16, 2:01 PM Page 1 of 23).

Parsons, A. (1964). Is the Oedipus complex universal? *The Psychoanalytic Study of Society*, III: 278–328. W. Muensterberger, & A. Axelrad (Eds.). New York: International Universities Press.

Pascal, B. (1669). *Pensées*. Trans. A.J. Krailsheimer. Harmondsworth, Middlesex: Penguin, 1966.

Pine, F. (1990). *Drive, Ego, Object, and Self: A Synthesis For Clinical Work*. New York: Basic Books.

Pine, F. (1995, March). *One psychoanalysis composed of many*. Unpublished paper presented to the Toronto Institute of Contemporary Psychoanalysis.

Plato (380 BCE). *Republic.* Trans. G.M.A. Grube. New York: Hackett Classic, 1974.

Pope, T.P. (2009). When sex leaves the marriage. *New York Times Magazine*, June 3, 2009.

Popper, K. (1972). *Objective Knowledge: An Evolutionary Perspective.* Oxford: Clarendon Press.

Pound, M. (2007). *Theology, Psychoanalysis and Trauma.* London: SCM Press, Veritas.

Pound, M. (2014). *Lacan.* Video-lecture on Lacan. https://youtu.be/0IxKzk8JHO0

Prochnik, G. (2017). The curious conundrum of Freud's persistent Influence. *New York Times.* Book Review, August 14, 2017. www.nytimes.com/2017/08/14/books/review/freud-biography-frederick-crews.html?emc=eta1

Putnam, H. (2002). *The Collapse of the Fact/Value Dichotomy and Other Essays.* Cambridge, MA: Harvard University Press.

Racker, H. (1957). The meaning and uses of countertransference. *Psa. Q.*, 26: 303–357.

Rangell, L. (1980). *The Mind of Watergate: An Exploration of the Compromise of Integrity.* New York: W.W. Norton.

Rank, O. (1932). *Art and Artist: Creative Urge and Personality Development.* With a Preface by Ludwig Lewisohn. Translated from German by C.F. Atkinson. New York: Agathon Press, 1968.

Rank, O. (1936). *Truth and Reality: A Life History of the Human Will.* New York: Knopf.

Rank, O. (1958). *Beyond Psychology.* New York: Dover.

Reiff, P. (1959). *Freud: The Mind of the Moralist.* New York: New York: Doubleday.

Reik, T. (1948). *Listening With the Third Ear.* New York: Arena, 1972.

Reiner, A. (2009). *The Quest for Conscience and the Birth of the Mind.* Foreword J. Grotstein. London: Karnac Books.

Renik, O. (1993). Countertransference enactment and the psychoanalytic process. In M.J. Horowitz, O.F. Kernberg, & E.M. Weinshel (Eds.), *Psychic Structure and Psychic Change.* Madison, CT: International Universities Press, pp. 13–158.

Remmling, G. (1967). *Road to Suspicion: A Study of Modern Mentality and the Sociology of Knowledge.* New York: Appleton-Century-Crofts.

Richards. A.D. (2016). The left and far left in American psychoanalysis: psychoanalysis as a subversive discipline. *Contemporary Psychoanalysis* 52, 1: 111–129.

Richardson, W.J. (1986). Psychoanalysis and the God-question. *Thought* LXI (1986), 68–83.

Ricoeur, P. (1970). *Freud and Philosophy: An Essay on Interpretation.* Trans. D. Savage. New Haven: Yale University Press.

Rieff, P. (1959). *Freud: The Mind of the Moralist.* New York: Doubleday.

Rieff, P. (1966). *The Triumph of the Therapeutic: Uses of Faith After Freud.* New York: Harper & Row.

Riesman, D., Glazer, N., & Denney, R. (1950). *The Lonely Crowd.* New Haven: Yale University Press, 1961.

Roazen, P. (1996). Lacan's first disciple. *Journal of Religion and Health* 34, 4: 321–336.

Roazen, P. (2005). *Edoardo Weiss: The House that Freud Built.* New Brunswick (USA) & London (UK): Transaction Publishers.

Robinson, W.I. (2011). Global capitalism and 21st century fascism. *Al Jazeera*, May 8, 2011. Accessed February 12, 2017. www.aljazeera.com/indepth/opinion/2011/04/201142612714539672.html

Rothenberg, A. (1989). *The Emerging Goddess: The Creative Process in Art, Science, and Other Fields.* Chicago: University of Chicago Press.

Roudinesco, E. (1999). *An Outline of a Life and a History of a Thought.* Trans. B. Bray. Cambridge: Polity Press.

Rousseau, J.-J. (1754). *Discourse on Inequality.* Whitefish, MT: Kessinger Legacy Reprints, 2010.

Rousseau, J.-J. (1762). *Émile, or Education.* Trans. B. Foxley. London & Toronto: J.M. Dent and Sons, 1921.

Roustang, F. (1976). *Dire Mastery: Discipleship From Freud to Lacan.* Trans. N Lukacher. Baltimore: Johns Hopkins University Press.

Safán-Gerard, D. (1998). Bearable and unbearable guilt: a Kleinian perspective. *Psychoanal. Quart.*, 67: 351–378. Reprinted in Akhtar, S. (Ed.) (2013), *Guilt: Origins, Manifestations, and Management.* Margaret S. Mahler Series. New York: Jason Aronson, chapter 4, pp. 41–57.

Sagan, E. (1974). *Cannibalism: Human Aggression and Cultural Form.* New York: Harper.

Sagan, E. (1988). *Freud, Women and Morality: The Psychology of Good and Evil.* New York: Basic Books.

Sagan, E. (2001). *Citizens and Cannibals: The French Revolution, The Struggle for Modernity, and The Origins of Ideological Terror.* Lanham, Maryland: Rowman & Littlefield.

Sandler, J. (1960). On the concept of the superego. *Psychoanalytic Study of the Child* 15: 128–162.

Sandler, J., & Rosenblatt, B. (1962). The concept of the representational world. *Psychoanalytic Study of the Child* 17: 128–145.

Sandler, J. (1976). Countertransference and role-responsiveness. *Int. R. Psycho-Anal.*, 3: 43–47.

Sartre, J.-P. (1943). *Being and Nothingness: A Study in Phenomenological Ontology.* Trans. H.E. Barnes. New York: Philosophical Library, 1953.

Sartre, J.-P. (1944). *No Exit: A Play in One Act.* Trans. P. Bowles. New York: Samual French, 1958.

Sartre, J.-P. (1946). *Existentialism Is a Humanism.* Trans. P. Mairet. New York: World Publishing Co., 1956.

Sartre, J.-P. (1960). *The Critique of Dialectical Reason.* Trans. A. Sheridan-Smith. London: New Left, 1976.

Schaar, J.H. (1961). *Escape from Authority: The Perspectives of Erich Fromm.* New York: Basic Books.

Schafer, R. (1960). The loving and beloved superego in Freud's structural theory. *Psychoanalytic Study of the Child* 15: 163–188.

Schafer, R. (1976). *A New Language for Psychoanalysis.* New Haven: Yale University Press.

Schneiderman, S. (1983). *Jacques Lacan: The Death of an Intellectual Hero.* Cambridge, Mass.: Harvard University Press.

Searles, H. (1965). *Collected Papers on Schizophrenia and Related Subjects.* New York: International Universities Press.

Searles, H. (1975). The patient as therapist to his analyst. In P.L. Giovacchini (Ed.), *Tactics and Techniques in Psychoanalytic Therapy*, Vol. 2. New York: Aronson, pp. 95–151. Also in *Countertransference and Related Subjects.* Madison, CT: International Universities Press, 1979, pp. 380–459.

Segal, H. (1957). Notes on symbol formation. *Int. J. Psycho-Anal.*, 38: 391–397.

Seneca. L.A. (n.d.). *Seneca's Morals by Way of Abstract. To which is Added, a Discourse, Under the Title of An After-thought.* By Sir R. L'Estrange, Knt. The Ninth Edition (Google eBook. https://archive.org/details/senecasmoralsbyw00senerich, accessed 3 January, 2015).

Showalter, E. (1997). *Hystories: Hysterical Epidemics and Modern Media.* New York: Columbia University Press.

Singer, P. (1980). *Marx.* Oxford: Oxford University Press.

Singer, P. (1983). *Hegel.* Oxford: Oxford University Press.

Smith, H.F. (2000). Countertransference, conflictual listening, and the analytic object relationship. *J.A.P.A.* 48: 95–128.

Smith, J.H., & Kerrigan, W. (Eds.). (1983). *Interpreting Lacan. Psychiatry and the Humanities*, Vol. 6. New Haven & London: Yale University Press.

Snippe, A. (1988). Erich Fromm over de mens. Ph.D. thesis, University of Leiden.

Soler, C. (2016). *Lacanian Affects: The Function of Affect in Lacan's Work.* Trans. B. Fink. New York: Routledge.

Spence, D. (1984). *Narrative Truth and Historical Truth.* New York: Norton.

Spotnitz, H. (1969). *Modern Psychoanalysis of the Schizophrenic Patient: Theory of the Technique.* Second Ed. New York: Human Sciences Press, 1985.

Steiner, G. (1969). The language animal. *Encounter*, August: 7–23. Reprinted in *Extra-Territorial: Essays on Literature and the Language Revolution*. New York: Atheneum, 1971.

Steiner, G. (1974). *Nostalgia For the Absolute*. Massey Lectures, Fourteenth Series. Toronto: CBC. Publications.

Steiner, J. (1987). The interplay between pathological organizations and the paranoid-schizoid and depressive positions. *Int. J. Psychoanal.*, 68: 69–80. Reprinted in *Melanie Klein Today: Developments in Theory and Practice*. Vol. 1: Mainly Theory. Ed. E. Bott Spillius. London: Routledge, 1988, pp. 324–342.

Stern, K. (1975). *Love and Success and Other Essays*. New York: Farrar, Straus and Giroux.

Stern, D. (1985). *The Interpersonal World of the Infant: A View From Psychoanalysis and Developmental Psychology*. New York: Basic Books.

Stoller, R. (1975). *Perversion: The Erotic Form of Hatred*. New York: Pantheon.

Stoller, R. (1979). *Sexual Excitement*. New York: Pantheon.

Stoller, R. (1985). *Observing the Erotic Imagination*. New Haven: Yale University Press.

Stolorow, R.D., Brandchaft, B., & Atwood, G.E. (1987). *Psychoanalytic Treatment: An Intersubjective Approach*. Hillsdale, NJ: Analytic Press.

Stolorow, R.D., & Atwood, G.E. (1992*). Contexts of Being: The Intersubjective Foundations of Psychological Life*. Hillsdale, NJ: The Analytic Press.

Stolorow, R.D. (2002). Impasse, affectivity, and intersubjective systems. *Psychoanal. Rev.*, 89: 329–337.

Strachey, J. (1934). The nature of the therapeutic action of psycho-analysis. *International Journal of Psycho-Analysis* 15: 127–159.

Sullivan, H.S. (1940). *Conceptions of Modern Psychiatry*. New York: Norton.

Sullivan, H.S. (1950). The illusion of personal individuality. In *The Fusion of Psychiatry and Social Science*. New York: Norton, 1964, pp. 198–206.

Sullivan, H.S. (1953). *The Interpersonal Theory of Psychiatry*. New York: Norton.

Suttie, I.D. (1935). *The Origins of Love and Hate*. London: Free Associations, 1988.

Sykes, J.B. (Ed.). (1982). *The Concise Oxford Dictionary of Current English*. Oxford: Clarendon Press.

Symington, J., & Symington, N. (1996). *The Clinical Thinking of Wilfred Bion*. London & New York: Routledge.

Szasz, T. (1961). *The Myth of Mental Illness: Foundations of a Theory of Personal Conduct* (rev. ed.). New York: Harper & Row, 1974.

Szasz, T. (1965). *The Ethics of Psychoanalysis: The Theory and Practice of Autonomous Psychotherapy*. New York: Macmillan.

Szasz, T. (2004). Remarks at the 35th Anniversary and Human Rights Award Dinner, Citizens Commission on Human Rights International. Beverly Hilton Hotel, Beverly Hills, California, February 28, 2004. Accessed June 24, 2017: www.szasz.com/cchr.html

Tarnopolsky, A. (1995). Understanding Countertransference. *Psychoanalytic Psychotherapy* 9, 185–194.

Thurston, L. (Ed.). (2002). *Re-Inventing the Symptom: Essays on the Final Lacan.* New York: Other Press.

Tillich, P. (1952). *The Courage to Be.* London: Collins.

Tillich, P. (n.d.). Quoted by D. Mackenzie Brown in *Ultimate Concern: Tillich in Dialogue.* http://media.sabda.org/alkitab-2/Religion-Online.org%20Books/Brown,%20D.%20Mackenzie%20-%20Ultimate%20Concern%20-%20Tillich%20in%20Dialogue.pdf

Trilling, L. (1955). Freud: within and beyond culture. In *Beyond Culture: The Work of Lionel Trilling.* New York: Harcourt Brace Jovanovich, 1978.

Turkle, S. (1978). *Psychoanalytic Politics: Freud's French Revolution.* New York: Basic Books.

Twain, M. (1885). *The Adventures of Huckleberry Finn.* Raleigh, NC: Hayes Barton Press, 2005.

Vahanian, G. (1957). *The Death of God: The Culture of Our Post-Christian Era.* New York: Braziller.

Vaihinger, H. (1911). *The Philosophy of "As If".* New York: Harcourt, Brace, 1924.

Vercors. (1952). *Les Animaux Dénaturés.* Boston: Little, Brown.

ver Eecke, W. (1983). Hegel as Lacan's source of necessity in psychoanalytic theory. In J.H. Smith, & W. Kerrigan (Eds.), *Interpreting Lacan, Psychiatry and the Humanities*, Vol. 6. New Haven & London: Yale University Press.

Weber, M. (1922). *The Theory of Social and Economic Organizations.* Trans. A.M. Henderson, & T. Parsons. New York: The Free Press, 1947, pp. 358–392. Concept is defined online in the *Encyclopedia of religion and Society* here: http://hirr.hartsem.edu/ency/Routinization.htm

Weber, M. (1953). *From Max Weber.* H.H. Gerth, & C. Wright Mills (Eds.). New York: Oxford University Press.

Weil, S. (n.d.). *Pensées sans ordre concernant l'amour de Dieu (Thoughts without order concerning the love of God).* Accessed June 18, 2017. http://simoneweil.net/fauxdieux.htm.

Whitehead, A.N. (1925). *Science and the Modern World.* New York: Free Press, 1997.

Winnicott, D.W. (1953). Transitional objects and transitional phenomena—a study of the first not-me possession. *Int. J. Psycho-Anal.*, 34: 89–97.

Winnicott, D.W. (1954). Metapsychological and clinical aspects of regression within the psychoanalytical set-up. *Through Pediatrics to Psycho-Analysis*. London: Hogarth Press, 1987.

Winnicott, D.W. (1958). Psycho-analysis and the sense of guilt. In *The Maturational Processes and the Facilitating Environment*. London: Hogarth Press, 1965.

Winnicott, D.W. (1960a). Ego distortion in terms of true and false self. In *The Maturational Processes and the Facilitating Environment*. London: Hogarth Press, 1965, pp. 140–152.

Winnicott, D.W. (1960b). The theory of the parent-infant relationship. In *Maturational Processes and the Facilitating Environment*. London: Hogarth Press, 1965, pp. 37–55.

Winnicott, D.W. (1962). Ego integration in child development. In *Maturational Processes and the Facilitating Environment*. London: Hogarth Press, 1965, pp. 56–63.

Winnicott, D.W. (1963a). The development of the capacity for concern. In *The Maturational Processes and the Facilitating Environment*. London: Hogarth, 1965, 73–82.

Winnicott, D.W. (1963b). Communicating and not communicating leading to a study of certain opposites. In *The Maturational Processes and the Facilitating Environment*. London: Hogarth Press, chapter 17, pp. 179–192.

Winnicott, D.W. (1968a). Comments on my paper "The use of an object." In C. Winnicott, R. Shepherd, & M. Davis (Eds.), *Psycho-Analytic Explorations*. London: Karnac, 1989, pp. 238–240.

Winnicott, D.W. (1968b). The use of an object in the context of Moses and Monotheism. In C. Winnicott, R. Shepard, & M. Davis (Eds.), *Psycho-Analytic Explorations*. London: Karnac, 1989, pp. 240–246.

Winnicott, D.W. (1971a). *Playing and Reality*. London: Tavistock.

Winnicott, D.W. (1971b). The use of an object and relating through identifications. *Playing and Reality*. London: Tavistock, chapter 6.

Winnicott, D.W. (1971c). Mirror-role of mother and family in child development. *Playing and Reality*. London: Tavistock, chapter 9.

Winnicott, D.W. (1974). Fear of breakdown. *Int. Rev. Psycho.-Anal.*, 1: 103–107.

Winnicott, D.W. (1989). *Psychoanalytic Explorations*. C. Winnicott, R. Shepard and M. Davis (Eds.). London: Karnac.

Wrong, D.H. (1961). The oversocialized concept of man in modern sociology. *American Sociological Review* 26: 183–193.

Würmser, L. (1998). "The sleeping giant": a dissenting comment about "borderline pathology." *Psychoanalytic Inquiry* 8: 373–397.

Žižek, S. (2000). *The Fragile Absolute or, Why is the Christian Legacy Worth Fighting For?* London: Verso.

Žižek, S. (2003). *The Puppet and the Dwarf: The Perverse Core of Christianity.* Cambridge, MA: MIT Press.

Žižek, S., & Milbank, J. (2009). *The Monstrosity of Christ: Paradox or Dialectic?* Ed. C. Davis. Boston: MIT Press.

Žižek, S. (2015). Interview. www.youtube.com/watch?v=JkpRqxKbgF8

Žižek, S. (2017). Interview. www.youtube.com/watch?v=2ZUCemb2plE

Films

Flight from Death is a 2003 documentary film about death anxiety and the quest for immortality based on Ernest Becker's (1973) *The Denial of Death.* It was directed by Patrick Shen, produced by Greg Bennick, and narrated by Gabriel Byrne.

Gorillas in the Mist is a 1988 American drama film directed by Michael Apted starring Sigourney Weaver as naturalist Dian Fossey. It tells the true story of her work in Rwanda with mountain gorillas. Universal Pictures.

Hacksaw Ridge is a 2016 biographical war drama film written by Andrew Knight and Robert Schenkkan and directed by Mel Gibson. It tells the story of Desmond Doss, the first conscientious objector to be awarded the American Medal of Honor for service above and beyond the call of duty, while refusing to bear arms during the Battle of Okinawa. Summit Entertainment.

Manchester by the Sea is a 2016 American drama film written and directed by Kenneth Lonergan. Roadside Productions.

Index

Page numbers in *italics* denote tables.

Abraham (biblical character) 51–2
absence, metaphysics of 21, 22, 23, 149, 154–5, 158–9
abstract others 39–40
abuse victims, as abusers 36–7
Adorno, T.W. 34, 103, 105, 216–17, 218
Adventures of Huckleberry Finn, The (Twain) 51
aggression 22, 26–7, 27, 30, 33, 144–5, 147, 233; identification with the aggressor 38; and narcissism 152; scapegoating 235; and victims 37
Aichhorn, August 61, 87
Alexander, F. 222, 223
Alford, C.F. 39
American Psychoanalytic Association 5
anality 161, 163
Anderson, Hans Christian 132
anthropocentrism 24, 28, 227–9, 234
Antigone (Sophocles) 46, 52
anxiety 14; castration anxiety 24; death anxiety 161–7
Arlow, J. 42, 173
atheism 78, 138, 139, 226
attachment 32, 46, 48, 57, 110, 217
Attacks on Linking (Bion) 206, 208
Atwood, G.E. 112–15, 116–29, 129–30, 188

authoritarianism 118–19, 128–9; authoritarian superego 24, 53; authoritarian vs. humanistic conscience 222–4
authorization 55–6

Bacal, H.A. 76, 184–5
Bachofen, J.J. 224, 228
Badiou, Alain 103
Becker, Ernest 22, 23, 158, 161–7, 190; *The Birth and Death of Meaning* 161; *The Denial of Death* 161, 164; melancholic existentialism 161–7
Before and After the Depressive Position (Britton) 198
being-in-the-world 23, 53, 109, 181, 190
Beit-Hallahmi, B. 15, 77, 139, 226, 227
Berger, Peter 22, 23, 158, 162, 163, 166, 190, 216
Bergman, A. 213
Bible, the 19, 27–8, 140, 164–5, 213, 227
biologism 214–18
Bion, Wilfred 1, 3, 7–8, 9, 18, 23, 36, 48, 70–1, 82, 89, 96, 137, 197–8, 200, 206, 207, 208
Birth of Tragedy, The (Nietzsche) 216

Black, M.J. 67
Bohannan, Laura 86, 87
Bonhoeffer, D. 78
Borromean knot 21, 102–3, 137, 159
Bowlby, John 66, 195
Brandchaft, B. 117, 121
breast 208; breast envy 185, 195; breast mother 153; good/bad breast 35, 194–5
Brenner, Charles 88, 141, 143, 145
Brentano, Franz 67, 207–8
Britton, R. 23, 97, 195, 198–200
Brook, A. 208
Brown, Norman O. 161
Buber, Martin 40, 203, 221
Buechler, Susan 59–60
Burston, D. 40, 99, 137, 138, 215

Carveth, Donald L. 36, 44, 197
castration 20, 21, 32, 144, 152, 158, 159, 231; acceptance of castration 149, 155–6; castration anxiety 24, 91, 141, 143; double castration 148
centaur model of man 30, 38, 145, 146, 165
charisma 3, 140
Chasseguet-Smirgel, J. 132, 211–12
Chesterton, G.K. 37
children 32, 46, 97–8, 217; desire to be the phallus for the mother 147–8, 150, 151, 153–4, 158; mirror image 147–8, 150, 151, 152; sense of the real 120
Chomsky, N. 218
Choosing Life: Fromm's Clinical Values (Buechler) 59–60
civilization 26–41, 48; abuse victims as abusers 36–8; characterization of humans as animalistic 26–30, 32; differentiation between superego and conscience 35–6; dual drive theory of *Eros* and *Thanatos* 27–8, 31–2, 38; and inhibition 26–7; mind/body dualism 12–13, 30–1; mob psychology 33; superego as the source of law and order 33–4
clinical vignettes: countertransference 1, 170–7; countertransference 2, 177–80; disillusion 82, 90–1; structural theory 62–5
Collapse of the Fact/Value Dichotomy, The (Putnam) 54
concern 52–4, 187, 229
condensation (metaphor) 84, 116, 145–6, 147
conflict 43–4, 45, 103–4, 105; conflict model's association with the drive model 108–9; conflicts among id, ego, superego, ego-ideal and conscience 49–52, 146–7, 168, 230
connection *see* maternal function
conscience 9–10, 24, 32, 44, 52–3; authoritarian vs. humanistic conscience 222–4; conflicts among id, ego, superego, ego-ideal and conscience 49–52, 146–7, 168, 230; definition of 45; differentiation from superego 19–20, 35–6, 45–6, 47, 49, 59–60, 222–4, 230–1, 234; as love 55–6; socialism of 234; as a training requirement 57–8
constructionist/deconstructionist 20, 66, 67, 71–2, 75–6, 79–80, 94–5
consumption 34, 42
Contexts of Being (Stolorow and Atwood) 112–15, 116–20, 121–2, 122–6, 129–30
core self notion 22, 23
correspondence theory of truth 120, 121, 123
countertransference 17, 22, 69, 86, 87, 97, 108, 168–80, 233; clinical vignette 1, 170–7; clinical vignette 2, 177–80; complementary countertransference 169–72, 173–5, 176–7, 178–80; concordant countertransference 169, 170–4,

countertransference *continued*
175, 176, 177–80;
countertransference identifications 168–9; distinction between conscious and unconscious countertransference 178–9; internal object relations concept 172, 173, 174; rationality 178; trial identifications 168–9
Crews, Frederick 7, 8
critique 1–25, 77–8; decline of 1–6; dialectical deconstruction 18; ideological vs. critical psychoanalysis 14–17; illness metaphor 10–14; and psychoanalysis 7–10

Darwin, Charles 28, 31
Dasein 109
death 22, 31; death anxiety 161–7; death instinct 186; necrophilia 55, 220–1
deconstruction *see* constructionist/deconstructionist; "In defence of splitting: progressive politics in the twentieth century" (Gabbert) 193
Deleuze, Gilles 103
depression 22, 23, 76, 82, 163
depressive/reparative position 39, 82–3, 153, 164–5, 187, 211; and Ps→D 193, 197–9, 200
Derrida, J. 67, 154
desire 144–5, 147, 148; as desire of the other 149–50, 152, 154, 158
destructiveness 18–19, 28–9, 183–6
Deutsch, Helene 22, 170
dialectical deconstruction 18, 67, 108, 232
dialectical logic 103
dialectical thinking 103–6, 129, 230–6; dialectical revision of neo-Kleinian theory *see* Klein, Melanie; as evolutionary thinking 233–4
dichotomies: analytic/synthetic 54;
constructionist/deconstructionist 20, 66, 67, 71–2, 75–6, 79–80, 94–5; disintegration/reintegration 23, 197–200, 201, 207; fact/value 54–5, 221; gnostic/agnostic 77–82, *81*; identifying/disidentifying 20, 71–2, 79–80, 94–5; illusioning/disillusioning 20, 66, 68–74, 75, *81*, 94–5, 232; similarity/difference 106–7; validation/invalidation 75–6, 119, 120, 122–3, 125–7, 128, 129
difference *see* similarity/difference
Dilthey, W. 109
disidentifying *see* identifying/disidentifying
disillusion 66–98; analytic vs. non-analytic psychotherapy 67–8; case vignettes 82, 90–1; frozen metaphors 82–7; future of 95–8; gnostic/agnostic 77–82, *81*; illusioning/disillusioning 20, 66, 68–74, 75, *81*, 94–5, 232; as theory or ideology 91–5; therapeutic iconoclasm 87–90, 91–2, 93–5; *via negativa* 70, 74–6, 79
disintegration/reintegration 23, 197–200, 201, 207; disintegration product concept 102–3
displacement 69, 84, 116, 145–6, 147, 235
disruption-repair cycle 21, 102
dissociative identity disorder 84
distortion 73, 119, 123–8
Dostoevsky, F. 166
Drive, Ego, Object and Self (Pine) 92
drive theory 6, 72; conflict model's association with the drive model 108–9; of *Eros* and *Thanatos* 27–8, 31–2, 38, 55, 104, 107–8, 210–12, 233
dualism 104–5, 106, 123, 129
Durkin, K. 227, 228

Eagle, Morris 5–6

ego 19, 21, 30–1, 45, 48–9, 57, 79; birth of the ego notion 182; conflicts among id, ego, superego, ego-ideal and conscience 49–52, 146–7, 168, 230; ego-identity 100; ego-organization 190; imaginary ego 23, 139; Lacanian theory of 150–1; specular ego 95; structural ego 95
ego-ideal 19, 53–4, 57; concept of 44; conflicts among id, ego, superego, ego-ideal and conscience 49–52, 146–7, 169, 230
Elements of Psychoanalysis (Bion) 197
Eliot, T.S. 76, 80, 166
empathy 22, 28–9, 39, 168, 169; and countertransference 170, 171–2, 173–4, 175, 176, 179; empathetic-introspective method 110–11; and observation 110
Empedocles 31
Endless Deferment of Meaning: The Media's Inequitable Melee of Events and Words (Natoli) 195–6
Enlightenment, the 27, 45, 78
environmental illness 86–7, 91
Epstein, M. 79, 172
Erikson, Erik 4, 30, 99, 145, 163, 165, 166, 190, 233–4
essentialism 24, 118, 218–19, 225, 229, 233
ethics 55, 56–7; naturalistic ethics 219–22
existentialism 22, 23; and anthropocentrism 227–9; authoritarian vs. humanistic conscience 222–4; existential humanism 24; Fromm's existentialism 214–29; humanistic religion 225–7; melancholic existentialism 161–7; and the Oedipus complex 224–5; productive activity 227–8; qualified essentialism 218–19; sociologism, biologism and humanistic existentialism 214–18
Existentialism Is a Humanism (Sartre) 55

Faces in a Cloud (Stolorow and Atwood) 120–1, 128, 188
fact/value dichotomy 54–5, 221
Fairbairn, W.R.D. 4, 58, 149
feelings 55–6
Feiner, A.H. 172
Ferenczi, S. 4, 222, 223
Feuer, L. 180
Fichte, Johann Gottlieb 103, 201
Fink, B. 7
First World War 27, 31
Fisher, H. 202–3
Fliess, R. 133
Flight From Death: The Quest for Immortality (film) 161
Fonagy, P. 7
fort!/da! concept 144, 154, 159, 160
Fossey, Dian 61
Foucault, M. 217, 218
fragmentation 21, 22, 23, 107, 149, 162, 190, 197, 231; of the self 31, 91, 99, 100, 102–3
Frattaroli, E. 57
Freud and Beyond (Mitchell and Black) 67
Freud, Anna 33, 73, 141–2, 168
Freud, Sigmund 1, 3, 5, 10, 24, 37, 43–4, 57, 60, 61, 67, 91, 92, 98, 99, 105, 116, 127, 129, 131–2, 133, 187, 202, 209, 215, 222, 227, 229, 230; and anxiety 165; and "borrowed" guilt 58; centaur model of man 30, 38, 145, 146, 165; and the central human problem 140; characterization of humans as animalistic 26–30, 32, 48; and Christian culture 136–40; *Civilization and Its Discontents* 18–19, 26, 32, 47, 78–9, 165;

Freud, Sigmund *continued*
 "Civilized" Sexual Morality and Modern Nervous Illness 26; dialectical nature of Freudian theories 207–8; dictatorship of reason notion 69–70; and disillusion 68–70; dual drive theory of *Eros* and *Thanatos* 6, 27–8, 31–2, 38, 55, 104, 107–8, 210–12, 233; *The Ego and the Id* 44, 45; faults and blunders 7–8; Freudian discourse, deliterization of 140–4; *The Future of an Illusion* 77, 165; *Group Psychology and the Analysis of the Ego* 33; as an hysteric 12; *Inhibitions, Symptoms and Anxiety* 165; *Instincts and Their Vicissitudes* 30; *The Interpretation of Dreams* 141; *Jokes and Their Relation to the Unconscious* 141; as a liberal 32–3; libido theory 104; mind/body dualism 12–13, 30–1; *On Narcissism* 53; and narcissistic neuroses 100–1; oedipal resolution 180; primary process 69–70, 84, 115–16, 117–18; psychoanalysis and science 56–7; *The Psychopathology of Everyday Life* 141; reductionist theory of the drives 218; on religion 226; self-observation 49; sociopolitical ideology 147; structural ego 95; structure metaphor 73; sublimation 56, 233; superego, views on 46–7, 224; theoretical parallels *181*; *Three Essays on the History of Sexuality* 145; *Totem and Taboo* 224; *triebe* 144–5; truth therapy 74–5, 86, 96

Friedman, L. 228

Fromm, Erich 24, 40, 46, 53, 55, 99, 101, 109, 230, 233; authoritarian vs. humanistic conscience 222–4; *Beyond the Chains of Illusion: My Encounter with Marx and Freud* 70; existentialism 214–29; *To Have or to Be* 227; humanistic religion 225–7; *Man For Himself: An Inquiry into the Psychology of Ethics* 219–20; naturalistic ethics, fallacy of 219–22; Oedipus complex theories 224–5; productive activity 227–8; qualified essentialism 218–19; sociologism, biologism and humanistic existentialism 214–18

frustration 26, 48, 53, 72, 100, 108–9, 114, 149, 194–5, 223, 232

Gabbert, M. 193, 205
Gallop, J. 133
Gilligan, C. 208–9
gnostic/agnostic 20, 77–82
Gorillas in the Mist (film) 61
Grand Inquisitor concept 166
Greenberg, J. 6, 215
Grinberg, L. 86
Grotstein, J.S. 94
Grunberger, B. 132, 133, 134–5, 148–9, 156
guilt 42–3, 168, 223; central importance of 34; guilt-evasion 61–2; persecutory guilt 14, 19, 35, 37–8, 47; real and induced guilt 58; reparative guilt 14, 19, 35, 47, 58
"Guilty Man" 20, 99, 104, 108, 110, 129, 232
Guntrip, H. 73, 145

Hackshaw Ridge (film) 51
Hanly, C. 145
Hartmann, Heinz 10, 73, 95
hate 6, 38–9, 55–6, 223, 234
Hegel, G.W.F. 46, 103, 105, 110, 152, 201, 202, 208, 232
Heidegger, M. 23, 131, 181, *181*
Hillman, J. 210
Homer 230
Horkheimer, M. 218, 221
Horney, Karen 214

human condition 8, 108, 149, 156, 163, 167, 218
human/cultural sciences 109–10
Hume, David 54, 55, 221
Huxley, Sir Julian 28
Huxley, Thomas Henry 28

iconoclasm 87–90, 91–2, 93–5
id 45, 48, 56, 70, 145, 169–70; conflicts among id, ego, superego, ego-ideal and conscience 49–52, 146–7, 168, 230
idealization/idealism 102; dialectical idealism 103
identifying/disidentifying 20, 71–2, 79–80, 94–5
illness metaphor 10–14
illusioning/disillusioning 20, 66, 68–74, 75, *81*, 94–5, 232
Imaginary, the 93, 94, 160, 210, 231–2; Imaginary experience 151–3; Lacanian Imaginary 9, 20, 21, 23, 79, 89, 91, 106, 135, 137, 139–40, 156–7
Immoral Superego, The (Carveth) 44
incest 152, 155, 225
Ingleby, D. 218, 220, 229
internal object relations concept 172, 173, 174, 231
internalization 17–18, 35, 72–3, 74, 107, 114, 117, 150–1, 231
International Psychoanalytic Association 3, 5, 16, 33, 50
intersubjectivity theory *see* self psychology, intersubjective perspectives
intimacy, retreat from 189–91
invalidation *see* validation/invalidation
isolated mind, myth of 112, 115

Jacobson, Edith 4, 113, 114
Jacoby, Russell 34, 43
Jakobson, Roman 84, 146
Janus 18

Kant, Immanuel 9, 103, 201, 221
Kellner, D. 228
Kernberg, Otto 4, 6, 102, 113, 174–5, 179–80, 202, 203
Kierkegaard, S. 51–2, 110, 161, 202, 232
Kissinger, Henry 33
Klein, Melanie 4, 6, 19, 35, 38, 47, 49, 53, 82, 88, 92, 93, 94, 101, 105–6, 137, 140, 154, 165, 187, 190, 231, 232; beyond Ps→D 193–205; and disillusion 68–70; *Envy and Gratitude* 195; good object preservation from the bad object 194–5; internalization 150–1; linking 206–13; neo-Kleinian theory, dialectical revision of 23, 193–213; sexual love 202–4; splitting 193–4, 195, 204, 205, 206–13; theoretical parallels *181*; thesis-antithesis synthesis formula 201–2
Knots (Laing) 207
Kohut, Heinz 20–1, 61, 73, 87, 92, 93, 99, 100, 101, 102–3, 105, 109–10, 112, 113, 129, 150, 152, 155, 168, 231, 232; dialectical method of argument 103; monistic theory of motivation 104, 108
Kojève, A. 201
Kris, Ernst 43, 199
Kristeva, Julia 21, 136–7

Lacan, Jaques 7, 15, 16, 22, 23, 33, 79, 84, 88, 91, 93, 109, 131–60, 181, 190, 210, 216, 225, 231; birth of the ego notion 182; Borromean knot 21, 102–3, 137, 159; Freud and Christian culture 136–40; Freudian discourse, deliterization of 140–4; humanization of the unconscious 144–7; Lacanian Imaginary 9, 20, 21, 23, 79, 91, 106, 137, 139–40, 151–3, 156–7; *le corps morcelé* 22,

Lacan, Jaques *continued*
  147–8, 162; mirror stage 147–53; obscurantism 132–6; phallocentrism 153–6; psychopathology 156–9; *sinthome* 20, 21, 103, 137, 159; theoretical parallels *181*; *The Triumph of Religion* 131
lack, sense of 144, 155–6
LaFarge, L. 172–3, 176–7, 179
Laing, Ronald 44–5, 207
Langs, R. 74–5, 116, 118, 209
Lasch, Christopher 34, 99, 215
Law of the Father 152, 158, 234
Lenin, Vladimir 5
Leon, Paola 58
Levene, J.E. 93
Levinas, Emmanuel 40, 53
libido 4, 49, 55, 104, 148, 149–50, 203, 233
Lifton, Robert 36, 57
linking 206–13, 233
Loewald, H.W. 17, 180, 199, 204
Lonergan, Kenneth 19, 40–1
love 10, 31, 52–3, 55–6, 222–3, 229, 234; sexual love 202–3
Lucius Annaeus Seneca 33–4
Luckmann, T 216
Luther, Martin 51

McWilliams, Nancy 6
Mahler, M.S. 101, 187, 211, 213
Malinowski, B. 225
Man Against Himself (Menninger) 34
Manchester by the Sea (film) 19, 40–1
Marcuse, Herbert 20, 34, 99, 215, 216–17, 218
Marshall, R.J. 85
Marx, Karl 24, 43, 70, 103, 218, 225–6, 227, 229
Maternal Care and Maternal Health (Bowlby) 66
maternal function/mother 20, 37, 39, 106–7, 131, 137, 224, 232, 234; child's desire to be the phallus for the mother 147–8, 150, 151, 153–4, 158
Mead, George Herbert 28, 88, 112, 131, 150, 214, 216
Menand, Louis 8
Menninger, Karl 34
mental illness 11–13
metaphors 82–7, 147; case vignette 82; "dead" and "live" terminology 82–3; environmental illness 86–7; identification with the patient's belief system 86–7; "joining" the patient's concretized metaphor 84–5, 87; psychic reality 85–6
metaphysics: of absence 21, 22, 23, 149, 154–5, 158–9; of presence 21, 154
metonymy 84, 116, 146, 147
mind/body dualism 12–13, 30–1, 38
mirror stage, theory of 21, 147–53
mirroring 61, 85, 87, 101–2, 104, 111–12, 155, 232
Mitchell, S.A. 6, 67, 215–16
mob psychology 33
monism 103–5, 106, 108, 129
Moore, G.E. 221
morality 10, 19, 29, 32, 37, 44–5, 155, 170, 175–6, 224; of animals 29, 46; moral conflict 45; moral judgement 59; and the rational ego 222; and the superego 45–6, 47, 48, 51, 57, 60, 230–1, 234
Muller, J.P. 157–8
multiple personality disorder 84–7
Mussolini, Benito 33

Name-of-the-Father 157, 158
narcissism 4, 6, 19, 23, 53, 85, 101, 102, 140, 187, 225, 229; and aggression 152; culture of 34, 42–3, 99; and the ego-ideal 44; as libido 148–9; narcissistic neuroses 20, 101–2; narcissistic personalities 102
Natoli, J. 195–6

natural sciences 109–10
necrophilia 55, 220–1
neoliberalism 4, 42–3
neoteny, theory of 162
neutrality 19–20, 59–60, 87, 147, 168
New Language of Psychoanalysis, A (Schafer) 113–14
Nietzsche, F. 18, 70, 76, 163, 216
Nineteen Eighty Four (Orwell) 50

object relations 4, 23, 42, 111, 117, 149, 170, 172, 173, 187
obscurantism 132–6
Obsolescence of the Freudian Concept of Man, The (Marcuse) 99–100, 215
Occupy movement 43
Oedipus complex 17, 24, 101, 141, 147, 151, 154, 180, 188; Fromm's theories 224–5
Ogden, T.H. 76, 79, 197, 201, 204
One Psychoanalysis Composed of Many (Pine) 92
optimal responsiveness 72, 76
Orwell, George 50

Paglia, C. 2
Paradise Lost 8
paranoid-schizoid position 23, 39, 53, 82–3, 93, 96, 97, 137, 151, 153, 190, 211; and dialectical thinking 105–6; and Ps→D 193, 197–9, 200
Parsons, Anne 225
Pascal, B. 78, 161
paternal function 20, 21, 37, 39, 106–7, 137, 148, 153, 232, 234
Paul, Saint *181*
penis 153; distinction from phallus 143–4; penis envy 91, 141–2, 143
perversion 203–4
Perversion and the Universal Law (Chasseguet-Smirgel) 211–12
phallus 21, 93, 137, 141, 142, 143–4, 152; child's desire to be the phallus for the mother 147, 148, 150, 151, 153–4, 158; phallocentrism 153–6
phantasy 69, 86–7, 88–90, 91, 92, 117, 141–2, 183; and death 165–6; fearful phantasy 188
Pine, Fred 92, 187, 213
Plato 45, 146
Popper, K. 75, 101, 120, 122, 187
Pound, M. 138, 139
presence 21, 149, 154
primary process 69–70, 84, 115–16, 117–18, 146–7, 199, 204, 211
Prochnik, George 7–8
projective identification 4, 19, 20, 38, 58, 69, 86, 87, 88–9, 96
Ps→D 193–213, 233
psychiatry 12, 13
psychoanalysis: analytic vs. non-analytic psychotherapy 67–8; definition and understanding of 7–10, 14; ideological vs. critical psychoanalysis 14–17; and mental illness 13–14; paradigm dispute 92; resistance to 145–6; and the science *Weltanschauung* 56–7; therapeutic substitute faiths 77–8; as a truth therapy 74–5
psychoanalysts 14–15; analytic attitude 88; complementary countertransference 169–72, 173–5, 176–7, 178–80; concordant countertransference 169, 170–4, 175, 176, 177–80; and conscience 9–10; definition and understanding of 16–17; discredited analysts 15; and distortion 123–4; as mirrors 111–12; non-judgemental yet conscientious approaches of therapists 58–60; objective observation 110–11; as the patient 118; patient's trust in 39–40; role responsiveness 170; training 9, 93–4; trial identifications 168–9;

psychoanalysts *continued*
and understanding viewpoints of the other 112–15, 117; validation of patient experiences 75–6, 119, 120, 121–3, 125–8, 129
Psychoanalytic Study of Falsehood, A (Chasseguet-Smirgel) 132
psychopathology 23, 69, 94, 99, 206–7; "forbidden mixture" conception of 211–12; and Lacan 156–9
psychopaths 57
punishment 33–4, 35, 168
Putnam, H. 54

Racker, Heinrich 17, 22, 47, 169, 170–2, 173, 175, 176, 179–80
Rangell, L. 43
Rank, Otto 161, 166
rationality 19, 69, 97–8, 178
reality 164; objective reality 111, 113, 119–21, 123, 124–5, 127–8, 129; subjective reality 121–2, 124–5
reason 54–5; dictatorship of reason notion 69–70
regression 33, 39, 94, 105, 111, 134–6, 159, 199
Reiff, P. 77
religion 14, 15, 40, 45, 58–9, 161, 162, 164–5, 166, 205, 232–3; Anglicans 189–90; Buddhism 79, 226–7; Catholicism 21; Death of God theology 78; Freud and Christian culture 136–40; humanistic religion 225–7; religionless Christianity 78; secular Christianity 138, 139; secularization hypothesis 77
Renik, O. 169
reparenting 73, 74
repression 26, 99, 115–16, 147, 151, 155, 161, 209
Richards, A.D. 5
Richardson, William 164

Ricoeur, P. 211
Riesman, D. 99, 215
Roazen, Paul 137
Robinson, W.I. 43
Roudinesco, E. 138–9
Rousseau, Jean-Jacques 55, 148
Russell, Bertrand 221

sadism 27, 28–9, 35, 60, 97
Safán-Gerard, D. 39, 60, 62
Sagan, Eli 17, 31, 40, 51, 180, 234
Sandler, J. 42
Sapir-Whorf hypothesis 50
Sartre, Jean-Paul 40, 55, 56, 76, 110, 131, 144, 152, 189, 207, 210, 216, 218–19
Schafer, Roy 4, 19, 49, 113–14
Searles, H. 116, 118
secondary process 83, 84, 116–17, 199, 204, 207, 212
Segal, H. 82
self-esteem 44, 65, 100, 114, 186
self-observation 49, 57–8
self psychology 2, 20–1; analysts and understanding viewpoints of the other 112–15, 117; conflict model's association with the drive model 108–9; connection/separation 106–7; dialectical thinking 103–6, 129; disruption repair cycle 102; distinction between natural and human/cultural sciences 109–10; distortion 119, 123–8; dualism 104–5, 106, 123, 129; empathetic-introspective method 110–11; fragmented self 31, 91, 100, 102–3; idealization 102; intersubjective conjunction 113; intersubjective disjunction 113; intersubjective perspectives 99–130; and mirror stage theory 147–53; monism 103–5, 106, 108, 129; object-instinctual transferences 100–1;

objective observation 110–11; objective reality 111, 113, 119–21, 123, 124–5, 127–8, 129; primary process 115–16, 117–18; self representation 172, 173; selfobject 101–2, 108, 109–10, 112, 129; similarity/difference 106–7; subjective reality 121–2, 124–5; Tragic Man 99, 100, 104, 108, 109–10, 129; unconscious mental processes concept 115–16
self-reflection 97–8
selfobject 20, 93, 101–2, 108, 109–10, 232; theory of 112, 115–16, 129; transference 125
separation (paternal function) *see* paternal function
sexual abuse 90–1, 117, 121–4, 127
sexuality 31; bisexuality 209, 210–11; perversion 203–4; sexual love 202–4
similarity/difference 106–7
sinthome 20, 21, 137, 159
Smith, H.F. 169, 173, 174, 179
Snowdon, Edward 43, 51, 52
social amnesia 34, 43
sociologism 214–18
Soler, Colette 136
Sophocles 46
splitting 23, 48, 94, 105, 106, 149, 151, 152–3, 157, 166, 190, 193–4, 195, 197, 198, 201–2, 204, 205, 233; attacks on splitting 206–13
Spotnitz, Hyman 61, 87
Steiner, G. 195
Stern, Karl 58–9
Still Small Voice, The (Carveth) 36
Stoller, Robert 202, 204
Stolorow, R.D. 112–15, 116–29, 129–30, 174, 188
Strachey, James 30, 223
structural theory 42–65; and authorization 55–6; case vignette 62–5; concern, capacity for 52–4; conflicts among id, ego, superego, ego-ideal and conscience 49–52; conscience 45, 57–8; ego 48–9; non-judgemental yet conscientious approaches of therapists 58–60; psychoanalysis and the science *Weltanschauung* 56–7; real and induced guilt 58; and reason 54–5; repudiation of 43–4; secular sacred 46; superego 46–8; technical implications 61–2; transcending the normative 45–6
sublimation 34, 56, 201, 208–9, 233
suffering 12–13, 29, 47
suicide 33, 34, 47, 220
Sullivan, Henry Stack 119, 214–15, 215–16
superego 32, 42, 46–8, 57–8, 114, 169–70, 171; authoritarian superego 24, 53; conflicts among id, ego, superego, ego-ideal and conscience 49–52, 146–7, 168, 230; differentiation from conscience 19–20, 35–6, 45–6, 47, 49, 59–60, 222–4, 230–1, 234; as hate 55–6; as internalized culture 44–5; loving superego 49; and self victimization 37–8, 40–1; as the source of law and order 33–4
suspicion 70, 71, 77, 162
Suttie, Ian 4
Sykes, J.B. 87–8
Symbolic, the 9, 13, 20, 21, 23, 91, 93, 94, 135, 136, 152–3, 156–7, 159, 160, 181, 182, 210, 232; symbolic forms 96, 97; symbolic functioning 89–90
Symington, J. and Symington, N. 23, 70–1, 208
sympathy 28, 29, 61–2, 168
Szasz, Thomas 10, 11, 12, 13, 203, 221

Target, M. 7
Tarnopolsky, A. 172, 179–80

terror management theory 22, 161, 167
thesis-antithesis synthesis formula 201–2
Tillich, Paul 78, 166
Titus Maccius Plautus 26–7
Toronto Institute of Psychoanalysis, Curriculum Committee 93
"Tragic Man" 20, 99, 100, 104, 108, 109–10, 129, 232
training: conscience as a training requirement 57–8; lack of, in research 2–3; psychoanalysts 9; tensions and problems 93–4
transference 14, 20–1, 39, 61, 64, 69, 97, 100, 133, 134, 135–6, 207; merger transference 101; selfobject transference 125
transitional phenomena 204–5
triebe 30
Trilling, Lionel 216–17
Trobriand culture 225
Trump, Donald 42
truth 2, 7, 8, 70–1, 77; and competing values 3–4; correspondence theory of truth 120, 121, 123; and distortion 127–8; and science 9; truth therapy 74–5, 86, 96
Truth Therapy/Lie Therapy (Langs) 74–5
Twain, Mark 51

Unamuno, Miguel de 166
unconscious, the 172; humanization of 144–7; unconscious mental processes concept 115–16
Understanding Countertransference (Tarnopolsky) 179–80
Uniqueness of Man, The (Huxley) 28

validation/invalidation 75–6, 119, 120, 121–3, 125–8, 129
values 24; fact/value dichotomy 54–5, 221; health values 10–11; and truth 4; value choices 55–6
via negativa 70, 74–6, 79

Weber, Max 3, 109, 112, 140
Weil, Simone 70
whistleblowing 43, 51, 52
Why Freud Survives. He's Been Debunked Again and Again—And Yet We Still Can't Give Him Up (Menand) 8
Winnicott, Donald 7–8, 22–3, 53, 66, 73, 79, 80, 88, 98, 150, 181–92, 204, 211, 216, 231; clarifying Winnicott 181–7; *Comments on My Paper "The Use of an Object"* 186; Communicating and not communicating leading to a study of certain opposites (paper) 188–92; death instinct 186; deconstructing Winnicott 188–92; destructiveness 183–6; fearful phantasy 188; organized regression 199; *Psychoanalytic Explorations* 185–6; retreat from intimacy 189–92; subject/object theories 182–7; theoretical parallels *181*; true self/false self 182, 188; *The Use of An Object and Relating Through Identifications* 182–5; *The Use of an Object in the Context of Moses and Monotheism* 186
Wrong, Dennis H. 214, 216
Würmser, L. 42

Žižek, S. 234